The Civil War Abroad

The Civil War Abroad

*How the Great American
Conflict Reached Overseas*

CHARLES PRIESTLEY

McFarland & Company, Inc., Publishers
Jefferson, North Carolina

LIBRARY OF CONGRESS CATALOGUING-IN-PUBLICATION DATA

Names: Priestley, Charles, 1945– author.
Title: The Civil War abroad : how the great American conflict reached overseas / Charles Priestley.
Description: Jefferson, North Carolina : McFarland & Company, Inc., Publishers, 2022 | Includes bibliographical references and index.
Identifiers: LCCN 2022013834 | ISBN 9781476687094 (paperback : acid free paper) ∞
ISBN 9781476645155 (ebook)
Subjects: LCSH: United States—Foreign relations—1861-1865. | Confederate States of America—Foreign relations. | United States—History—Civil War, 1861-1865—Influence. | United States—History—Civil War, 1861-1865—Foreign public opinion. | United States—Politics and government—1861-1865. | BISAC: HISTORY / Military / United States | HISTORY / United States / Civil War Period (1850-1877)
Classification: LCC E469 .P75 2022 | DDC 973.7/2—dc23/eng/20220323
LC record available at https://lccn.loc.gov/2022013834

BRITISH LIBRARY CATALOGUING DATA ARE AVAILABLE

ISBN (print) 978-1-4766-8709-4
ISBN (ebook) 978-1-4766-4515-5

© 2022 Charles Priestley. All rights reserved

No part of this book may be reproduced or transmitted in any form or by any means, electronic or mechanical, including photocopying or recording, or by any information storage and retrieval system, without permission in writing from the publisher.

On the cover: artwork *The Battle of the USS "Kearsarge" and the CSS "Alabama,"* 1864, Édouard Manet, French (1832–1883), oil on canvas, 137.8 × 128.9 cm (The John G. Johnson Collection, Philadelphia Museum of Art, cat. 1027). *Inset* Crew of the USS *Kearsarge* at their battle stations, shortly after her June 1864 action with CSS *Alabama* (Naval History and Heritage Command)

Printed in the United States of America

McFarland & Company, Inc., Publishers
Box 611, Jefferson, North Carolina 28640
www.mcfarlandpub.com

For Christine,
whose idea this was

Civil War, 48 BC

I sing of something more than civil war
Across the fertile plains of Thessaly,
Of lawlessness made law, a mighty people
Turning its conquering hand against itself,
Kin against kin, the nation's compact broken,
A shocked world feeling the full force of war,
All sharing guilt, flag against flaunting flag,
Standard clashing with standard, spear with spear.
Why so much madness, citizens, such slaughter?
—From Lucan: *De Bello Civili*, Book I
(translation: Charles Priestley)

Table of Contents

Preface   1

1. Alexander Beresford Hope and the Civil War   7
2. A Philosopher's Defense of the Confederacy   17
3. A Lively Meeting in Burnley   25
4. Yancey and the Fishmongers   35
5. A Civil War Grave in Turkey   41
6. On the Cleburne Trail in Cork and Cumbria   49
7. France's Opportunity   59
8. Death in Paris   68
9. The Last Days of the *Alabama*   85
10. Three Accounts of the Battle Off Cherbourg   104
11. The Prince Offers His Services   116
12. From Calais to Cairo   132
13. Three Union Veterans' Overseas Graves   149
14. An Officer's Payslip   167
15. A Postmaster in the Cavalry   182

Chapter Notes   199
Bibliography   213
Index   215

Preface

As far as I can remember, I first became interested in the American Civil War at about the age of 11. How much this was due to my having cousins in Chattanooga, Tennessee, I am not sure, but perhaps less so than one might suppose; most of those of my British friends who share my interest in the war have no American connections, family or business, whatsoever. What is certainly true, however, is that going over, at the age of 16, to spend two weeks staying on Missionary Ridge with my aunt and uncle turned what had been an interest into something more like an obsession, which it has remained ever since. Five years later, a series of extraordinary coincidences led to my being able to spend a year, directly after graduating from Cambridge University, as Visiting Lecturer in Classics at what was then the University of Chattanooga. Since then, I have returned whenever possible to tour the battlefields and to see my cousins. Inevitably, though, the demands of work and family meant that such visits gradually became less and less frequent. In the increasing gaps between trips, I continued to take every opportunity to study the Civil War at home. I read what I could, watched videos, attended lectures, discussed with fellow enthusiasts and so on, until one day I suddenly conceived the idea of writing about the war as well.

I decided from the start that there was little point in trying to compete with historians in the U.S. by writing about the military and political developments of the war in America itself. After all, the Civil War is on their doorstep; the battlefields, libraries and archives are all within easy reach. Instead, I deliberately determined to concentrate on researching and writing about various different aspects of the war as it affected foreign countries, first of all my own country, the United Kingdom, and then France, as the two countries most closely involved in the war. The more I began to look, though, the more I realized what a huge quantity of material there was on my own doorstep.

Most of us know of Liverpool's connection with the Civil War. The city and its surroundings have an enormous number of sites with Civil War associations, while the Merseyside Maritime Museum has a rich collection of Civil War documents, as well as paintings, models and artifacts illustrating the naval side of the war. If London cannot quite compete with Liverpool, a little investigation soon reveals how many buildings and monuments with Civil War associations still survive in the capital, too. All over Britain, from Scotland to Cornwall, can be found the graves of Civil War veterans from both sides, and town libraries and county archives frequently turn out to offer the researcher unexpected treasures. Across the English Channel, Paris is now little more than two hours from London by train. Judah P. Benjamin, John Slidell and Dudley Mann are all buried there, and the number of surviving buildings associated with the Civil War, while less extensive than London's, is still impressive. Cherbourg, three hours by ferry from Portsmouth, has numerous traces of the *Alabama*'s visit and the battle of June 19, 1864, as well as the very useful naval archives. In Frankfurt, Germany, is the tomb of the only foreign national to reach the rank of major general in either army. A little further afield, in Istanbul, is the grave of perhaps the most successful blockade-runner captain in the war, while yet further afield is Cairo, where one can still follow in the footsteps of those Civil War veterans who served in the Egyptian Army in the 1870s.

In the last 100 years, there have been a number of books dealing with the international dimensions of the Civil War. E.D. Adams's *Great Britain and the American Civil War* finally appeared (initially only in England) in 1925, even though its author had actually begun work on it in 1913. It was followed in 1931 by Frank Owsley's *King Cotton Diplomacy*. Rather more recently, Dean Mahin published *One War at a Time* in 1999. Howard Jones's *Blue and Gray Diplomacy* came out in 2010, the same year as Amanda Foreman's *A World on Fire*, which started life, according to its author, as a history of the British volunteers in the Civil War but swiftly turned into an account of the British-American experience during the war. In 2011, two books by the young French historian Stève Sainlaude, *Le Gouvernement Impérial et la Guerre de Sécession* and *La France et la Confédération Sudiste*, looked at the reaction to the war of Napoleon III's government. Finally, 2015 saw the publication of Don Doyle's *The Cause of All Nations*, which is actually subtitled *"An International History of the Civil War."*

These volumes, and several others, set out to provide a general history of such subjects as Union and Confederate diplomatic efforts and relations with foreign powers, primarily Britain and France, the response to the war of the foreign powers—again, primarily Britain and France, although Don Doyle looks rather further afield—and so on. This book, however, is not one of them. What it is, rather, is a compilation of separate pictures of specific individual aspects of the international side of the Civil War, snapshots or vignettes which, when looked at together, may add some pieces to the overall jigsaw puzzle.

In researching and writing the chapters which make up this book, I have tried to keep in mind two basic principles. When I was at Cambridge University, one of our lecturers was the great Professor Denys Page. Whenever he was talking about a Greek play, and when there was some doubt about the interpretation of a passage, his response was always the same: "Let us see what is in the text." In other words, it is important not to rely on someone else's commentary but to see what the person actually wrote; what does he actually say? What is he telling us? Secondly, many of us will know, from experience, how very difficult it is to understand a battle without walking the field, no matter how good the maps of the battle may be and how vivid the accounts are. I had read many detailed reports of the battle of Gettysburg, but it was not until I finally visited the battlefield in 2002 that I was able actually to understand the battle. In the preparation of this book, then, I have tried, in every case, to "see what is in the text" and, wherever possible, also to "walk the field," whether it be the walk up from the Bosphorus ferry to Hobart Pasha's last resting place or the long climb which the Civil War veterans in the Egyptian Army made daily from downtown Cairo, where they stayed, up to the Citadel, where they worked.

If we take Chapters 9 and 10 as an example, there have been numerous accounts in English over the years of the CSS *Alabama*'s arrival at Cherbourg and the sea battle of June 19, 1864. Why is this one different? From the moment that the *Alabama* arrived off the Cherbourg breakwater until at least two days after the battle, the local Préfet Maritime, Vice-Admiral Augustin Dupouy, sent detailed dispatches to the Minister in Paris informing him of the latest developments and asking for orders. Copies of all of these are in the naval archives (Service Historique de la Défense) in Cherbourg, as is the very full report of the French naval doctor who treated the wounded from both ships. No one writing in English, however, appears to have made any use of these at all—with the curious exception of the authors of the catalogue accompanying an exhibition at the Metropolitan Museum of Art, New York, in 2003 titled "Manet and the American Civil War."[1] In addition to all the sources in English, then, known and not so well known, I have made full use of all the various French sources, including a professional naval officer's report and a novelist's breathless account. In addition, over the last ten years I have made eight visits to Cherbourg, taking the three-hour ferry across the English Channel in order to spend two or three nights in the town. On these visits, apart from consulting the naval archives, I have tramped the streets of Cherbourg in search of more sites associated with the battle, taken the boat out several times to the fortified breakwater, climbed the Montagne du Roule above the town, where many of the populace gathered to watch the battle, and walked the five miles along the coast to Querqueville, up to the Chapelle de St-Germain, the favored vantage point of those who could afford a carriage, and then down again and out to the West Pass, through which the *Alabama* sailed on the morning of the battle.

I should like to think, then, that this book will add to our knowledge of the Civil War. I should also like to think, though, that it might inspire readers to go out and search for themselves for traces of the Civil War overseas. Many will not be aware that there is still substantial interest in the war beyond the shores of the United States. In Britain, we have the American Civil War Round Table (United Kingdom), which traces its origins back to 1953. The Belgian equivalent is the Confederate Historical Association of Belgium, which, despite its name, is a nonpartisan study group. Australia, which saw the visit of the CSS *Shenandoah* in early 1865, has not one but two Round Tables: the American Civil War Round Table of Australia and the American Civil War Round Table of Queensland. There are also Civil War enthusiasts in Italy, Norway and elsewhere. At the Pickett's Mill visitor center, in 2002, I was amazed to come upon a German family asking for information on the battle, and in 2018 the name just above mine in the visitors' book at the Mississippi Final Stands Interpretive Center at Brice's Crossroads was that of a French couple.

There is thus still significant overseas interest in the Civil War, even if on occasion the war is viewed through the prism of local political prejudices. The U.S. literary critic Leslie Fiedler, for example, recalled once attending a showing of *Gone with the Wind* in Athens, Greece. Throughout the performance, the audience of Greek leftists alternately cheered the Confederates and booed the Yankees. Similarly, the cover of a French book about the *Alabama* published in 2001 summarizes the author's view: "The Civil War is not over and it directly affects Europe today, threatened by the globalist dreams of Yankee imperialism."[2]

There are also still numerous physical traces of the Civil War both in Europe and beyond. Some of them will appear in the following chapters, but there are many others besides, and they often emerge unexpectedly. In the port of Ciudadela, for example, the beautiful former capital of the Spanish island of Minorca, is a bust of David Farragut, with an inscription in Catalan and English, his father having emigrated from the island. In Stockholm, right across from Sweden's Royal Dramatic Theater (Kungliga Dramatiska Teatern), stands a fine monument to

Bust of Farragut, Ciudadela, Minorca (author's photograph).

John Ericsson, designer of the original *Monitor*, while in Bombay the visitor to the Prince of Wales Museum is surprised suddenly to come upon a portrait of Lincoln by the American artist Daniel Huntington.

Earlier versions of the bulk of the chapters in this book appeared in *Crossfire*, the magazine of the American Civil War Round Table (United Kingdom). Two started their lives as talks given by me to the Round Table, and two or three were published, in English or French or both, in *CHAB News* in Belgium. All have been revised, extended and, where necessary, rewritten. Chapter 2 originally appeared, in its entirety, in July 2006 in the magazine *North and South*.

At this point, a word of apology is probably in order. First of all, I must apologize for the intrusion, here and there in this book, of the personal. That was, unfortunately, unavoidable in the account of my journeys on the trail of Patrick Cleburne in Ireland and England, but it was also difficult to avoid on a number of other occasions. Secondly, I hope that I will be forgiven for, in the final two

Monument to Ericsson, Stockholm (author's photograph).

chapters, breaking my own self-imposed rule and crossing the Atlantic in order to tell the story of two individual soldiers from North Carolina: an infantry officer and a private in the cavalry. My only justification is that, in each case, the inspiration came from a document which I had bought in England: a payslip belonging to the officer and a letter written by the private. Nevertheless, they are interesting stories in themselves, and stories which have not been told before, while the second one has a curious and intriguing twist to it.

In researching and writing this book, I have received help, advice and support from a number of individuals and institutions both in the United States and elsewhere. At the risk of sounding like an Oscar winner, I should like to thank the following in particular:

In the United States: Alabama Department of Archives and History; Dr. Chester (Chet) Bennett, M.D., Dublin, Ohio; Dr. Germain Bienvenu, Hill Memorial Library, Louisiana State University; Dr. Norman C. Delaney; Professor Don H. Doyle, University of South Carolina; Elizabeth Dunn, David M. Rubenstein Library, Duke University; Professor John Dunn, Valdosta State University; Dr. Norman B. Ferris; Robert L. Folstein, the Jacques Offenbach Society; Mauriel Phillips Joslyn, the Patrick Cleburne Society; Dr. William Kurtz, Nau Center for Civil War History, the University of Virginia; Princeton University Library; David M. Rooks III, Chapel Hill, North Carolina; Michael Schreiber, the Nicaragua Study Group; Kathy Shoemaker, Rose Library, Emory University; Bruce Vail, Baltimore; the late Glen Wiche, Chicago, a friend for over 50 years; the Wilson Library, the University of North Carolina at Chapel Hill; Sharon Wolff, Cammie G. Henry Research Center, Northwestern State University, Louisiana.

In Britain: my friends and colleagues in the American Civil War Round Table (United Kingdom) Robin Ansell, Greg Bayne, Michael Hammerson, Tony Margrave and Maurice Rigby; the Bank of England Archive; the late Gordon Batchelor; Burnley Library, Lancashire; Dr. Amanda Foreman; Lincolnshire Archives; the late Dr. Peter Odgers; Dr. Simon Rennie, the University of Exeter; Geoff Watts, Southampton; the Wren Library, Trinity College, Cambridge University.

In Ireland: Daniel J. Murphy, Killumney.

In Belgium: Daniel Frankignoul, Gérard (Gerald) Hawkins and Hubert Leroy, the Confederate Historical Association of Belgium.

In France: the late Christopher Dickey, Paris; Joë Guesnon, one of the original divers on the wreck of the *Alabama*; François Zoonekyndt, Service Historique de la Défense, Cherbourg.

Finally, I owe a special debt of gratitude to my wife, Christine. Not only has she tolerated my Civil War obsession for more than 40 years; she has actually indulged it. Three times she has sent me back to the battlefields as a birthday present, while yet another birthday present was a flight to Frankfurt to visit the two Civil War graves there. Some years ago, when we were over in Chattanooga for a family wedding, she even allowed me to drag her round the battlefield of Chickamauga (an experience which she assures me is unfortunately unlikely ever to be repeated). I owe her enormous and eternal thanks for everything.

1

Alexander Beresford Hope and the Civil War

The traditional view of British support for the Confederacy is that it was largely the preserve of the upper classes, who felt greater kinship with an agrarian and aristocratic South than with the industrial North, while the broad mass of the population, hating slavery, supported the Union. Yet it has been known for some time that the true picture was very much less simple. The almost universal support for the South in Liverpool, for example, however embarrassing this may be for some of the present-day inhabitants of that city, is attested to by friend and foe alike. As later chapters will indicate, it is clear that the Confederacy could count on the sympathy of a much more representative cross section of British society than is usually admitted even today. One prominent sympathizer who exemplifies perfectly the traditional pattern, however, is A.J.B. Beresford Hope.

Beresford Hope was born on January 25, 1820, the third son of Thomas and Louisa Hope, and was christened Alexander James Beresford, Beresford being the name of his mother's family. The Hopes were of Scots descent but had been residents for some 200 years in Holland, where they had a successful mercantile and banking business. With other members of the family, Thomas Hope left Holland in 1796, after the occupation of the country by the armies of Revolutionary France, and settled in England. Here, his wealth enabled him to live the life of a country gentleman and to pursue his interest in art. He accumulated an outstanding collection of paintings, sculptures and vases and wrote several learned monographs on aspects of art and architecture. He is better known today, however, for the highly successful romantic novel *Anastatius*, which was published anonymously in 1819. So untypical was this work of the staid and respectable Hope that it was immediately attributed to Byron—who later declared himself furious, first, that he had not written it and, second, that Thomas Hope had.

Thomas Hope died in 1831, whereupon his widow married her first cousin, William Carr Beresford, Viscount Beresford, famous as the commander of the Duke of Wellington's Portuguese troops during the Peninsular War against Napoleon. Relations between Lord Beresford and his stepson seem to have been close and affectionate. On Louisa's death, Alexander took over responsibility for the care of his stepfather in his declining years. When Beresford himself died, in 1854, he left the estate of Bedgebury Park, in Kent, and the remainder of his extensive possessions to his stepson, who at once added the marshal's name to his own, thus becoming Alexander James Beresford Beresford Hope. (Although others tended later to hyphenate the name, Beresford Hope himself does not appear ever to have done so.)[1]

Beresford Hope was educated at Harrow School and at Trinity College, Cambridge, at both of which he won several prizes, in particular for Latin composition. In this connection, it is interesting to note that Richard Washington Corbin, the Franco-Virginian author of *Letters of a Confederate Officer to His Family in Europe*, who also attended Trinity College (albeit some years after Beresford Hope), sent his sons to both Harrow and Trinity.[2] Given Beresford Hope's strong Confederate sympathies and his close lifelong links with the University in general and his own college in particular, it is not inconceivable that the two men met at some stage and even that Beresford Hope suggested the choice of school.

Alexander Beresford Hope (author's collection).

On graduating from Cambridge in 1841, Beresford Hope, like many another Victorian gentleman, was free of the need to work for his livelihood. He inherited from his stepfather a substantial income and from his father a passion for art; possession of the one made it possible for him to indulge in the other. He was particularly interested in church architecture and decoration. A prominent member of the Ecclesiological Society, which championed the Gothic Revival in England, he restored, at his own expense, St. Augustine's Abbey, Canterbury, and commissioned the building of All Saints, Margaret Street, London, perhaps the supreme example of Victorian religious architecture.[3]

Unlike his father, however, Beresford Hope did not neglect more mundane matters. As early as 1841, he was elected to Parliament from Maidstone in the Conservative interest, and he remained a member of Parliament, with two brief intervals, for the rest of his life. In 1842, he married Lady Mildred Cecil, daughter of the Marquess of Salisbury and elder sister of Queen Victoria's later prime minister; the marriage linked Beresford Hope to one of the most important noble families in England and can only have encouraged his political ambitions. It was as an Independent Conservative, however, that he was elected, and independent he remained throughout his career. When voting, he invariably ignored the blandishments of the party whips in order to follow the dictates of his conscience—which tended to take a robustly reactionary line on most questions. Thus, we find him, in 1859, stating his "undying, undeviating, and unmitigated opposition" to a bill permitting a widower to marry his dead wife's sister. In 1867, he equally fiercely opposed the Reform Act introduced by the Conservative government, accusing Disraeli of being more liberal than the Liberals and referring to him scathingly as "the Asian mystery." Disraeli, in return, congratulated his opponent in a mocking allusion to Beresford Hope's Dutch origins and clumsy delivery on his "Batavian grace."[4]

The outbreak of the war in America coincided with one of the two periods in Beresford Hope's life when he was not in Parliament, since he failed to win a seat in the 1859 election and was not reelected until July 1865. This was unfortunate for the Confederacy, since he was thus deprived of a natural platform for his views, which were decidedly pro–Confederate from the start. Lacking his usual forum, then, Beresford Hope resorted to giving public lectures on the war, delivering three lengthy talks on the subject in Kent in November 1861, January 1862 and January 1863, and afterwards publishing these as pamphlets in order that they might reach the widest audience possible.

The earliest of his lectures, *A Popular View of the American Civil War*, starts with a general history of North America and an outline of the federal system of government. Beresford Hope points out the resemblance of the American Constitution to that of Great Britain, "having its two Houses of Legislature, its old Saxon privileges, its common and statute law, and its trial by jury" but laments, "all these glorious bulwarks of freedom, all these well poised safeguards of order, are alike overruled and trampled down by that miserable, levelling democracy and universal suffrage which is so rapidly landing the Northern States in a perfectly Assyrian despotism." In the South, on the other hand, while there is "the same universal suffrage among the whites," "owing to the large landed proprietors and the condition of the country, the mob has not the same power." He goes on to discuss in some detail the events leading up to the war, justifying secession by reference to 1776 and, in a nod to his own Dutch ancestry, to the "Glorious Revolution" of 1688 which brought William of Orange to the throne of England. He attacks the "abominable acts of tyranny" of the government of Abraham Lincoln, whom he labels "an incapable pretender" and dismisses as "a bargee, rail-splitter, and attorney" (the first two being clearly less reprehensible, in Beresford Hope's eyes, than the last), contrasting Lincoln's physical appearance unfavorably with that of the "bold ... daring, yet politic statesman" Jefferson Davis. He states his conviction: "The inevitable design of Providence appears to be that the country should be divided into at least four great commonwealths" and finishes by comparing the North, "the hotbed of anarchy," with the South, "fighting with one heart and mind for its independence from a hateful thraldom."

Returning to his theme some two months later in a lecture at Hawkhurst, Beresford Hope developed his arguments in favor of the South's right to secede. He repeated his view that the North had "violated private liberties" and condemned "that barbarous method of offensive warfare, unparalleled in history and revolting to humanity, which destroys for ever a great mart of trade and harbour of refuge open to the ships of the world, by sinking a stone fleet at its mouth." This time, he also stressed that it was in Britain's interests that the South should win—"the interests of England are what I care for in entering upon the argument." Reminding his hearers of "the lawless and piratical outrage which was perpetrated by Capt. Wilkes on the British flag," he ended by outlining his vision of the future. A Southern victory, aided by British recognition, would result in "gradual freedom for the slave, a liberal conservative constitution growing out of unbridled democracy, free trade with a boundless expanse of the richest soil, from which English mills and English ships will reap a golden harvest, the high civilization of old Europe pervading a people prepared and grateful for its influence, and a true ally, not only for England on the Channel, but for England on the St. Lawrence." In the event of a Union victory, however, he could see "the worst passions of an unchained democracy let loose to work out its dream of universal insult and promiscuous conquest, or else a military despotism placing its iron yoke upon an enslaved people."[5]

No British supporter of the Confederacy, however, could hope to avoid for long the question of slavery, and Beresford Hope made no attempt to do so. His third lecture, indeed, given at Maidstone in early 1863, concentrated largely upon this subject. He had already referred, in his earlier lectures, to "the unhappy, the abominable institution of slavery" and expressed himself as "hating … in common with all my countrymen, from the bottom of my heart, that detestable system." Like other British sympathizers with the Confederacy, however, such as James Spence and Colonel Fremantle, he was able to reconcile his dislike of slavery with his admiration and support for the South. His own attitude towards the workers on his Bedgebury estate was paternalistic in the extreme—he planned at one stage, for example, to build a model village for them in the neighboring woods, with a chapel, a "good cheap shop" and, in addition, a reformatory school, whose reluctant occupants would be encouraged to "create a fresh farm in the heart of the woods while reclaiming the moor and bog, an ideal training for future emigrants"[6]—and he undoubtedly saw the typical Southern plantation owner as having the same sense of responsibility towards his charges.

His chief arguments were that the South had inherited the system of slavery through no fault of its own, that slavery, as practiced in the South, was "not so generally cruel as many believe," that the Negro was treated a great deal worse in the Northern States than in the South and, finally, that a Southern victory would lead to gradual emancipation. In support of the second of these points, while repeating that slavery is "a curse and a misfortune," he states that nevertheless "the best of the slaveowners make its chains as light as possible—they educate their blacks, they make them Christians." "In the South," he tells us, "the slave … is well treated; in social matters he is regarded as a fellow creature; he kneels at the same altar as the white man, and travels in the same train." Compare this with the situation in the North where "the church, the tavern, the railway car, which the white man frequents, are prohibited to the free black, who is treated with as much aversion and loathing as if he were a loathsome reptile." For this reason, "the slaves have stood by their owners, and are zealous for Dixie." Of course, there were slaveholders who abused their power, but such occurrences were rare. One such abuse was the separation of families; this was "in practice an exception, … seldom carried out," but "the bare possibility of such an iniquity ought to be stopped altogether." Here, however, Beresford Hope was able to adduce a recent pastoral of the Confederate Episcopal Church in which the bishops made precisely this point and proclaimed the duty of "the masters of the country" to arrange things so as to "prevent all necessity for the separation of parents and children, and of husbands and wives."

On the question of emancipation, while Beresford Hope wanted "as much as any one to see the Negroes free," it "must be gradual, not sudden." "Immediate emancipation" would mean "bloodshed, outrage, destruction of property, and perpetual starvation over the South." Lincoln's Emancipation Proclamation (which Beresford Hope refers to sarcastically as "a noble document!") "enfranchises all the slaves over whom the United States have no authority, and keeps in bondage all the slaves in the Border States, and those portions of the Confederate States over which the United States' armies are dominant." In fact, "the enfranchisement of the slave is not a question to be settled off in an emancipating proclamation nor a sensation novel" but something which could "only be dealt with by men who have lived in the country where it [i.e., slavery] prevails, men who have felt its evils while they understand its workings." A Confederate victory would allow the people of the South to be free of the pressure of the abolitionists in the North "by embarking upon the gradual liberation of their slaves, to place themselves in full accord with English feeling." An independent South would "perforce be brought into intimate relations with Europe," and the force of European public opinion would "irresistibly compel it to change its course with regard to slavery." "I honestly and entirely believe," he tells us, "that the cause which will tend to the confirmation of all the evils of slavery, is that of the North, and that the cause which is most likely to prove a benefit to the slave, and in the end relieve him of his shackles, is that of the South."

Finally, Beresford Hope appeals to his audience's feeling of kinship with the South. While "the Southern States are to a great extent communities of Englishmen still living in the 18th century," "the Northerners are by this time Englishmen of no century at all, but a nationality partly original and partly a tessellation." He ends his third and last lecture with a plea for immediate recognition of "the independence and sovereignty of the Confederate nation on its own merits." His concluding sentence, with its biblical reference, is curiously reminiscent, to a modern ear, of Martin Luther King: "They have passed the Red Sea—shall we never give them a hand that they may reach the promised land?"[7]

Beresford Hope did not, however, confine his rhetorical efforts on behalf of the Confederacy to his home county of Kent. On October 16, 1863, for example, he addressed a crowded meeting of the Southern Club at Liverpool, the event being fully reported in *The Times* of London the following day. Claiming that his speech was "intended for the Confederate ear," he devoted the greater part of it to refuting a recent statement by the Foreign Secretary, Earl Russell, that the majority in England now sympathized with the United States. He disagreed with "the noble Earl" and challenged those who denied "the sympathies of England were unmistakably with the Southern States of America" to "perform the most difficult of all logical operations, the proving of a negative." In support of his view, he adduced the reaction in the country to the death of "Stonewall" Jackson, "which had excited almost as much regret, and his life as much admiration, as that of our own Havelock"[8] and the universally favorable treatment in the British press of Southern statesmen and generals. Furthermore, if Lord Russell had been in the House of Commons, "he would have heard his political chief, Lord Palmerston, brand the acts of Butler as 'infamous' … the strongest word that had ever been used in the Legislature by a Prime Minister of England against the chosen General of an ally with whom we had not quarrelled." Although the speaker suffered, on three or four occasions, from the attentions of a lone heckler, his sallies were greeted by the rest of his hearers, according to *The Times*, with "cheers" and "laughter," and his introduction at one point of an Irish joke with "great laughter."

Turning to "the ticklish question" of slavery, he congratulated his "Confederate friends present" because "the practical working of the system … was better understood in England now than it was some years ago." "All the newspapers of the day" admitted "the black peasant of the Southern States of America was as well clothed, as well fed, as well sent to church, as any peasant in the world," although this did not mean "the condition of those peasants" could not be improved. In short, the "intellectual channels" of England had decided "whether … slavery was or was not defensible in itself, there was no blame to the actual inheritors of the system" who, "taken all round, were men who generally did work out that system in a spirit of philanthropy and of wisdom."

Finally, Beresford Hope, mindful of his audience, mentioned the Laird rams. "There had been certain questions about certain very magnificent ships that were building, it was said for a French house. He knew no more of those rams than this…. He had read that they were for a French firm, and had very Mahomedan appellations. [Cheers.] That was all he knew of them; and that was all anybody knew of them. [Roars of laughter.] These ships with Mahomedan names were supposed by some as likely to lead to a change in the system of our international law…. It was impossible that such could be the case [Cheers], and he could give them the very best authority for saying that such could not be the case. [Cheers.]" Here Beresford Hope proceeded to read out extracts from a speech by the same Russell in February 1858, vehemently opposing the Conspiracy to Murder Bill. The government of the time had introduced this bill under pressure from France, and Russell had expressed himself "shocked by some of the declarations made in the course of this debate, by which it seemed that the favour of a foreign Power was of more value to England than the maintenance of her ancient prestige…. It is easy to ask for a mild measure at first to satisfy a foreign Power. At the same time, even any demand of this kind naturally rouses the jealousy and susceptibility of the British people…. If I were to vote for the introduction of this Bill I should feel shame and humiliation." Having thus cunningly turned Russell's own words against him, Beresford Hope assured his audience, "England would brook contempt from Seward, and Sumner, and Lincoln, and the Northern States still less than brook it from that France whom she had often hated, but whom in the battlefields of Europe she had never ceased to respect. [Cheers.]"

He concluded by saying "he had detained them long, but he felt that he had not occupied them fruitlessly if he had contributed one iota to that object which was his hope and prayer,—the consolidation of the kindly feeling and the good understanding which had grown up between England and those most ancient British colonies, her dearest and eldest children, Virginia and the Carolinas [loud and reiterated cheers]." James Spence then moved for a vote of thanks, which occasioned more cheers, and the meeting broke up.[9]

Meanwhile, a Southern Independence Association had been formed in Manchester shortly before this, on October 5, 1863, with Lord Wharncliffe as president. When a London branch was organized two months later, Beresford Hope, as one of the prime movers behind this, was a natural choice for chairman.[10] Almost exactly a year after his address to the Southern Club, he was back in Liverpool for the Southern Bazaar, more properly the Bazaar in Aid of the Southern Prisoners Relief Fund, which was held at St. George's Hall from October 18 to October 22, 1864, under the auspices of the Southern Independence Association. Beresford Hope's wife, Lady Mildred, was one of the "lady patronesses" of this affair, and she and Beresford Hope stayed for the five days of the bazaar with Mr. and Mrs. Frederick Hull on Rodney Street. The 12 stalls at the bazaar had each been given the name of a Confederate State (including Kentucky but not Missouri), and Lady Mildred and Mrs. Hull, with the aid of the female members of their families, were responsible for Tennessee. According to *The Liverpool Daily Post*, Beresford Hope, an early visitor on the opening day, "made extensive purchases." Since the Tennessee stall had, in the opinion of the reporter, "one of the best collections of goods in the room," it seems probable that Beresford Hope's purchases contributed to the stall's total takings for the day of £200. The bazaar raised, in all, nearly £21,000.[11] Six months later, the Confederacy collapsed.

Beresford Hope was now free to concentrate on British politics. On July 12, 1865, he was returned to parliament from Stoke-on-Trent, and three years later he achieved his ambition of being chosen by the electors of the University of Cambridge, whom he continued to represent until his death. He was thus able, once again, to give Parliament and country the benefit of his thoughts on a wide range of issues and was prominent enough to merit, in 1870, a caricature by "Ape" in the pages of *Vanity Fair*. This picture, inevitably titled "Batavian Grace," shows a stout Victorian gentleman with a bushy beard, a monocle and a somewhat irritable expression. The ironic tone of the accompanying text suggests that, to some at least of his contemporaries, Beresford Hope's tendency to see himself as an expert on almost any subject was a source of some amusement. He was not, however, without a sense of humor himself. Turning to fiction late in life, he produced two successful novels, *Strictly Tied Up* (1880) and *The Brandreths* (1882), of which *The Times* said that they gave "many smartly-written and amusing descriptions of society in the present day."[12]

St. George's Hall, Liverpool, scene of the Southern Bazaar of October 1864 (author's photograph).

Beresford Hope's support for the Confederacy did not end, however, with Appomattox—or even Durham Station. He had decided at the outset that the South's cause was just and saw no reason to change his mind simply because Fate appeared to disagree. His London residence, Arklow House, Connaught Place, had been a rendezvous for Confederate officials, agents and sympathizers throughout the war; Yancey, Mason, Bulloch, Hotze, Spence and Edwin De Leon had all been welcomed there.[13] With the end of the war, "broken-down Confederates found their way in swarms to England," and Beresford Hope continued to offer them the hospitality of his home.[14] He was also very much concerned at this time with a project to produce a statue, paid for by British sympathizers, of "Stonewall" Jackson. This was something which, in fact, he had suggested soon after Jackson's death; 4,000 guineas had been subscribed and a sculptor found, but the end of the war, together with the artist's other commissions, caused the work to be suspended. Former Confederates now encouraged Beresford Hope to revive the plan, and the statue was finally shipped over to Virginia and unveiled in Richmond on October 26, 1875, before an enthusiastic crowd. There was a balance in the fund of £243, which Beresford Hope, as treasurer, sent to Virginia to be invested as seemed best. This was eventually used to produce two gold medals to be presented each year to the two most distinguished graduates of the Virginia Military Institute. The medals, each bearing the inscription "Jackson-Hope

Medal, the Gift of English Gentlemen," are still awarded today.[15] It was perhaps as a result of this that Beresford Hope received honorary doctorates from both Washington and Lee University and what *The Times*, in his obituary, referred to as "the University of South Tennessee" (in fact the University of the South at Sewanee, Tennessee).[16]

It is hardly surprising, then, that when Jefferson Davis landed in Liverpool in August 1868, at the start of his trip to England, Beresford Hope hastened to put his house at his disposal. His offer was declined, but the two men were able to meet when Davis arrived in London in early September, staying initially, according to *The Times*, in lodgings at No. 36 Clarges Street, off Piccadilly, a short carriage ride from Connaught Place. From this time on, they maintained a friendly, if sporadic, correspondence which lasted until Beresford Hope's death in 1887.[17] On July 4, 1869, for example, Beresford Hope wrote to Davis, by then living at 18 Upper Gloucester Place, begging him not to worry about "the conventional hour for visiting" ("for we are always glad to have the pleasure of seeing one for whom we have so high an admiration & regard"), regretting that Lady Mildred had been "really very ill" and, therefore, unable to see the former president a few days earlier and, finally, pressing Davis to agree to a date for his family's visit to Bedgebury and suggesting the second week in August—"& we expect a *good* visit."[18] Some 12 years later, on August 7, 1881, we find Beresford Hope writing to thank Davis for sending him a copy of *The Rise and Fall of the Confederate Government*, which Beresford Hope had already reviewed in his weekly magazine, *The Saturday Review*. Lady Mildred had died in Nice in March of that year, and Beresford Hope had brought out a second edition of *Strictly Tied Up* as a memorial to her; he begged Davis to accept a copy.[19] One of the last letters Beresford Hope ever wrote, indeed, was to Jefferson Davis. In this, dated July 10, 1887, and written from Arklow House, Beresford Hope thanks

Arklow House, Beresford Hope's London residence (author's photograph).

Davis for a newspaper which the former president of the Confederacy had sent him, complains of his recent "serious illness," refers to "that maniac Gladstone" and asks to be "most kindly remembered" to Mrs. Davis.[20]

Alexander Beresford Hope died on October 20, 1887, and was buried at Christ Church, Kilndown, a short distance across the fields from Bedgebury, six days later. He was laid to rest next to his wife in an ornate Victorian tomb just outside the South wall of the church which his stepfather, Marshal Beresford, had built, and he had embellished. A special train was commissioned to bring mourners down from London, and *The Times*, in its account of the funeral, published a list of the more important of these—a list which it had hastily to emend the following day, having omitted three of the most important.[21] There are no obviously Confederate names on the list, but it would be pleasant to think that those Southerners who heard the news and who knew of Beresford Hope spared a thought and a prayer for an Englishman who had never wavered in his support for the Confederacy and who had done all that was within his power to advance the cause of Southern independence.

2

A Philosopher's Defense of the Confederacy

Among the papers of the Cambridge philosopher Henry Sidgwick in the Library of Beresford Hope's alma mater, Trinity College, are seven letters, ranging in date from September 1863 to March 1867, from Sidgwick's friend Jermyn Cowell, son of the British economist and Confederate sympathizer John Welsford Cowell. The elder Cowell, who will appear prominently in a later chapter, had represented the Bank of England in the United States from the autumn of 1837 until the middle of 1839; during this time, he had become acquainted with John C. Calhoun and other prominent Southerners, and on the outbreak of the Civil War he lost no time in urging on the British government and people the need for recognition of the Confederacy, writing several pamphlets on the subject. From his son's letters to Sidgwick, it is clear that Jermyn Cowell fully shared his father's views on the rights and wrongs of the conflict. Four of the seven letters deal with the war, and the first of them is a long and carefully argued exposition of the writer's reasons for siding with the South.

John Jermyn Cowell was born in London on January 30, 1838, some three months after his father's arrival in Philadelphia. He was educated at Westminster School, where he was a Queen's Scholar,[1] and (like a number of other Confederate sympathizers) at Trinity College, Cambridge, from which he graduated in 1860. It was at Trinity that he met and became friendly with Henry Sidgwick, a brilliant scholar who, although a few months younger than Cowell, had gone up to Cambridge a year before him, at the age of 17. The two young men shared an interest in philosophy and a youthful desire to put the world to rights. They were also deeply interested, like so many other Victorians, in spiritualism, attending a number of séances together, although they were properly skeptical of the more extravagant claims of some of the fashionable mediums of the day. Cowell at least, however, found time also for more active pursuits; he was a keen climber, being elected to the Alpine Club in 1860 and serving as secretary in 1863–1864.[2]

Immediately upon his graduation in 1859, Sidgwick was elected a Fellow of Trinity; he remained at the college until his death in 1900. Cowell, graduating a year later, was admitted to Lincoln's Inn and then called to the bar in 1864.[3] As will be seen, however, he had little time to practice as a lawyer.

Trinity College, Cambridge; John Jermyn Cowell, his father and Beresford Hope all studied here (author's photograph).

As mentioned above, in the first of his letters to Sidgwick he sets out in detail his reasons for supporting the South and opposing the North's war of invasion. Knowing his audience, Cowell argues from a legal and philosophical standpoint. Since his objective is, if possible, to convince his friend, he attempts throughout to maintain a calm, rational tone, but he is unable to prevent his emotions from breaking through from time to time. The letter is worth quoting in full, both for the light which it throws on British attitudes to the war in general and as an example of the views of a young Cambridge graduate, a professed liberal in politics. The American Civil War aroused in Britain feelings no less passionate than those excited by the Spanish Civil War nearly three generations later—and probably a great deal more widespread, given the country's closer connection with America. Cowell's views may not have been universally shared, but he was certainly far from unique in holding them.

The letter covers 18 sides of paper and is written in a clear, legible hand. So far as I am aware, it has never before appeared in print. It is reproduced here by kind permission of the Master and Fellows of Trinity College. In preparing it for publication, I have made no changes to the text, even where, at one point, Cowell repeats a word. Similarly, I have not attempted to alter his somewhat idiosyncratic system of punctuation, preferring to let him speak for himself as much as possible. Here, then, is the authentic voice of a young Englishman, a passionate supporter of the Confederacy, speaking to us from 1863:

2. A Philosopher's Defense of the Confederacy

Royal Hotel. Deal. Kent
Tuesday, September 15; 1863.

Dear Sidg,

We had after all to give up our intended fishing trip to Scotland, as my father was taken ill with the gout so severely, that he was advised not to go very far from London, and to try some sea air. So we are here on a 3 weeks visit.

In my leisure time here I have been reflecting upon our difference of view as to the invasion and devastation of the Southern States; and I have regretted that I did not go more fully into the subject with you, during the pleasant 4 days that we passed together. But my chief reason for not doing so was my belief that, owing to our entire opposition of opinion as to the fundamental facts of the question, a reference to documents of admitted validity, was a necessary preliminary to any satisfactory discussion of the legal pleas, which you allege to justify that invasion. For a proper discussion of those pleas, the following three classes of documents are most available,—because they are of admitted validity on all sides—& they are probably sufficient.

1st. The Constitution of the United States.
2nd. The Interpretations of that Constitution pronounced by the Supreme Court of the United States.
3rd. The Constitutions of the individual States, and the Conditions upon which they severally entered into a Union with each other.

The first & third I have got at home, and I studied them when the invasion began. The second I have, in an imperfect form, in Story's (The American Judge's) works; these I have not studied, but I now intend to do so. Let us both study them, and at our next meeting thoroughly discuss the question.

I make this proposal for the following reason.

You and I each of us believe the other to be actuated by a sincere desire to benefit mankind; to ascertain their wants—especially their religious and moral wants, and to learn how best to direct his efforts to assist in satisfying those wants. On general principles we were agreed; (as all men must be who think of acting together;) we wished to strike at the passions which curse the world; which tempt men to sacrifice other men to their rapacity and ambition; to neglect justice, and subsist by violence. The horrible despotisms of the middle ages, and their modern representatives in Italy, Austria, & Russia, were our abomination. We were liberals—we execrated those who presumed anywhere to abase or maltreat, under the pretence of respect for "religion" or "order," people who only wished to be let alone, & be happy in their own way. We had no difficulty then in agreeing to condemn the French, for destroying the Roman Republic by violence in 1849; in spite of their pretence that that Republic had established a profoundly immoral & irreligious Government; to condemn Nicholas, for invading the Principalities on pretence that the Christianity of those, and other Turkish provinces, was in danger of destruction by an infidel & barbarian power[4]; or to condemn Austria in tyrannizing over Hungary, on the pretence that it was resisting God, who had authorized Franz Joseph to govern it. We condemned the attempts of England & Spain to conquer and maltreat their injured subjects in America, in 1777, & 1819.

Now arrives a new war—of appalling magnitude—among civilized people—creating indescribable slaughter & desolation—a war of invasion—to conquer people who only ask to be let alone within their own borders. I condemn this war, of course, as an inhuman aggression—but—to my indescribable confusion & disappointment, this crucial test divides us—and you admire what I execrate. The sense of this great gulf existing between the respective verdicts of our moral sentiments, on a question of overwhelming importance to mankind, has been a permanent discomfort in my mind, and a discouragement to my philanthropic hopes & aspirations. I say to myself; "here is going on a transaction productive of fearful evil; that evil results from a fearful crime on one side or the other; Sidgwick & I disagree as to which side is the guilty one; then how can we expect to agree on questions of less importance to humanity? & if he and I cannot agree—each being sincerely desirous of deciding right—how can any men ever be expected to agree? how can any good be done? what a thing is man?! &c &c" So I feel this startling divergence of our opinions to be a severe stumbling-block *in limine*[5] (—and you must feel the same on your side—) on our starting in our tentative career of hostility to the abuses that debase mankind. It will be a permanent discouragement in my mind, if our moral sentiments remain permanently in direct antagonism on this point; and I cannot but think that a more complete investigation of the question on both sides, might to some extent reconcile our views. It is for this reason that I suggest our studying the above-mentioned documents; which probably are to be found in the U. Library. I wish I could lend you our copies but I cannot do so, because my father is constantly in want of them for purposes of reference.

Another object of this letter is to submit to your notice the accompanying papers— (which I beg you will keep as long as you like—and then return to me). The Article in Barker's Review[6] gives a concise view of many most important details which I should be glad to hear your opinion upon. If you will fraternally pardon a candid confession on my part, I will tell you that my impression has all along been, that you took your side in the beginning, after a merely superficial view of the subject; that your sympathies were enlisted by the cry about slavery, so that you now find yourself committed to particular doctrines, on vastly important political questions which you have not examined for yourself. This impression was strengthened during our last conversations on the legality of secession, by your proposing to regard the States of the Union as "Municipalities," and your disposition to make light of their Titles of *Sovereign* States, as if it were only a question of words, and not of realities. Now of course I admit that on the whole question of the War you are as likely to be right as I am; but on this particular point I am sure you are wrong. De Tocqueville,[7] which you have read, carefully recognizes & records the Sovereignty of each State (one example of which you may find quoted in the Sat. Rev.[8] of Sept. 12, page 360). This question of Sovereignty is *the* fundamental question of the whole case; and to discuss American politics without appreciating the distinction between a municipality & a Sovereign State, is like discussing the British Constitution, and confusing the legislative power with the judicial. Everett[9] has been able to give you detailed accounts of the (newly invented) doctrine of the Republican party, who have been doing their best to falsify history on this point; and there has been nobody at Cambridge sufficiently well-informed on the specialties of the case, to refute him. To do so satisfactorily documents are necessary—but a general common-sense explanation of the nature of sovereignty is a simple affair. All communities are primâ facie, either Sovereign or Subject; a Sovereign Community possesses (within its own confines) possesses [*sic*] *every* Power, & every Right, except those which it has, by its own act, shared with, or delegated to, some other Person or Community: a Subject Community possesses *no* Power or Right, except those which have been allowed or given to it, by an antecedent Sovereign authority. An ordinary Municipality is such a Subject Community. England is a Sovereign State, and therefore no other State has any Power over individuals in England; but, by treaty with France, England has given France a Right to reclaim French criminals who are on English ground. When that Right is exercised England ceases to be in that case Sovereign *sole*; France is in that transaction equally, or rather superiorly, Sovereign; because her demand *must* be complied with. But that does not make England a Subject State; she is a Sovereign State, who has, on one particular subject, divested herself of her Sovereignty and granted it to some one else. Exactly analogous is the position of Virginia. In 1787 she was (you will admit) a Sovereign State; she then divested herself of certain specified parts of her Sovereignty, and granted them to an Agent, called the Federal Government; which, to that extent—but no further—acquired exactly the same kind of Sovereignty over Virginia, that France acquired over England by demanding and obtaining the arrest of a criminal. The Sovereign Grantor, Virginia, declares (please read the Act of Secession,) that all Powers not *expressly granted*, remain with her; and the Agent, the Federal Government, admits (please read the Constitution,) that it possesses no Powers except those which are *expressly granted*. All other Sovereign Powers *therefore* remain with Virginia alone, & she is *therefore* a Sovereign State. To make her out to be a Municipality, or a Subject State, is therefore hopeless. But before proceeding further—into the question of Secession—we must study those 3 classes of documents.

To turn now to the general question. I want you clearly to realize to yourself the principles of political morality to which (as it seems to me,) you are committing yourself. There are in reality *two separate* questions, which the Federals have designedly entangled, so as to confuse the public mind; but which the philosopher is bound to disentangle, and discuss separately, each on its own merits.

First Question. (if addressed to the Political jurist) Is it lawful? (if addressed to the liberal Philosopher) Is it moral? for the Federal Government to make War on a State which secedes?

Second Question. Is it Moral to Make War on a People because it will not abolish slavery?

These two Questions are entirely distinct; and each requires an answer, independently of the other. We will therefore, if you please, keep them distinct. We will discuss Q. First, without reference to Slavery; just as if it were the case of the State of Massachusetts, which attempted to secede in 1815; or of the Six New England States, which for 15 years the Abolition party urged to Secede; or of Illinois, for which State its Senator, one A. Lincoln, claimed the Right of Secession at pleasure, in a speech now lying before me. Q. Second, we will discuss without reference to any other causes of War—let us first find out whether the existence of slavery *alone* is a sufficient cause of War.

The first part of Q. First, "Is it lawful?," we must, as I have said, defer till a future meeting; but this much I assume you will at once concede to me. However lawful it may be for the Federal Gov. to make war upon a seceding Virginia; it cannot be more lawful than it was for England to make war upon rebelling Virginia in 1777, or than it would be for her to make war upon rebelling Canada or Australia now.

Now I ask you, "is it Morally right to make war on a large community of men because—threatening no one—they desire only to be left alone, and govern themselves." Surely a Liberal—one who seeks only the happiness and progress of mankind must answer—No. Surely every hater of tyranny must answer—No. What is the test to apply? This one—does making War in such a case tend to increase or diminish human happiness? if to increase it—then let all Liberals die the death, & let King Philip the Second & the Duke of Alva[10] rise up, and reign over us.

Whatever political institutions men establish, it is certain that, at some time, they will require to be altered; and if they are not altered then, human happiness will be diminished. The men who have striven to prevent alterations, desired by vast numbers of men, by fire and sword, have been the enemies & curses of the human race. ***In primis***[11] Charles V, Philip II, Louis XIV, George III. In America, after the experience of two clear generations, 8 millions of men desire to alter their political arrangements, and establish a new government, without threatening any other community or government. As usually happens, it is the interest of certain other men to thwart their desire; for which purpose they invade the country—and more—they destroy it—they destroy its harbours, burn its cities, break its agricultural instruments, drive out its population from their homes, slaughter their horses and cattle, cut down their orchards, throw burning naphtha into their houses *at midnight*, and, most horrible of all, let loose the Mississippi over regions as large as Scotland, and drown every living thing. For every one of these barbarities I will (if you please) give you, date, place, and authority. Is it a Liberal, is it a benevolent philosopher?

who will say it is *morally right* to subject a people to these horrors, or merely the ordinary horrors of invasion, because that people insists on its Natural Right to govern itself! Then—King Philip was a Liberal, & Alva benevolent; and miserable humanity is as far as ever from peace and goodwill towards men, on an earth where the best of men approve such deeds.

If you approve this invasion for this reason, you render it for ever necessary that political reformation should be effected only at the risk of a fearful & demoralizing war. The morality of the middle ages had progressed nearly as far as that. If you justify the conduct of the North in desolating a continent, because the rights of the Federal Gov. have been technically violated, much more easily can I justify such minor massacres as those of St Bartholomew, & the Macdonalds of Glencoe, in each of which cases the victims had undoubtedly violated the technical rights of their murderers.

No improvement on a large scale can ever be made without violating the technical rights of somebody. It is not the part of a well-wisher to mankind, to encourage that "somebody," to set the world on fire rather than waive his rights; the philosopher rather seeks to persuade men to waive their rights, and abate their selfish passions for the sake of others; "*Mollitque animos et temperat iras*."[12]

Therefore, by answering "Yes," to the 2nd part of Question First, a man declares himself the enemy of all peaceful political progress.

The answer to Question Second is a much more difficult one; and could probably be given with authority, only by a man with vast knowledge of history, & of men, and things. Still, as a matter of practical common-sense, it must be admitted that 9 men out of 10 would decide in the negative. In general I should urge arguments such as are devoted to this part of the subject in the Article in Barker's Review. I should say; it is not Moral to make War upon People who refuse to abolish Slavery, because the War is pretty sure to make more misery than it removes; it injures the general prosperity of both masters & slaves, and of all communities related to them. If the War fails, it does vast harm, & no good; if it succeeds, it does harm more vast, some theoretical good, but of practical good a very small amount indeed. It disorganizes Society—a most fearful evil–; it creates hatred on the part of the whites against the slaves; and, by a sudden liberation it demoralizes the slaves, who are unaccustomed to independent action, and their industry comes to an end. In fact the evils of a sudden military emancipation on a large scale are so obvious, that I suppose you will admit it is the worst possible way of emancipating slaves.

If any Power had made war on England in 1803, for refusing to abolish Slavery is it not certain that Emancipation would have been retarded by 30, 40, or 50 years? Do we make War on Brazil for not abolishing slavery at six months notice? Would not every wise man stigmatize such an act as a crime? What we do is to influence Brazil by persuasion & example; and she has made conventions with us, improving the condition of her slaves, and paving the way for emancipation 50 years hence. *That* is the only temperate and prudent way, & therefore (in dealing with interests so immense,) the only Moral way. Making war, is the way of furious fanatical men, who prefer the apparent triumph of a principle, to the real success of a measure. It is not Moral to run so fearful a risk of doing *unmitigated* harm. The Liberal Philosopher must condemn this attempt to play pitch & toss with the happiness of 8 millions of men against that of 4 millions.

Q. second is answered, as far as I can answer it in the limits of a letter; but I have only entertained it thro' deference for your (mistaken) opinion that the War was begun in order to free or benefit Slaves. Mr Lincoln's declarations to the contrary are repeated, and emphatic, & I know very well that only a few Northerners wish well to the negro. The rest of them who tout for European sympathy, are abandoned hypocrites beyond the reach of invective. But if you will only—if you will only—read the Declaration of Independence, and the solemn affirmation, "Governments derive their just Powers only from the Consent of the governed," you will hardly be surprised at my thinking that even those pretended emancipators are outdone, by the indescribable hypocrisy of the men, who, after devoting their voices for 50 years to the worship and glorification of that noble affirmation, and claiming for it and themselves the respect of the civilized world, now claim the respect of the world for repudiating their principles, and for attempting to impose a detested government upon 8 millions of men. Posterity will be aghast at an apostacy so unparalleled, & so revolting. Only by a thoroughly depraved people could such an inexpiable crime have been consummated—a people lost to every sense of honesty, *decency, and shame.*

Perhaps my dear Sidgwick I have written too vehemently—I have indeed written from the fullness of my heart; forgive me if I have said anything which pains you—you know such was not my intention. But it *is* my wish to rouse your earnest attention, and startle you into reviewing the whole matter from the beginning, in your own mind.

I have heard from Tawney[13]; he sails from Gravesend on Monday for India.

On Wednesday next I go down to stay a week on a visit in Norfolk and after that I spend ten days in Shropshire; so I shall be in London about the 15th of October when I begin reading with an Equity lawyer. So if you are in town about then come & look for me.

Ever yours affectionately
Jermyn Cowell

It is pleasant to record that the two young men did not allow their difference of opinion over the Civil War to affect their friendship. They continued to meet regularly, and Cowell continued to write to Sidgwick until his death. (Unfortunately, none of Sidgwick's letters to Cowell appears to have survived.) On January 30, 1864, for example, we find him writing to his friend as follows:

> Ten minutes after I saw you I met Tommy,[14] just returned from Chattanooga where he saw the battle of Nov. 26. 27. 28. He says the South is being conquered—but I am not a bit frightened.

On April 9, 1864, Cowell returns to the subject:

> I heard yesterday on good authority a piece of news which will please you; the mighty ones have determined to discountenance the South. Francis Joseph Maximilian & Napoleon have agreed that Mexico is not to recognize the Confederate States. I regret this because it may prolong the war; but it cannot now affect the final issue since the Confederates like the United Netherlands long ago and the Danes now have had to abandon all hope of assistance from their natural allies and have learned the painful lesson that "Who would be free *themselves* must strike the blow."
>
> I am making a collection of tit-bits of atrocity for my future history. I have Colonel Dahlgren's instructions, and also a choice morsel from New O.

The shock, when it came, was considerable. On April 23, 1865, Cowell wrote to Sidgwick:

> As to the cause of Southern independence I cannot trust myself to speak after to-day's news—my heart is too full of pity and admiration; and of horror and burning indignation against the most wicked and hypocritical tyrants known in modern history of whom you will I think some day feel ashamed when you see for what purpose they destroy thirteen sovereign republics and subjugate 8 millions of civilized men.

Still, however, he signs himself "Yours affectionately."

The final letter in the series is dated March 13, 1867, and written from 21 Grand Parade, a lodging house in St. Leonards on the Sussex coast. Cowell's father had died there suddenly a month earlier, and Cowell thanks Sidgwick for his letter of condolence, explains that he, too, has been very ill and expresses his aim to stay on in St. Leonards for the time being. It is not clear whether he ever returned to London, but on December 16 he himself died, a little further along the street at 3 Grand Parade; a few years earlier, this had been a private residence, but by now it had probably become another of the many lodging houses on Grand Parade.[15] Cowell was apparently buried in his father's grave[16] in the beautiful municipal cemetery high on a hill above Hastings, although the inscription on the grave, well enough preserved today, mentions only the elder Cowell. The cause of death was given as heart disease and congestion of the lungs, from both of which the doctor who examined the body diagnosed that Cowell had been suffering for several years.[17] Jermyn Cowell was 29 years old.

3

A Lively Meeting in Burnley

The myth of universal British working-class support for the North during the American Civil War, believed by even such a normally astute witness as Henry Hotze,[1] was punctured more than 60 years ago by the socialist historian Royden Harrison in his article "British Labour and the Confederacy."[2] The picture of the strength of pro–Southern sentiment among industrial workers which emerges from Harrison's study is a surprising one. There were almost certainly a number of possible reasons for this sympathy, but one factor appears simply to have been the opposition of some of the more radical elements in Victorian Britain to the kind of capitalism which they saw as represented by the North. Why, then, has the traditional myth persisted in spite of the evidence? Harrison explains this as at least partially the result of wishful thinking on the part of certain middle-class observers with an idealized view of international working-class solidarity. In the words of Peter d'A. Jones, "It told people what they wanted to believe." A little more recently, Mary Ellison's *Support for Secession* demonstrated the very widespread support for the Confederacy in Lancashire, the British region most affected by the war.[3] Finally, a brief but very useful article by Michael Brook, "Confederate Sympathies in North-East Lancashire, 1862–1864," looks more specifically at Burnley and the surrounding area.[4]

Brook's main source is *The Burnley Advertiser*, which, in his words, "stood both for Southern independence and the abolition of slavery. Its pro–Southern attitude was not extreme, and it was fair in giving space to the opposing view." The files of the paper in Burnley Library continue to provide a valuable source for the Civil War researcher, since they contain full reports of the numerous local meetings and lectures on what the paper invariably refers to as "the American question." The *Advertiser*'s accounts of these various gatherings reveal considerable support for the Confederacy right through 1863. When the American-born singer Henri Drayton gave his "comic and musical entertainment," titled "Federals and Confederates," in the Mechanics' Institution in Bacup in November 1863, his performance of "Dixie" with Albert Pike's words ("Southrons, hear your country call you") was "tremendously applauded." By the spring of 1864, however, this enthusiasm had waned, and Union speakers for the first time faced only minimal opposition.

The most detailed report in the paper of any of these meetings is that of the one held in Burnley on April 9, 1863, a few weeks after the arrival at Liverpool of the U.S. relief ship *George Griswold*. This was the result of an editorial in *The New York Times* the previous November, which had inspired a group of prominent New York merchants to set up an organization to collect aid for "the suffering operatives of Lancashire." There is little doubt that the initial impulse behind it was a charitable one. Nevertheless, it would be unrealistic to ignore the propaganda advantages of such an effort. Both Charles Francis Adams, U.S. Minister to Britain, and John Bright saw it from the start as a valuable means of countering Confederate influence and bolstering support in Britain for the North, while a New York minister (the Rev. Theodore Cuyler) justified it as "a war measure."

The committee had assumed that support for the project would be forthcoming from other major cities, such as Boston, and in particular from the grain-producing states, but in the event only Philadelphia showed any enthusiasm and it thus remained almost exclusively a New York enterprise. The response there, though, was very positive indeed. Contributions poured in, the use of the *George Griswold* was offered free of charge by her owners, and tugboat captains, pilots and stevedores volunteered their services without payment. On January 10, 1863, laden with barrels of flour, pork, bread, bacon and corn, the ship was ready to sail, and on February 9 she docked at Liverpool in order to start distributing her cargo. Not surprisingly, this generous gesture was met with a warm reception in Britain. At meetings in all parts of the country, people expressed their gratitude to the sponsors and to the United States in general, and tribute was paid in parliament. On occasion, though, where an over-obvious attempt to make political capital out of the gift was detected, the reaction was rather less positive. The organizers of a meeting held in March in Manchester, for example, had planned that, after listening to the speeches, the local operatives would form up and march in procession behind floats bearing a model of the *George Griswold* and a black shape supposedly representing the *Alabama*, after which 15,000 loaves of bread would be distributed to them. The workers, however, who may well have been incited by pro–Confederate elements from Liverpool, strongly resented being patronized, as they saw it, in this fashion. Hardly had the meeting begun when the crowd surged forward, seized the loaves of bread and started hurling them at the platform. A flying loaf caught the Rev. C.W. Denison, chaplain of the *George Griswold*, on the side of the head, and the meeting broke up in disorder.[5]

It is against this background that we need to see the meeting which took place in Burnley on April 9, 1863, and which was reported in such detail by the *Advertiser*. The meeting in question was held in the Mechanics' Institution, a fine old building of 1855 still in use today as a theater. The objective was to present the Union point of view of the war in America, and the two main speakers were the Rev. C.W. Denison and Peter Sinclair. Charles Wheeler Denison was born in Connecticut in 1809. He was the first editor of *The Emancipator*, the New York abolitionist journal, and later served as U.S. Consul in British Guiana. After arriving in England on the *George Griswold*, he spoke and preached energetically in Lancashire on behalf of the Union, often in conjunction with George Thompson, the British anti-slavery orator. Peter Sinclair, a Scotsman summarized by Dr. Amanda

Foreman as a "social reformer,"[6] had been living in the United States for six years but returned to Britain in 1861, apparently specifically in order to counter any tendency towards British support for the South. He settled in Manchester and immediately made his name as a convinced and tireless champion of the Union. As such, he quickly came to the notice of the U.S. Consul in London, Freeman H. Morse, who made use of his substantial State Department budget to fund Sinclair's activities and to pay for the publication and distribution of his pamphlet, *Freedom or Slavery in the United States*.[7]

Among the figures named by the *Advertiser* as being present at the meeting are two prominent local speakers on behalf of the Confederacy, Joseph Barker[8] and the Rev. Edward Arundel Verity. *The Dictionary of National Biography* summarizes Barker as "preacher, author, and controversialist." Born near Leeds in 1806, he was a man of decided but frequently changing opinions, at various times Chartist agitator, Methodist preacher, freethinking secularist and abolitionist. Emigrating to the United States in 1851, he bought land in Nebraska and became associated with William Lloyd Garrison in the anti-slavery movement. He returned to England in 1860 and by 1862 was living in Burnley. One constant throughout Barker's life was that he was an extremely powerful and effective public speaker. Abandoning his earlier sympathies, he now placed this gift at the service of the South, speaking regularly and with great success on "the American war" throughout the Northwest. Verity, who was born in Bridgend, Glamorgan, in 1822, was one of those outsize Victorian characters like the writer and traveler George Borrow or the soldier and explorer Colonel Fred Burnaby. He was a large man who lived a life full of events, although he was not above embellishing these events to make a better story. He came from a medical family and started to train as a doctor but then decided to go into the Church, although he continued to carry a surgeon's knife with him on all occasions in case of emergency. He had spent part of his medical studies in Paris and claimed to speak almost every European language, as well as Turkish. He served briefly as an army chaplain in the Crimea, although the story of his having been at Balaclava and worked with Florence Nightingale is, unfortunately, apocryphal. He was vicar of All Saints, Habergham Eaves, outside Burnley, where he quickly distinguished himself by his championship of the local workers. His support for the Confederacy was presumably the natural development of this, and his commanding presence and powerful voice must have been an asset to the cause.[9]

Although both Barker and Verity spoke at the end of the meeting, Barker's main response came four days later at a lecture in the Public Hall (also still standing today), at which he dealt in detail with the various points made by the two Unionist speakers. An immediate intervention, however—and a most effective one, as will be seen below—came from a young workingman called William Cunliffe. Cunliffe appears elsewhere in the files of the *Advertiser* as having intervened similarly in discussion on the war, but it is clear that his contributions were not limited to public speaking. In the course of his recent research into the large body of poems written in dialect during the Lancashire Cotton Famine, Dr. Simon Rennie of the University of Exeter has come upon a number written by a "Williffe

The Mechanics' Institution, Burnley, scene of the meeting of April 9, 1863 (author's photograph).

Cunliam." There can be no doubt at all that this was William Cunliffe. Dr. Rennie's preliminary investigations show that he was born in 1833 and was at one time a blacksmith, although Mary Ellison describes him as a cotton operative.[10]

The *Advertiser*'s report of the meeting appeared two days later, on April 11. In transcribing it below, I have been careful to leave the original text and punctuation unchanged in order to retain the immediacy of the narrative. I have merely noted three or four small errors or misprints. The following, then, is a direct, contemporary account of a meeting in Burnley to discuss the Civil War.

THE AMERICAN QUESTION

———

MEETING
IN THE MECHANICS' INSTITUTION

It was announced by placard last week that a public meeting would be held on this question in the Assembly room of the Mechanics' Institution, on the evening of the 9th instant, which would be addressed by the Rev. C.W. Denison, chaplain of the relief ship George Griswold, Peter Sinclair, Esqr., and others, the chair to be taken by Mr. Councillor Kay. Mr. Denison preached twice in the town on Sunday last; in the morning at Westgate Chapel [independent] and in the evening at Salem Chapel [independent]. Admission to the public meeting was to be by ticket, and as the day approached great anxiety was manifested to obtain the privilege; and there was considerable grumbling at this arrangement, and much injury as no one seemed to know where the tickets were to be obtained.

3. A Lively Meeting in Burnley

We know not how far this plan of admission was carried out, but long before the time stated for the opening of the meeting, the spacious room was crowded. Opposition was anticipated, and indeed freely spoken of in the town. The first to mount the platform—nearly half an hour before the commencement of the proceedings—was the Rev. E.A. Verity, where he sat a long time by himself. At the appointed time—half past seven—the chairman and speakers, with others ascended the platform and were received with cheers. Among those around the chair besides the speakers, and the Rev. E.A. Verity, were the Revds. J.T. Shawcross, J. Stroyan, O. Hargreaves, J. Alcorn, G. Gill; Mr. R.R. Davies, Mr. Joseph Barker, Mr. J. Gaukrodger, Mr. G. Graham, Mr. T. Willis, Mr. H. Hargreaves, &c., with a number of strangers. Silence having been obtained.

The Chairman requested the audience to refrain from stamping in the expression of their approbation of anything that was said, on account of the readers in the Exchange below, and that if they did not agree with any statement made by the speakers they would show a charitable spirit, and listen patiently. He took the question before them that night to be an important matter. They ought to have a right conception of the quarrel now raging in America. First, as to its cause; unless they knew this, they could have no conception how soon the war would be settled. The settlement of the quarrel had frequently been predicted, but he saw no hope as yet of the prophesy being fulfilled. It struck him that they must look back for a great number of years for the cause of the quarrel. Its groundwork was older than the constitution of America, for the constitution was the result of a compromise; and therefore they found the Constitution and Declaration of Independence antagonistic. In the constitution there was a provision for some being held in bondage. Out of this arose this question. It was the love of Union which led the framers of the constitution to make this concession; but they never expected that this concession would be permanent in the constitution, as might be found from their writings. Had slavery not been conceded there had been no constitution. It was the love of the Union that led men to make a sacrifice of their convictions on this great question. They had been told that slavery had nothing to do with this quarrel. He thought slavery had something to do with it; that slavery was at the bottom of it. Those who had come to address them that night would be able to show them much better than he could that this was the case. He would call them before the meeting, and try to keep order during the proceedings. [Cheers.]

James [sic] Sinclair, Esq., presented himself at the call of the chairman. He said he came as a stranger among them, yet he was a countryman of their own. He had travelled some five years in the United States. He went to acquaint himself with the people and their institutions, the resources and capabilities of the country. He did not go to find fault with the people, to discover their weak points; but to find out what was good, and he was glad to shut his eyes to what was bad. He had gone through the free states, the border states, and as far South as he could go without being elevated [a laugh]. Seeing he could not go South and exercise the right of a freeman without exposing himself to this, he refrained. He could have gone South if he had put a padlock on his mouth; but as he was not a dog and did not fancy a padlock, he did not go South. He told them honestly that no freeman could go and exercise the rights of a freeman in the South, and he challenged contradiction. If a freeman would consent to be silent he might visit the slave states; but he would then become a participator in the most damnable form of expression the world ever saw [cheers]. He remembered some clergymen having gone South, and they came home and spoke about the sunny South, but they were silent as to what they saw of slavery. They did not lift up their voice against it. Perhaps it would be said, as he did not go South because of the danger, that he was as bad as the clergymen. He did not think so. William L. Garrison by living away from the slave states was able to shake the whole fabric of slavery to its foundations; and so it was possible to overthrow oppression and not put themselves in the hands of the tyrant. The great question at issue in America was in their hands. He was quite aware of the position the people of America occupied. He was not ignorant of the sympathy the South got in this country. But for this sympathy they would not have been deprived of cotton. If it had not been for the money the South got to sustain them, the state of things in this country would not have lasted three months. He did not speak what he could not prove. He was going to deal chiefly with facts. He would refer them to the words of the great father of the constitution, George Washington, in his farewell address to the people of America. He [Mr. Sinclair] would just remind them that previous to the Constitution there were two forms of union. There was during the struggle for independence first a confederation of colonies, and then a confederation of states. These were sufficient during the war, but as soon as peace came, then a more perfect union became necessary, and then a constitution was formed, not by the states, but by the people. It was the sovereignty of the people. There were two principles,—the principle of the sovereignty of the people, and of the states. He wished them to bear this in mind, because it was for the sovereignty of the people the people of America were now contending. They say "We the people." The seceding states were going back to the exploded doctrine of "We the States." General Washington, in his farewell address did not address the states, but the people. [Mr. Sinclair read from the address.] He urged the maintenance of the union as the palladium of political prosperity and safety, of the Federal constitution and of the public credit: he abjured them to avoid sectional jealousies, and the baleful effect of party spirit, and of permanent inveterate antipathies against particular nations, or passionate attachments to others, dwelling at length on the polity of an impartial neutrality and of disconnection with the nations of Europe so far as existing treaties would permit, together with the dangers of foreign influence. In his anxiety for the union, he seemed to have some knowledge of what was coming. That good man seemed to be aware of the danger that was in his country, and it had come from the quarter he feared. The union of America had constituted its safety. United he knew they would stand; divided he knew they would fall. No men knew better than the men of this country the evil effects of division. It was the downfall of liberty. We said that union is strength. Did any freeman ever fear a free press, a free platform, and a free pulpit [Cheers]. The constitution of America was the voice of the people, and because it was so, it had been the terror of despots. With its enemies, covertly or openly, freedom was the point of attack. [Mr. Sinclair again referred to official documents before him which spoke of a general government with auxiliary state governments.] Where, he asked, was the doctrine of State sovereignty? Whoever heard of an auxiliary being superior to the parent? The states were made by the union, not the union by the states. Government over the whole was necessary and to the power of the government union was indispensable. George Washington had for ever destroyed the idea that any portion of the country had a right to take a portion without consent of the supreme Government. The father of his country knew what he was speaking about. The people that made the constitution had a right to change it, and a right to amend it, and his had been done on three different occasions. If the men of the South had cause of complaint, why did they appeal to the people to amend the constitution? They had no right of secession; but they had a right of amendment. He denied altogether the right of secession. The people had a right to amend; and if the south had any grievance, there was provision for redress, and provision was made for the education of the people. There were free schools, so hated by the South, in these states, in which there was a seat for every child of five and fifteen free of charge to the people. They believed in America that if the people had a right to punish crime, they had a right to prevent it. They believed if the people were well educated the majority would be good, and hence entitled to claim the rights of freemen. In some countries, it was only the select few who were thought worthy of the elective franchise. In America they thought the whole people worthy of the franchise, because they believed the people the source of power. He had proved the foundation of a perfect union of the people, not of States, and the exercise of all rights, not of States, but of people. [Mr. Sinclair then read the opinions of Chief Justice Marshall,

Jefferson, Hamilton, Patrick Henry, and Chancellor Kent on the doctrine of secession, shewing that the States had no such right as was claimed by the South.] He would turn to the opinions of the South, because he wanted his countrymen to know what the slaveholders had to say for themselves. John C. Breckenridge, vice-president under Buchanan, and the candidate of the slave party for the presidency, stated that the following were the designs of the party of freedom: "I charge that the present and ulterior purpose of the Republican party are, 1st To introduce the doctrine of Negro equality into American politics, and to make it the ground of positive legislature hostile to the Southern States. 2nd To exclude the slave property of the South from all territory now in the Union, or which hereafter may be acquired. 3rd to prevent the admission, in any latitude, of another slave holding state. 4th To repeat [sic] the Fugitive Slave Law, and practicably refuse to obey the constitution on that subject. 5th To refuse to prevent or punish by state action the spoliation of slave property; but, on the contrary, to make it a criminal offence in their citizens to obey the laws of the Union in so far as to protect property in American slaves. 6th To abolish slavery in the district of Columbia. 7th To abolish it in the forts, arsenals, dockyards, and other places in the South where Congress had exclusive jurisdiction. 8th To limit, harass, and frown upon the institution in every mode of political action, and by every form of public opinion. 9th and finally. By the executive, by the Congress, by the postal service, the press, and in all other accessible modes, to agitate without ceasing until the Southern States, without sympathy or brotherhood in the Union, worn down by the unequal struggle, shall be compelled to surrender ignominiously, and emancipate their slaves."

These were the whole charges brought. Was there anything about the tariff? No! He [Mr. Sinclair] had to come to England to learn that the tariff had anything to do with the question. In all the charges against the North there was not one word about the tariff. Mr. Sinclair quoted many other documents in support of his views in favour of the North. Towards the conclusion of his remarks he referred to Abraham Lincoln, the President. The first time he met him was in a ragged school. He was addressing the children. From his own knowledge of life, he could say that he was an honest man. He hated slavery as much as any abolitionist. There were two parties in America on this question—the abolitionists and the Anti-slavery men. The latter believed in giving compensation for the slaves; the abolitionists, at the head of whom was W.L. Garrison, believing that liberty was the right of all, were determined to have it for all let what would come. When Lincoln was a private citizen he stated that were he in Congress, and a vote should come up on a question whether slavery should be prohibited in a new territory, he would vote that it should. He said also "he would like to know," if taking the old declaration of independence, which declared that all men were equal upon principle, and making exceptions to it, where would it stop? If one man said it did not mean a negro, why not another say it did not mean some other man? If that declaration was not the truth, let them get the statute book, in which they found it, and tear it out; but if true, stick to it, and stand firmly by it. Let them discard all the grumbling about that man and the other man, that race and the other race being inferior, and therefore they must be placed in an inferior position; regarding the standard left, they would discharge all those things, and unite as one people throughout the land, until they should once more stand up declaring that all men were equal. He hoped the lamp of liberty would burn in their bosoms, until there should no longer be a doubt that "all men were created free and equal." Those were the sentiments of the Republican party. All that Lincoln could do as an anti-slavery man he had done, and he was ready to take any other justifiable course possible. Why did they not get cotton in Lancashire? He told them from the words of slaveholders themselves that it was all settled before rebellion began. Having quoted the language of slaveholders, who wished to obtain our interference by the stoppage of cotton and the effect such a course would have upon England, the speaker said "Poor Old England is down upon her knees to slaveholders." When he said this there was loud dissent; "No, no" was shouted from every side followed by a perfect storm of hissing and hooting. It was a long time before he could be heard to utter another sentence. When the hubbub had subsided a little, Mr. Sinclair said "I see that pinches some folk." Some one cried out "Prove it," and he replied "I'll prove it." The hissing and hooting again commenced, and notwithstanding that the chairman succeeded in calming the meeting for a minute or two, Mr. Sinclair could not succeed in proceeding further. He sat down after having spoken for nearly an hour and a half.

The Rev. C.W. Denison, whose name had been called out several times as the last speaker was vainly endeavouring to continue his speech, presented himself to the meeting. After looking at those before him for a short time, he said they were all a set of jolly good fellows. The English were good at hearing others, and quite willing to be heard themselves; they were willing to attend to a speaker, and they wanted to be heard themselves. He had heard it said that of all people in the world John Bull was the best at grumbling. If they took away this privilege—of making things go right when he thought they were going wrong, they took away a great privilege. They had then a real Yankee before them who would yield to anyone who desired it the privilege of speech. He believed that every man had a right to his opinions, and to express those opinions. He was prepared to speak, and he was also willing to hear any who were desirous of expressing their opinions. The previous speaker had been in America for five years. He had been in all the free states, and in the states on the borders of the slave states. They might safely rely upon what he had stated to them. He had been in the habit of adducing the same facts himself. Every word was true. It was the slave power that begun the war. They made the discovery twenty years ago of what the end would be if the states were allowed to go on increasing in population, and in intelligence. Referring to the common schools. In the state of Massachusetts there were but eight men in a hundred but what could read, write, and do arithmetic. In the place where he lived there were about 8,000 inhabitants, every man, woman and child above eight years of age could read, write, and do arithmetic. Besides this, there was not a place in that town where a single drop of intoxicating drinks were sold. Each one was living under his own vine and fig tree, none daring to make them afraid. In that town they had a model of what America should be. They were doing as well as they could to this end. He did not say they had done all well, but they were doing the best they could for the overthrow of slavery, the great curse and evil of their land. If the South was ready to fight for their slavery, the North was equally ready to fight for the slave [cheers]. Their government was a compact associated government, not an association of state. The motto on their shield, "One among many" represented the states. Mr. Denison proceeded to state that in his country were certain land*s* called territories, which until they were made into states were subject to the nation. With respect to states, the constitution gave them no power to interfere; but in the territories they had the right. [We understand that some one in the meeting sent a note to Mr. Denison in which it was stated that the sincerity of Lincoln was questioned, on which he proceeded in a very animated strain to produce proofs that the American President was no hypocrite in his professions in regard to slavery]. One of the things Abraham Lincoln had done for the abolition of slavery was, that in the territory known as the district of Columbia he had emancipated 3,000 men, women, and children. He [the speaker] saw them set free. And the money paid for them the poor freed slaves would never be able to give them back. Compensation had been offered to the border slave states for the freedom of their slaves, to one ten millions, of dols. to another one million to another 800,000. As fair a price had been offered as the slave owners in Columbia got. They had no more right to set the slaves free than those in the meeting had. All they had the right to say was, if you will set the slaves free yourselves, we will compensate you. He asked if that was not fair. Was not that a proof of Abraham Lincoln's sincerity? Whenever they had the opportunity of striking for liberty they had gone into the slave states and

3. A Lively Meeting in Burnley

offered to pay them for the freedom of their slaves. More than 300,000 slaves had been set free on the march of the republican army during the last eighteen months. Immediately after the inauguration of Abraham Lincoln, a pirate was arrested, tried, and condemned. Every effort was made by Cuban, Portugese [sic], and other merchants to save this man. But Abraham Lincoln said "No, he has been guilty of stealing a man, and law says he shall die for the crime." And die he did. The first slave thief executed in America. Another point would show this sincerity. The black republics of Hayti, in the west Indies, and Liberia, on the west coast of Africa had for the last 25 years been trying to get into the American family. These had been admitted; they had sent representatives and ambassadors and old Abe had walked up to one of them and said "Give me your hand." Referring to what was said of the prejudice against the negro in the North he remarked on the advertisements often seen in our English papers with the words at the conclusion, "No Irish need apply." He thought the English had better get rid of this prejudice before finding fault with the Americans. The Americans might say to them "Physician heal thyself." They could not get rid in a day of an evil of 200 years. Slavery had originated the prejudice. They must help them to get rid of slavery, and they would help them to get rid of the prejudice. It was said they had established the blockade. Well the English had recognised the blockade. They must settle that manner with their foreign secretary. He predicted that before eight weeks had elapsed they would have cotton on its way from America. It was stated that Lincoln had said he was willing to maintain the Union if he maintained slavery with it. [A Voice: To be sure he is.] He [Mr. Denison] said it was false, and the man who said so knew it was false. No such passage could be found in anything he had said. He wanted to maintain the union for the purpose of abolishing slavery. This had been proved, and he who said otherwise was either a knave, a rogue, or a liar. The utterance of these words roused the meeting, and again there was hissing and hooting. Mr. Denison in vain tried to proceed after this, and at last retired.

Mr. Joseph Barker and the Rev. E.A. Verity both presented themselves to the meeting, but after a while sat down.

At the call of the Chairman, Mr. R.R. Davies, moved the following:

That the secession of the Southern states of America from the Federal government having avowedly originated in the determination not only to maintain, but to extend slavery, this meeting indignantly repels the assumption that the English people sympathise with a rebellion that thus violates every principle of political justice, or with institutions framed in defiance of the moral sense of civilised mankind, and which are an outrage upon the religion whose sanction has been claimed in their support.

The resolution was seconded by a gentleman whose name we did not learn.

A young man named William Cunliffe, who some time before had risen in the body of the meeting to object to what had been stated, now appeared on the platform. He said he was a working man like themselves. He had been in the United States. He had been West, and he had been South too. He was not not [sic] like Mr. Sinclair. He had no fear of hanging. He went to the States in love with them. He thought the States a model government. When he heard these men speak as they did, his English blood rose in his veins. He was astonished at them. Evidently they did not want anyone to have an opinion contrary to themselves. They told them that this was a question of slavery; he thought it was a question of domination over the South. The South had a right to secede. They were told that the North had all along been struggling for the freedom of the negro. They might listen to their sentiments about the negro, but they kicked him out of the carriages in some parts, in others, however, he was suffered to ride with his master. One of the speakers told them that the negro had a right to vote in the free states; but he had to have a certain amount of property in order to acquire the right, which was not the case with the white man. He found in the Northern States the strongest prejudice against the negro. In their theatres, the negro had to sit with the worst characters thieves, prostitutes, and disreputable persons all in one box. "God defend me," said the speaker, "from ever becoming a subject of the United States" [great cheering].

In the Northern their aim was self aggrandizement. In the North, he found all rotten and corrupt. Everyone was ready to put his hand in the public purse for his own ends. He found, in order to get power, politicians ready to give voting papers to anyone, although five years' residence was required in order to entitle them to vote. Mr. Denison had referred to the advertisement found in English newspapers in which the words "No Irish need apply" were found. He had himself seen the same words in advertisements in United States' papers. They told them to let the States alone, and yet these men came here to interfere with them. It seemed to him that the North wanted them to hold the South while they thrashed him. John Bull liked to see fair play. Mr. Cunliffe then referred in a telling way to the outcry of the North about the Alabama, but they said nothing about the hundreds of thousands of muskets and rifles which had gone from this country to them. They had been shipping men in Ireland for the North. During the Russian war, the states resented the attempt to enlist men for England, of which he believed the English government knew nothing, and at the same time subjects of the States went out openly to help Russia against England. After a few more pertinent remarks, Mr. Cunliffe concluded by moving the following amendment: "That this meeting while it deplores the civil war in America and its attendant evils, does consider as unwarrantable and unjust, and as a breach of strict neutrality any public demonstration of sympathy with either of the contending factions in this war; and that this meeting especially views with indignation the attempt of Northern agencies to interfere with the free sentiments and judgement of the people of England." [Cheers.]

Mr. Joseph Barker seconded the amendment in a long and able speech in the delivery of which he was frequently applauded. We regret that we have no space left for an outline. Mr. Barker took up every point and statement of Messrs. Sinclair and Denison in his effective way. The Rev. E.A. Verity supported the amendment in a few pointed remarks, "in order," as he said, "that Mr. Davison [sic] might not go back without knowing something of the feelings of the Clergy of the Church of England." Mr. Sinclair first, and Mr. Denison afterwards said a few words in reply. The chairman then put the question before the meeting and the amendment was carried by an overwhelming majority, followed by immense cheering.

After a vote of thanks to the chairman, the meeting separated, it wanting but a few minutes to twelve.

4

Yancey and the Fishmongers

Jefferson Davis's choice of William Lowndes Yancey to lead the original Confederate commission to Europe has not generally been considered one of his wisest decisions. Writing at the time, Mary Chesnut gives the view of her circle: "Send a man to England who had killed his father-in-law in a street brawl! That was not knowing England or Englishmen, surely."[1] Frank L. Owsley's summary was, "the velvet gloves of diplomacy were not worn well by an outspoken agitator."[2] In his recent, very readable, volume on the international ramifications of the Civil War, *The Cause of All Nations*, Professor Don H. Doyle accuses Davis of "a certain tone deafness" in questions of diplomacy and quotes Edwin De Leon's description of Yancey as "not a winning or persuasive man" but "bold, antagonistic and somewhat dogmatical" and "not at all impressive in personal appearance, and decidedly negligent in dress." Professor Doyle also wonders "what the English made of Yancey."[3]

What Don Doyle fails to mention, however, is that De Leon also says of Yancey that he was "a great talker and a strong reasoner, and when brought into contact with Englishmen of marked note, never failed to make a strong impression on them."[4] Owsley, too, describes Yancey elsewhere as "a very able man ... possessed of poise and dignity," but "in private intercourse straightforward and pleasant mannered" and "a clear-sighted realist in most matters," who "might have been fairly well qualified to send to Europe" had he not been "so identified with the institution which both England and France hated."[5] Finally, we have solid evidence of what some, at least, of "the English" made of Yancey, as will be seen.

Yancey arrived in London on April 28, 1861, having left Montgomery, Alabama, on March 15. He put up initially at the Bath Hotel, Arlington Street,[6] where rooms had been engaged for the three Commissioners by William Thomson, United States Consul at Southampton.[7] Moving on May 4 to the Westminster Palace Hotel on Victoria Street,[8] Yancey finally, on May 16, settled into rooms at 15 Half Moon Street, "at 3½ guineas pr week for the season, fires, lights & attendance included."[9]

He appears to have become increasingly disillusioned with his post—understandably so, given the cool attitude towards the three Commissioners by the Foreign Secretary, Lord John Russell. Yancey's diary, which he had started on leaving Montgomery, comes to an abrupt end on June 18, following his return to

Half Moon Street from a short visit to Paris. He seems to have requested to be relieved of his duties sometime around the end of August 1861, his resignation being accepted by the Confederate Secretary of State, R.M.T. Hunter, on September 23.[10] From then on, Yancey was able to do little more than wait to be replaced, until the arrival at the end of January 1862 of the new Commissioner to Great Britain, James Murray Mason, finally allowed him to return to Alabama. Nevertheless, during the long months of waiting, Yancey did at least score one conspicuous success, albeit one on a relatively modest scale.

On Lord Mayor's Day (November 9), 1861, Yancey, Dudley Mann and the Confederate purchasing agent Caleb Huse were all invited to a banquet at the Fishmongers' Hall on London Bridge. In his brief memoir of his Confederate service, Huse describes what happened:

> I never heard [Yancey] address an audience but once, but that once convinced me he was a born orator. It was at a Fishmongers' Guild dinner, and the few representatives of the Confederate States were the guests of the evening. Mr. Yancey sat on the left of the Lord Warden. I sat four or five seats from him, on the opposite side, the tables being arranged in the form of a horse shoe. There was a large number present, and many were evidently Americans from the North.
>
> Very early in the list of toasts, the toastmaster,—a butler possessed of a ringing voice, and who stood just behind the chair of the Lord Warden, from whom he received his orders—called out: "Gentlemen, fill your *glah-ses*, the Lord Warden will take wine with you." The glasses being filled, the toast was announced. I do not now recall the words, but

Fishmongers' Hall, London (author's photograph).

4. Yancey and the Fishmongers

it had reference to the "new nation," and to Hon. William L. Yancey, and "our guests from the Confederate States of America." The Lord Warden made a short address of welcome and called on Mr. Yancey. All the Confederate guests were expected to stand while their spokesman replied. But I declined to make myself so conspicuous, fearing that in a company so entirely new to Mr. Yancey, as I felt sure this English company was, his speech would be anything but appropriate.

I could not have been more in error. What he said exactly fitted the place and the occasion; the audience was delighted, except some people at the lower ends of the tables, who, by rattling their glasses and moving their feet, did their best to disconcert the speaker. In this they failed. The speech was short, and at its conclusion the storm of applause clearly showed the pleasure it afforded the great majority of the audience. I remember well a barrister—a member of the city government—who after the dinner was over, commented enthusiastically on the eloquence of Mr. Yancey.[11]

Strangely enough, I have not so far been able to find any reference to the dinner in the Fishmongers' voluminous archives. Yancey's speech was printed in full, however, both in *The New York Times* of November 25 and in the November 23 issue of *The Illustrated London News*. It ran as follows:

Upon the part of Americans, I sincerely respond to the sentiment just expressed by the Prime Warden for the restoration of peace in America. Such a wish, proclaimed by a company of intelligent Englishmen, must kindle a corresponding feeling in the bosom of every enlightened and impartial American. The name American no longer represents a united people. There exist now two American nationalities—the Confederate and the Federal Americans. I—as you may, perhaps, be aware—am a Confederate, or—as the Federal American, unmindful of the character of our common forefathers, disdainfully terms me—a rebel. But the justice and the sense of right of this great Government, promptly coincided in by France and Spain, speedily wiped out that stigma from our brows, and my countrymen are acknowledged here, at least, to be belligerents. [Cheers.] Though indebted to an enlarged and enlightened view of public law, and not to the mere grace or favor of England for this acknowledgment of our unquestionable rights and *locus standi*, I must freely express here to-night, that deep sense of thankfulness, which I am sure all my countrymen feel, for its early public avowal—"*Bis dat qui cito dat*"—[prolonged cheers]. From no other Power could it have come so gracefully. In this—"the old country"—the principle of self-government is recognized and practiced, however blended with the prerogatives of the Crown and the rights of the aristocracy. To your institutions Americans are indebted for the chief of those vital principles which have caused them to style their Republic—
"The land of the free
And the home of the oppressed."
Such invaluable rights as the old English writ of habeas corpus, of a speedy trial by jury, of freedom of speech and freedom of the Press, are the main pillars of American Constitutional liberty; and I am both happy and proud to say are observed at least throughout the Confederate American States as vital and practical rights, even during their stern struggles to preserve their "national life." [Hear, hear, and cheers.] I feel how unbecoming it would be in me to intrude upon such an occasion as the present any merely partisan views of the causes which have broken up the late Federal Union. No matter what they may have been, one thing is clear, and that is that the contest now going on is upon the part of the people of the Confederate States for the right to govern themselves and to resist subjugation from the North. [Hear, hear.] They occupy a territory as large as England, France, Spain and Austria together—they are ten millions in number—they are chiefly producers of important raw materials, and buyers of every species, of all kinds of

manufactured goods. Their pursuits, soil, climate, and production, are totally different from those of the North. They think it their interest to buy where they can buy cheapest, and to sell where they can sell dearest. In all this the North differs, *toto coelo*, from them, and now makes war upon us to enforce the supremacy of their mistaken ideas and selfish interests. [Hear, hear, and Cheers.] In defence of their liberties and sovereign independence, the Confederate States and people are united and resolute. They are invaded by a Power numbering 20,000,000; yet for eight months has the Confederate Government successfully resisted—aye, repelled—that invasion along a military frontier of 1,000 miles. Though cut off by blockade from all foreign trade, their internal resources have been adequate to the equipment and maintenance in the field of an army of over 250,000 troops. Can all this be, and yet these 6,000,000 of whites be divided? The idea is preposterous. So much has been said about our efforts to obtain foreign intervention that I may be allowed to declare emphatically that the Confederate States have neither sought nor desired it. They can maintain their independence intact by their own strength. As to their recognition by the Powers of the world, that of course they desire. They are a people, a nation, exhibiting elements of power which few States of the world possess. But they have no reason to complain, nor do they feel aggrieved, because these great Powers see fit for a season to defer their formal recognition and reception into the family of nations. However they may differ with them as to the period when their recognition should take place, they fully understand that such action is purely a question to be determined by those countries each for itself and with reference to its own interests and views of public policy. Other nations having trading relations with us have quite as much interest to send Ministers and Consuls to us as we have to send such representatives to them. [Hear, hear.] Why, then, shall there not be peace? Simply because the North in its pride will not admit that to be a fact—a *fait accompli*—which Old England, followed by the first Powers of Europe, has recognized, and which the Confederate Government and armies have repeatedly demonstrated to be a stern and bloody fact—the fact that we are a belligerent Power. There can be no basis for negotiations, or for peace proposals or consultations, so long as the Confederates are deemed to be and are treated as rebels. [Hear.] But when our adversary shall become sufficiently calm to treat us as a belligerent power, the morning of peace will dawn in the horizon. When that hour shall arrive I think I may say the Confederate Government will be inflexible upon one point only—its honor and its independence. For the great interests of peace and humanity it will yield much that is merely material or of secondary importance. [Mr. YANCEY sat down amid loud and continued cheering.][12]

By a curious coincidence, Charles Francis Adams, the U.S. Minister to Britain, was dining at exactly the same time at the Guildhall, a guest of the Lord Mayor, William Cubitt. *The Saturday Review*, which tended to echo the views of its proprietor, Alexander Beresford Hope, reported in its issue of November 16 on both banquets, comparing Yancey's speech with that of his Unionist rival, to the great advantage of the former. After referring to "Mr. Adams's forced and stiff dignity of contemptuous indifference," the magazine continued:

> Mr. Yancey did not discuss London Bridge, nor did he dilate on Dr. Johnson's rooms in the Temple, or on the recent sale of Shakespeare's garden at Stratford. Such large themes he left to the orator at Guildhall. But he certainly went to the core of the matter when he publicly acknowledged the fair and upright conduct of England in recognising the belligerent rights of the South; and when he announced that Free Trade was the natural policy of the Confederate States, he did much more for his cause than if he had gone into a stirring oration on the tyranny of the North, or the demerits of the Morrill tariff. In Mr. Yancey, at any rate, we see one American public man who neither affronts our feelings by cynicism or our temper by swagger.[13]

4. Yancey and the Fishmongers

"Banquet at the Fishmongers' Hall on Lord Mayor's Day" (*The Illustrated London News*, November 23, 1861).

It was therefore with understandable delight that I discovered, a few years ago, that an old family medical friend was doctor to the Fishmongers and found myself invited by him to follow in Yancey's footsteps and attend a Livery dinner one evening in May.

The interior of the hall had been badly damaged by a bomb in 1940, but once the war was over the Fishmongers hastened to restore it to its original splendor, selling a number of their London properties in order to be able to ensure that the work was done to the highest standards and using the best materials. Since the 1835 exterior escaped the bombing relatively unscathed, the hall now looks, both internally and externally, exactly as it did in 1861. Of course there are women at these dinners now (Princess Anne, amongst others, at this particular one), but otherwise things can have changed very little since the three Confederate representatives were there, and it was easy to imagine oneself stepping back in time. To complete the illusion, the waiters pouring the champagne before dinner, uniformly dressed in tailcoats, appeared to have been chosen not merely for their skill and professionalism but also for their physiognomy, since two at least of them had faces which were pure Victorian. I had in fact brought a copy of Yancey's speech with me and was urged by my neighbors at dinner, one of whom had a daughter-in-law from South Carolina, to stand up and declaim it, but wisely refused.

In a final example of serendipity, a few days later I suddenly came across a copy of the engraving from *The Illustrated London News* accompanying the paper's report of the 1861 dinner. The banqueting hall appears today exactly as it is in the engraving, showing that the Fishmongers' postwar restoration of their hall was both careful and accurate. It would be pleasant to think that the two standing figures shown at the end of the room represent Yancey and the Prime Warden, but I suspect that it may be more likely that they and the rest of the diners in the engraving are merely standard figures, representing no one in particular. Whatever the case, though, engraving and report together remain a pleasing and valuable record of one of the few moments of real success in the brief diplomatic career of William Lowndes Yancey.

5

A Civil War Grave in Turkey

Even the keenest student of the Civil War may be forgiven for being unaware that one of the greatest of the blockade-runner captains in that conflict lies buried on a Turkish hillside overlooking the Bosphorus.

Augustus Charles Hobart, known to his Victorian contemporaries as Hobart Pasha, was born on April 1, 1822, at Walton-on-the-Wolds, Leicestershire, the third son of the Rev. Augustus Edward Hobart, rector of St. Mary's Church and younger brother of the fifth earl of Buckinghamshire.[1] Some confusion has arisen over the family name of the future naval hero, which is usually given today as Hobart-Hampden. This is because his uncle, the fifth earl, on inheriting the Buckinghamshire estates of the Hampden family in 1824, added their name to his own. However, although the rector of St. Mary's succeeded to the title in 1849, he did not change his name until 1878.[2] Augustus Charles, who died in 1886, was therefore a plain Hobart for all but the last eight years of his life.

The boy was sent to Dr. Mayo's famous school at Cheam, Surrey. He proved a most unpromising student, however, and in 1835, shortly before his 13th birthday, he abandoned his studies and joined HMS *Rover* at Devonport as a midshipman.

He spent the greater part of the next eight years on ships patrolling the coast of South America, as part of the Royal Navy's efforts in the suppression of the slave trade. In the course of this, while serving on HMS *Dolphin*, he managed to capture a Brazilian slaver and brought her in triumph into the harbor of Demerara as a prize. He also found time, while back in England between voyages, to pass his navy examinations. As a reward for gallant conduct, he was next appointed to the royal steam yacht *Victoria and Albert*, then commanded by Captain Lord Adolphus FitzClarence. By September 1845, however, he was on duty in the Mediterranean as a lieutenant on board HMS *Rattler*, later transferring to the *Bulldog*, whose captain found him "full of zeal."

On the outbreak of the Crimean War in 1854, Hobart, now a first lieutenant, was still with the *Bulldog*, which formed part of the Baltic Squadron. For two weeks in August, he was in command of HMS *Driver*, taking part with her in the attacks on the Russian forts on the Finnish coast. For this he was mentioned in dispatches, his "ability, zeal, and great exertion" being particularly commended. In 1855, he was serving on HMS *Duke of Wellington*, the flagship of Admiral R.S.

Dundas and, with the French *Bretagne*, one of the most powerful warships at that time in the world. Commanding the mortar boats in the unsuccessful attack on the great naval fortress of Sveaborg, outside Helsinki, he was again mentioned in dispatches and promoted to commander.

After 20 years of almost continuous service at sea, Hobart spent the years 1855–1861 first as officer of the coast guard at Dingle, Co. Kerry, and then commanding the hulk HMS *Hibernia*, which served as receiving ship and guard ship for Malta. The latter part of 1861, however, found him back at sea again, commanding the gunboat HMS *Foxhound* in the Mediterranean. Promoted to captain in March 1863, he was retired on half-pay.[3]

It is difficult, when examining the lives of some of the more colorful characters of the Victorian era, to separate fact from fiction, to decide what is history and what is legend. In the case of Augustus Charles Hobart, this is particularly challenging. His autobiography, *Sketches from My Life*, published posthumously, is full of good stories.[4] The naval historian John Knox Laughton, however, who reviewed it for *The Edinburgh Review*,[5] having carefully examined all the relevant naval records, was able to show conclusively that Hobart, apart from confusing dates and places, had exaggerated some of his adventures, invented others and appropriated still others from brother-officers. (In justice to Hobart, it should be said that he wrote the book while suffering from the illness which eventually killed him and that many of the events he was referring to had taken place 40 or more years earlier).

Nevertheless, there is sufficient evidence to show beyond any doubt that Hobart was a born naval commander, fearless and resourceful. Reference has already been made to his two mentions in dispatches during the Crimean War. In its obituary of him, *The Times* asserted that his exploits both while running the blockade and while serving with the Ottoman Navy showed "the English Navy can still produce men who may be named with Nelson's captains,"[6] and he was described by Laughton as a "bold buccaneer of the Elizabethan period, who by some strange perverseness of fate was born into the Victorian."[7] Indeed, Hobart would probably have been far happier as one of Elizabeth I's sea dogs, given an independent command where he could best display his natural gifts rather than having to follow the orders of others. Like Nathan Bedford Forrest, with whom he had a certain amount in common, he was not by nature a good subordinate, being impatient of what he saw as the unnecessarily cautious attitude of his superiors and unwilling to show respect to those who, in his opinion, had not earned it. At the same time, though, as his energetic restructuring of the Turkish fleet showed, he had organizational skills worthy of Braxton Bragg. It is interesting to note that he found his greatest opportunity to display his talents first in the American Civil War and then in the Ottoman Navy.

A man of Hobart's character was never likely to be satisfied with a quiet life ashore on half-pay, and the Civil War in America had thus come at a providential time for him. Together with two or three other post captains, then, he applied for command of a blockade-runner, adopting the pseudonym "Captain Roberts." A desire for adventure was undoubtedly a key factor in this, and Hobart must also have been aware of the great profits to be made from blockade-running. On the other hand, it seems clear that his sympathies were with the South; he refers to himself and a colleague as "stanch Southerners in our opinions,"[8] while, according to *The Times*, the war "provided him with the opportunity of showing his sympathy with the Confederate cause."[9]

Seven of the 31 chapters of Hobart's autobiography deal with his blockade-running adventures. These were reprinted, virtually unchanged, from the account which he published as "Captain Roberts" in 1867, titled *Never Caught*. In contrast to much of the rest of his autobiographical writing, this was apparently judged by at least one American authority, according to Laughton, as substantially accurate.[10]

The summer of 1863 thus found him in command of the blockade-runner *Don*, in which he was to enjoy a number of successful runs into Wilmington. On August 7 that year, in a dispatch to the U.S. Secretary of State, William H. Seward, the U.S. Vice Consul in Bermuda, W.C.J. Hyland, noted the arrival of "steamer *Don* from London with merchandize for merchants here, and also for rebel agents."[11] According to Hobart, this included "one thousand pairs of stays ... five hundred boxes of Cockle's pills, and a quantity of toothbrushes" which he had brought out on his own account; the rest of the vessel's cargo consisted of "blankets, shoes, Manchester goods of all sorts, and some mysterious cases marked 'hardware,' about which no one asked any questions, but which the military authorities took possession of."[12] The following January, the U.S. Consul, Charles Maxwell Allen, reported: "Steamer *Don*, Capt. Roberts, from Wilmington with 561 bales cotton, came in on the 14th instant, screw boat 233 tons."[13] According to his own account, Hobart made a total of six round trips in and out of Wilmington in the *Don* before handing her over to his First Officer, Fred Cory, and returning to England[14]; she was captured on March 4, 1864, by the USS *Pequot* while attempting the run into Wilmington from Nassau.

In an interview in January 1893 with *The New York Times,* Captain Grosvenor Porter, formerly of the Confederate blockade-runner *Phantom*, claimed to have met Hobart in London after the war and to have been told by him that he had temporarily retired from blockade-running at this stage because his identity had been discovered.[15] This seems probable, since on July 13, 1864, Allen, announcing to Seward the recent arrival at Bermuda of the *Falcon*, one of Alexander Collie's steamers, continued, "She is commanded by a person who was formerly master of the *Don*, who then went by the name of Roberts. He is said to be an English naval officer, son of some nobleman, is an intimate friend of Governor Ord. If captured will try to pass himself off as a deck hand."[16]

As Allen's intelligence was usually extremely accurate, this, incidentally, further disproves the theory, still often repeated as fact today, that Hobart commanded the blockade-runner *Condor*, which left the Clyde on August 16, 1864. It was, in fact, under the command of another Royal Navy officer, Captain (later Vice Admiral) W.N.W. Hewett, V.C., whose nom de guerre was Samuel Ridge, that the *Condor*, having reached the safety of the guns of Fort Fisher on her first run from Halifax, ran aground on October 1, 1864, apparently while trying to avoid the wreckage of the blockade-runner *Night Hawk*.[17] In the shadowy world of the blockade-running captains, though, identities were frequently confused.

Hobart himself tells us that he "could not rest long in England, … got the command of a new and very fast paddle-wheel vessel, and went out again." This vessel, he says, was "one of four built by R. and G., of Glasgow."[18] This must refer to the *Falcon*, one of five, rather than four, vessels built on the Clyde for Alexander Collie by Randolph, Elder & Company.[19] Hobart tells us that he "made one successful round trip in the new vessel," landing 1,140 bales of cotton at Bermuda but that yellow fever broke out among the crew just as he was starting out again, and he had to return to Halifax. Stricken with fever himself, he decided to give up blockade-running for good.[20] In fact, the *Falcon* appears to have made two successful runs into Wilmington from Halifax and Nassau.[21]

Exactly how many times Hobart ran the blockade is unclear. The subtitle of *Never Caught* refers to "twelve successful trips," while others have claimed for him as many as 18. What is certain, however, is that he was both one of the most successful and one of the most daring of all the blockade-running captains. In the *New York Times* interview referred to above, Captain Porter is quoted as saying, "Hobart's ship, the Don, took tremendous risks—greater, in fact, than was ever taken by any ship in the course of the war commanded by an Englishman," and the *Don* "would run into a whole fleet of war ships apparently for the mere fun of it, and, what was more, usually get through in safety."[22]

With the war in America over, it was not long before Hobart was looking for fresh challenges. These he now found in the East rather than the West. In the course of a tour of the Continent in 1867 he found himself, according to his own account, "more by accident than design," in what was then still called Constantinople. Here he had an interview with Fuad Pasha, the foreign minister, to whom, apparently, he had letters of introduction. At this time Crete, still part of the Ottoman Empire, was in revolt, and Turkish efforts to bring the island into submission were frustrated by blockade-runners from Greece, operating with the active support of the Greek government. Hobart "accidentally hinted" to Fuad Pasha that he could see a way in which this blockade-running "could be put a stop to without infringing any law." As a result, he was offered a naval advisory post in succession to Sir Adolphus Slade, who had just retired.[23]

When Laughton, in *The Edinburgh Review*, questions the veracity of much of Hobart's autobiography, he is really talking, as he says, about that part of the book covering Hobart's life up to the Civil War. If Hobart's tale of his blockade-running adventures can be taken to be largely true, his account of his service in the Ottoman Navy carries conviction and is generally confirmed by the historical evidence.

He entered the Ottoman service at the end of November 1867, and on January 19 of the following year, by imperial decree, he was officially appointed to the Board of Admiralty. In February, he was raised to the rank of rear admiral, which brought with it the title of Pasha, and was given command of the fleet stationed off Crete.[24] In this capacity, Hobart swiftly brought the island under Turkish control again by employing against the Greek blockade-runners precisely the same tactics which he himself had faced in America a few years earlier.[25] Although Greek representations to the British government resulted in his being struck off the Navy List,[26] in consequence of his success in resolving the Cretan problem he was promoted in January 1869 to vice admiral and put in charge of the newly established Naval Reforms Commission.[27]

It is not often realized that in the 1870s, as a result of the reforms instituted during the reign of Abdul Aziz, Ottoman Turkey had the third biggest navy in the world, only the British and French navies being larger.[28] Hobart now immediately embarked upon a thorough and far-reaching program of reorganization and improvement, establishing naval schools and training and gunnery ships and striving to maintain the efficiency of the new ironclads. As Dr. Dilara Dal puts it, "The naval modernization was directed by Hobart Pasha from his instatement to the end of the reign of Abdülaziz ... and the naval reforms made after 1869 were prepared and implemented under his direction."[29]

Hobart's name had been restored to the Navy List in 1874 through the influence of Lord Derby, only to be erased again when the Russo-Turkish War broke out in 1877, and he accepted command of the Turkish Black Sea Fleet. In this capacity, however, he had little chance to show what he could do. Whether through timidity or through jealousy, the Turkish high command was reluctant to make the aggressive use of his squadron which he proposed. Furthermore, by the Treaty of Paris at the end of the Crimean War, Russia had lost her own Black Sea Fleet. Although she had unilaterally abrogated the relevant clauses of the treaty in 1870, she had so far made little progress in building up her own naval forces there, which meant that no great naval battle could take place. Nevertheless, in an echo of his blockade-running days, Hobart successfully ran his ship, at the start of the war, from the Turkish headquarters at Rustchuk in Bulgaria down past the Russian batteries on the Lower Danube and out into the sea to rejoin the fleet.[30] He also proved that he had discovered an effective solution to the problem of the dreaded Russian torpedo boats (for which he personally showed only contempt), protecting his ironclads, when at anchor, with a system of guard boats linked by ropes.[31]

Hobart had always enjoyed the complete confidence of Sultan Abdul Aziz and in return had given the sultan his total loyalty. After Abdul Aziz had been deposed and (in somewhat mysterious circumstances) died in 1876, Hobart continued to enjoy the full confidence of his successor, Abdul Hamid II, and, once again, responded in kind. In 1881, Abdul Hamid raised him to the rank of Mushir (marshal), the first Christian to be so honored, and at some point he also named Hobart to be one of his aides-de-camp, in which capacity, in Hobart's words, "I have had at times and still have important duties."[32] Like many other Englishmen who have had anything more than merely superficial contact with the Turks, Hobart formed a great admiration and, indeed, affection for them. He was convinced that some sort of formal and lasting alliance between the British and Ottoman empires was vital to the interests and security of both and visited London in 1885, very possibly at the sultan's instigation, on a mission to try to bring this about. He failed, but had the satisfaction at least of seeing himself once more restored to the Navy List, with the rank of vice admiral.

Meanwhile, however, the exertions of a very active and adventurous life had begun to tell on him at last, and his health had started to fail. Advised to go to the Riviera to recuperate, he died at Milan on June 19, 1886, while on his way back to Turkey.[33]

Abdul Hamid sent a gunboat to Genoa to bring Hobart's body back to Turkey for burial. The official palace gazette, the *Osmanli*, describing Hobart's death as "an irreparable loss," commented:

> When the steamer Nedjid returns with the remains of the illustrious dead, there will certainly not be wanting Ottoman shoulders to carry the mournful burden to the heights of Scutari, where our departed friend may rest henceforth side by side with other heroes of his country, under the shadow of that column which Queen Victoria and her people raised there 30 years ago to the memory of those who fell in the sacred cause of their country and of the Sultan, their ally.[34]

Back in London, *The Daily Telegraph* opined:

> It was the good fortune of the distinguished maritime commander now deceased, to win golden opinions from all sorts of peoples, and his name and prowess will be as cordially remembered in his native land, and in the Southern States of America, as on the shores of the Bosphorus and the Golden Horn.[35]

Hobart Pasha's grave, Istanbul (author's photograph).

Hobart still lies in the British Cemetery but no longer, strictly speaking, in Scutari. Scutari (Üsküdar in Turkish), once used in reference to the whole area of settlement on the Asian side of the Bosphorus, now covers a slightly narrower area, and the cemetery is today in the suburb of Haydarpaşa. Since it contains a number of British and Indian graves from the First World War, it is in the care of the Commonwealth War Graves Commission, and two fairly recent visits, in 2007 and 2009, found the grass mown and the graves, whether military or civilian, beautifully maintained.

Although there are ferries from the European side to Haydarpaşa, these do not run all day, and anyone wishing to visit the grave would therefore do better to take one of the regular and frequent ferries to Kadıköy, a journey of about 15 minutes, costing (in 2009) the equivalent of $1. From there, it is a 30-minute walk to the cemetery, going left along the shore, then up the hill, over the railway-line, past a large military hospital on the left and then left at the traffic lights at the top of the hill. The narrow cemetery gates are some 30 yards ahead, down a path by the side entrance to the military hospital.

On the upper level are the Crimean graves and the tall and impressive Crimean War monument of 1857. To find Hobart's simple grave, which is on the lower level, one walks straight on, past the neatly arranged Commonwealth graves section on the left, towards a tall pink obelisk marking the grave of Charles Simpson Hanson (1874). Hobart's grave is the fourth one beyond this, next to the long, low, gray grave of Sir Philip Francis (1876).[36]

The grave on the hillside, however, is not quite the only memorial to Hobart Pasha in Istanbul. In the collection of the Naval Museum (Deniz Müzesi) in Beşiktaş is a portrait of him in full Turkish naval uniform. The painting is undated, but Hobart appears distinctly younger and slimmer than in the best-known photographs of him, and it therefore presumably dates from the earlier stages of his career in the Ottoman Navy. Although not normally on display, it fortunately formed part of an exhibition in 2009 at the Pera Museum and the Istanbul Research Institute, in the center of Istanbul, of pieces from the Naval Museum, while the Naval Museum itself was undergoing a major renovation and reorganization. Since the museum reopened, greatly extended, in 2013, the portrait should presumably now be on permanent display.[37]

Hobart Pasha; Portrait in the Turkish Naval Museum, Istanbul (author's photograph).

Finally, Hobart is not entirely forgotten in the village of his birth. Walton-on-the-Wolds is a pretty village just over four miles from Loughborough. St. Mary's Church, where Hobart's father was rector, is on a slight hill just south of the center of the village, with the rectory, Hobart's childhood home, next to it. Although the rectory is now a private house, the right-of-way from the center of the village up to the church goes right through the former rectory garden and passes within a few yards of the house. The church itself is normally locked, but an inquiry at the bar of the Anchor, the welcoming pub in the center of the village, quickly produces a key. There is a large memorial to Hobart's mother, Mary, on the north wall of the chancel, while back in the Anchor a modest wooden frame near the bar contains a brief synopsis of the life of a British naval officer who found his greatest fame as the master of a blockade-runner and as an Ottoman admiral.[38]

6

On the Cleburne Trail in Cork and Cumbria

On November 25, 1863, the Confederate Army of Tennessee was driven from a supposedly impregnable position on Missionary Ridge, in one of the most extraordinary assaults of the Civil War, by men from George H. Thomas's Army of the Cumberland. Only one Confederate division, on the right of the line, held firm all day, throwing back all attacks made against it and finally charging down the hill, routing its assailants and capturing some 500 prisoners and eight battle flags. Two days later, this same division, by its stand at Ringgold Gap, enabled the beaten Army of Tennessee to withdraw south unmolested. It is interesting to speculate how differently things might have turned out if the commander of this division, Major General Patrick Ronayne Cleburne, had not, 17 years earlier, failed the entrance examination to the Apothecaries' Hall in Dublin and thus been unable to follow his father into the medical profession.

Most British students of the Civil War, whether Unionist or Confederate in our sympathies, share an admiration for Patrick Cleburne, a Protestant Irishman from Cork with ancestral roots in England, who spent three years in the British Army, emigrated to Arkansas, cast in his lot with the South, became the greatest divisional commander in the Army of Tennessee and foresaw, more than a year before the Confederate authorities reluctantly accepted it, the need to arm the slaves if the South was to gain her independence. There are his extraordinary military achievements, of course, as well as his constant care for his men and his own "moral and upright" personal character, "bound by his honor and conscience in all things," as an old friend from his Arkansas days described him. These alone should be enough to endear him to us, but perhaps there is also something more. Many of us, and not only those with Irish family connections, tend to think of him as a sort of fellow-countryman—which, of course, in the Victorian era, he would have been. After all, he served for three years in the 41st Regiment of Foot and told Colonel Fremantle "he ascribed his advancement mainly to the useful lessons which he had learnt in the ranks of the British Army," joking that this also enabled him to keep his white facings cleaner than any other Confederate general.[1] Whatever the reason, though, he remains for a number of us one of our great Civil War heroes.

To view the scenes of Cleburne's greatest triumphs, of course, to see the site of his death and to pay our respects at his grave, we have no choice but to cross the Atlantic. Fortunately, though, there are surviving buildings associated with him and memorials dedicated to him very much nearer home. The majority of these are naturally in County Cork, where Cleburne was born in 1828 and where he grew up. First of all, there is Bride Park Cottage in Killumney, where he was born, and Grange House, a short distance away, where his family moved in 1836. Nearby is the now-disused St. Mary's Church, Athnowen, where the family worshiped and Cleburne was baptized and where his father, Dr. Joseph Cleburne, lies buried. Finally, there are the former barracks in Ballincollig, where Joseph Cleburne provided the medical services, receiving £6 a year for doing so. All of these were on my list when my wife and I set off in October 2008 on what was my first visit to Ireland. The reason for the visit was to meet a newly discovered 93-year-old second cousin of hers, as well as various other hitherto unknown cousins. Once I realized that we were going to be based in Cork, however, I naturally insisted on adding a Cleburne element to the trip.

Before leaving, of course, I did some research, going through Craig L. Symonds's 1997 biography of Cleburne and the 1998 series of essays on him edited by Mauriel Phillips Joslyn of the Patrick Cleburne Society, "A Meteor Shining Brightly."[2] Between them, the two books had photographs of the main sites, and the Symonds biography had in addition a very useful map, based on the Ordnance Survey map for 1845, showing their whereabouts. I had also obtained the relevant section of the modern Ordnance Survey Ireland map, on which I had marked, as closely as I could, their location. I was therefore as well prepared as I could be when, having met all the cousins, we set off at last on the road west out of Cork.

We started in Ballincollig, about five miles from Cork. Initial inquiries for "the old barracks" produced a bewildered shake of the head, until someone realized that I was looking for "the Barrack Square development" and directed us there. The barracks were originally built in 1810 in order to provide security for the supply of gunpowder from the nearby Royal Gunpowder Mills and were occupied by the British Amy continuously from then on until the advent of Home Rule. The last British troops left on May 17, 1922, when the barracks were formally handed over to the forces of the new Irish Free State. Damaged during the Irish Civil War of 1922–1923, they were finally restored and reoccupied in 1940 and remained in use until 1998, after which they were sold to a developer for conversion into a mixture of office and residential space. Fortunately, the developer was wise enough not to tamper with either the exterior of the buildings or the general layout, and as a result I felt confident, as I glanced around it, that the old barrack square would be clearly recognizable to Dr. Joseph Cleburne today for what it had been.

I had hoped also to be able to identify another building in the vicinity. This was the school started in Greenfield by the Rev. William Spedding, chaplain to the barracks, to which Cleburne was sent at the age of 12. Its location was shown on the Symonds map, but unfortunately it soon became clear that it must have been swallowed up in the expansion of Ballincollig. I later discovered that it had fallen into disrepair in the early 1900s and that there was now nothing left.

We had better luck with Grange House, a short distance beyond Ballincollig.

Ballincollig Barracks (author's photograph).

The building was apparently much reduced in size at some later stage in its history and is today only about a quarter as big as it was when Dr. Cleburne moved his family there, but there it was, still standing, at the end of a small side road. No one answered my knock, and although there were a number of people working in the farm buildings a little further back up the road, none of them showed any interest in us, so I was able to prowl around the outside of the house and take as many photographs as I wished before we moved on to St. Mary's.

This once fine old Church of Ireland (Anglican) building, also at the end of a side road, stood shuttered and boarded up, although the sturdy exterior was still in reasonably good condition. The churchyard was very overgrown, the graves at all angles, but I noticed that it contained a number of more recent graves and that it seemed no longer to be limited to members of the Church of Ireland, since many of the modern graves bore what appeared to be more typically Roman Catholic names. Anyway, I stumbled through the long grass and looked at every legible headstone that I could see but never managed to find Dr. Joseph Cleburne. There was, however, a rather nice old set of stone steps going over the low wall surrounding the churchyard, which I imagined that the young Pat Cleburne must often have enjoyed climbing.

We then drove on into the village of Killumney in search of Bride Park Cottage. In her list of acknowledgments, Mauriel Joslyn mentioned that the owner of the cottage was one Daniel J. Murphy. Cork Library had virtually nothing on Cleburne, and Cork Tourist Office had no more than a photocopy of his military

Grange House, Cleburne's boyhood home (author's photograph).

record; at the top of this, however, was a handwritten note saying that Cleburne was born in Bride Park Cottage, that a room there contained a memorial to him and that anyone interested should contact "D. J. Murphy, Bandon Garden Centre." Reasoning that this was probably the same Daniel J. Murphy, but being unsure how up-to-date the information was, I called the garden center that morning, before we set out, and was immediately put through to Mr. Murphy. I explained that I was a great admirer of General Cleburne ("Are you now?" was his response to this) and that I would very much like to see his birthplace—from the outside, of course, I added hastily. He then handed me over to his wife, whose first words were: "When were you talking about?" "Oh, 11:30, noon or so," I replied. "Oh, no, that time wouldn't be convenient," she said. "You see, we've got the builders in." I repeated that I only wanted to see the house from the outside and asked what time would be convenient. Well, no time that day, was the response. "But we're only here for today!" I pleaded. "Oh, no!" she exclaimed, but she was still adamant that today was "not convenient."

We continued on into Killumney, however, in the hopes of at least getting a glimpse of Bride Park Cottage from the road. Just inside the village, and in what looked to me to be about the right position, we saw on the right a modern gate and a modern stone wall, with a driveway beyond. My wife stopped the car, and I got out to have a look. Beyond the gate was an enclosed area with trees, rather overgrown, and beyond that a much earlier gate leading to what I recognized

Bride Park Cottage, Killumney, Cleburne's birthplace (author's photograph).

immediately from the photographs as Bride Park Cottage. There was a builder's van parked outside the house and bags of cement piled up on the lawn but no sign of life as I passed cautiously through the second gate. If I had not had that conversation with Mrs. Murphy, I would simply have gone straight up to the house and banged on the door. As it was, I naturally felt somewhat inhibited, so contented myself with moving around as unobtrusively as possible and taking some photographs of the front and side.

Almost exactly a year later, we were back in Cork once again. This time, I had taken care to obtain from Mauriel Joslyn detailed directions for Dr. Cleburne's grave in St. Mary's churchyard. I had also managed, on the day before we left for Ireland, to make contact with Daniel Murphy at Bandon Garden Centre. He was very friendly, told me that I could certainly see the house and suggested that I call him from Cork once I knew what our plans were. I called him on the Saturday, as we were just going up the drive of yet another distant cousin's house, and agreed with him that I would come over on the Monday. This was a holiday, but the garden center would be open, and he said that he would be home again from 10:30 after opening it up and that I was welcome to come any time after that. We were staying this time on the far side of Cork, but it took me less than 30 minutes to get to Killumney. I was a little too early so decided to go first to the church and look for Dr. Cleburne's grave. I found St. Mary's again without too much trouble and then started to search for the grave. This time I found it fairly quickly, thanks to Mauriel's excellent directions and because it was the only one fitting her description of "a stone table on legs"; the tombstone itself, though, was completely covered with layers of dirt and dead leaves and a thick growth of brambles and ivy. I cleared away just enough to be able to make out the name underneath and to confirm that it was Dr. Cleburne's before it was time for my appointment with Mr. Murphy.

He welcomed me very warmly, gave me a thorough tour of Bride Park Cottage and could not have been friendlier or more helpful. It was immediately apparent that he had preserved the house beautifully. Many of its original features had survived. The rooms were filled with period furniture; family portraits and other pictures covered the walls, and ornaments and plants adorned the side tables and mantelpieces. In other words, the house looked very much as it must have done in the nineteenth century. There was a large portrait of Cleburne in the hall, and one of the windows bore the Cleburne family coat of arms in stained glass, with the Anglo-Saxon motto "Clibbor ne sceame"; although this motto was apparently originally longer, the three remaining words translate roughly as "No shame attaches,"—"Clibbor" ("sticking") being obviously a pun on the family name. Finally, Mr. Murphy showed me the upstairs bedroom where Cleburne is supposed to have been born. The commemorative plaque on the outside of the house, just to the right of the front door, gives the general's date of birth as March 17, 1828—St. Patrick's Day. Both Mauriel Joslyn and Craig Symonds, however, agree that Cleburne was in fact born on St Patrick's *Eve*, March 16; the idea that he was born on March 17 is therefore probably an example of later wishful thinking on someone's part. The two authors disagree, however, as to the room where he was born. Mauriel Joslyn states that it was in the room on the left of the upper story as one faces the house, while Craig Symonds claims that it was in the room on the right. I cannot now be entirely

St. Mary's, Athnowen, where Cleburne was baptized and his father was buried (author's photograph).

sure, but I am fairly certain that it was the bedroom on the left which Mr. Murphy showed me in 2009.

Having thanked Mr. Murphy for his hospitality, I returned to St. Mary's, where I spent some 45 minutes cleaning the top of Dr. Cleburne's grave. I started by clearing away all the dirt and brambles, using my bare hands. It had been raining hard overnight and was still drizzling, and some water had collected in a hollow on one of the graves. Luckily, I found an empty water bottle in the car, and by refilling it frequently with water from the hollow and pouring this over the tombstone and then wiping it away with handfuls of grass, I was able at last to get the grave reasonably clean and the inscription clearly visible. I was watched throughout by a little robin, which clearly felt that I had no business to be there. Like all his kind, he was very territorial, and as soon as my back was turned he was back perching on the grave again. Presumably he had become used to feeding on the bugs that lurked in the dead leaves, which I had now ruthlessly swept away.

Altogether, then, it had been a very enjoyable and successful morning, even though for some time afterwards I was still picking thorns out of my hands.

The four sites can be reached very easily by taking the N22 west out of Cork city. (Sheet 87 of the Ordnance Survey Ireland Discovery Series, while not essential, is probably a worthwhile investment.) The road turns sharply to the left as it reaches Ballincollig, but a right turn at this point on to the R608 and into Ballincollig itself brings one very shortly to the old barrack square. The N22, meanwhile, continues straight down the east side of Ballincollig, to turn sharp right again at the bottom, at the junction with the N40. Shortly after this, a left fork at Greenfield leads off on a minor road towards Killumney. Barely a mile further on, Grange House lies at the end of a small road that runs down to the left. Once back on the Killumney road, the next turn on the right takes one to St. Mary's. The road comes to an end at the church, with a field and then the N22 lying beyond it. Entering the churchyard and continuing along the wall to the right, one comes upon Dr. Cleburne's large, raised tomb in a corner by the end, surrounded by iron railings. It looks as if my efforts in 2009 may have had some influence, since a recent photograph on the internet shows the slab clear of debris and a Hardee battle flag draped over the railings.

Finally, there is Bride Park Cottage a very short distance on beyond the church. It is probably a good idea to call Mr. Murphy at Bandon Garden Centre, even if it may not always be necessary. My colleague Robin Ansell of the American Civil War Round Table (UK), for example, turned up unannounced in June 2018 and was welcomed and shown round the house and grounds immediately. The house was in fact for sale in April 2017 and was advertised as such in *The Irish Times* with a guide price of €1.1 million. I thought briefly of trying to persuade my wife that we should try somehow to raise the money to buy it but reluctantly dismissed the idea, since she had earlier refused even to consider buying a farm on Perryville Battlefield which had been going for a mere $200,000 or so. As it was, Mr. Murphy told Robin that he had been unable to sell the house and had therefore taken it off the market. He had, however, made one significant change. On my two visits, the outside of the house was an unobtrusive pale ochre color—as, indeed, was Grange House. It was still the same color in the photograph in *The Irish Times* in 2017. Judging by Robin's photograph, though, it is now a rather more aggressive sort of Farrow & Ball blue-gray.

This is not quite the end of the Cork part of the Cleburne trail, however, since the Cork Public Museum in Fitzgerald Park in Cork city has a small Cleburne exhibit. In fact, it consists of no more than a photograph of a portrait of the general, together with the Confederate Medal of Honor and Order of the Southern Cross awarded posthumously by the SCV, and can be found in a display case next to the sword and Invalidity Pension application of another local man, Captain Patrick Joseph Brown of Co. I, 147th New York, who lost an arm at Gettysburg. Finally, the more dedicated Cleburne enthusiast might want to complete the tour by taking the boat trip out from Cobh (Queenstown) to Spike Island in Cork Harbour, where Cleburne was stationed on guard duty in the spring and summer of 1849. This has the advantage of an additional Civil War connection in that John Mitchel, Irish nationalist and, later, staunch supporter of the Confederacy, was held for three days on Spike Island while awaiting transportation to Bermuda after his conviction for sedition in May 1848.

It is not even necessary to cross the Irish Sea, though, to find a memorial to Patrick Cleburne, and for this we have to thank Dr. (later Rear Admiral) Christopher J. Cleborne, USN, despite the different spelling of the family name (another, very common, variant is Claiborne), the doctor and the general were first cousins. Christopher Cleborne was born in Edinburgh on December 16, 1838, emigrated to the United States, graduated from the University of Pennsylvania in 1860 and was appointed to the U.S. Navy in 1861 as assistant surgeon, rising in November 1863 to surgeon. He retired from the Navy in 1899 with the rank of rear admiral and died ten years later.[3]

From 1871 on, Dr. Cleborne appears to have spent all the time that he could spare from his naval duties researching the history of his family. His search led him eventually to the little village of Cliburn in Westmorland, now subsumed into Cumbria, and into a lengthy correspondence with Canon Burton of St. Cuthbert's Church there. The church underwent a major restoration in 1886–1887 under Canon Burton's incumbency, and it seems to have been at this time that Dr. Cleborne donated two windows to it in return for the hospitality which he had received during his visit.[4] One of these is in memory of his infant son, Cuthbert Lowther Cleborne, who had died in January 1870 at the age of six months. The other is a small lancet window in the north chancel, bearing the Cleburne arms. On the recessed stone ledge directly below this, Dr. Cleborne had a large brass plaque installed commemorating his distinguished cousin. The inscription reads:

> In Memory
> of Major General
> Patrick Ronayne Cleburne
> C.S.A.
> Born 17th March 1828.
> Killed at the battle of Franklin Tenn
> 30th November 1864

6. On the Cleburne Trail in Cork and Cumbria

Cleburne memorial, St. Cuthbert's, Cliburn (author's photograph).

I had been thinking for some time of making the pilgrimage up to Cliburn to see this. Having a few free days towards the end of January 2010, and fresh from my successful visit to Cork the previous October, I decided that the time had come. Rather than enduring the long drive up from London, I decided to take the train up to Penrith, base myself there for a couple of nights and do the 12-mile round trip to Cliburn on foot. The Agricultural Hotel, Penrith, turned out to be only a couple of hundred yards from the station and, more important, to be recommended in *The Good Beer Guide*, so I booked myself into it and set off on the train from London, which took only two hours. Arriving at dusk, I checked in and then reconnoitered the road out to Cliburn before sampling a couple of good pints at the hotel and a rather indifferent Indian meal at the only recommended restaurant in Penrith.

The next morning, after an excellent full Cumbrian breakfast at the hotel, I set out on the road to Cliburn. It was a clear day with some sun, although very cold, with traces of snow lingering on the tops. After walking two miles down the main road south, I turned left onto a much smaller and quieter road and reached the little village of Cliburn without incident. I had taken the precaution, before leaving London, of checking that St. Cuthbert's Church was normally open and found it without too much difficulty—a lovely little old church standing on its own on the edge of a slope, with a small avenue of yew trees leading to it. It did not take too long to spot the window with the Cleburne arms and motto and the brass plaque on the sloping windowsill in front of it commemorating the general, largely because someone had helpfully placed in front of it a jar containing two small, hand-painted flags, a First National and a Hardee battle flag, the latter complete with battle honors. The only difficulty I had, in fact, was in photographing the brass plaque, because of the angle and the reflection of the light from the window, but after several attempts I finally achieved a reasonable result.

I then set off again on the road back towards Penrith, turning off to the left, however, after a couple of miles to take the little road over the hill to Clifton in order to view the last battle fought on English soil. Here, in 1745, Lord George Murray with the rear guard of Prince Charles Edward's retreating Jacobite Army had lain in wait for Cumberland's pursuing dragoons while the prince and the rest of the army marched on to Penrith. The dragoons had attacked in the December dusk and been routed by a charge by the Macphersons on the Jacobite left. After viewing the various memorials in and around the village, I pressed on back towards Penrith, since it was now mid-afternoon and very cold indeed. I arrived just after darkness had fallen and made straight for a welcoming pub in the little square in the center of the town, where I rested my legs and relaxed with a good pint in front of the fire before hobbling up the hill to my hotel for a hot shower and a good local supper.

Cliburn is six miles from Penrith and can be reached by the minor road of Wetheriggs, which forks left off the main A6 South shortly after Eamont Bridge. St. Cuthbert's is just off this road to the right and should normally be open; the Cleburne window and memorial plaque are just to the left of the altar. Anyone wishing to follow this with a visit to Clifton will find it just off the A6, about four miles south of Penrith. The site of the battle was still open farmland to the south when I visited it (although it looks disturbingly likely that it may since have been encroached upon by a recent housing development), and the village contains several monuments and memorials to the battle, including the so-called Rebel Tree, which marks the burial place of the few Jacobite dead. The Cleburne trail itself, however, ends at Cliburn.

7

France's Opportunity

One of the more curious examples of Confederate propaganda in Europe is a pamphlet of 30 pages titled *La France et les États Confédérés* ("France and the Confederate States"). Published in February 1865, it was the work of John Welsford Cowell, father of John Jermyn Cowell (see Chapter 2). The author is described on the title page as *"agent et représentant, muni de pleins pouvoirs, de la Banque d'Angleterre aux États-Unis dans les années 1837, 1838 et 1839"* ("agent and representative, with full powers, of the Bank of England in the United States in the years 1837, 1838 and 1839"). It is of interest chiefly because its English author, despairing of any such action on the part of his own country, makes a sustained and, indeed, passionate plea for France to intervene on the side of the Confederacy.

John Welsford Cowell was born on March 30, 1796, the son of John Cowell of Bedford Square, London, and was educated at Eton and (like Beresford Hope) at Trinity College, Cambridge, from which he graduated in 1818. He had been admitted to Lincoln's Inn in 1815, but appears to have found the law less appealing than the world of economics.[1] He tells us that he helped David Ricardo and James Mill (father of the perhaps better-known John Stuart Mill) to set up the Political Economy Club in 1821, and we know that he served both on the Poor Law Commission and later, in 1833, on the Factory Commission, which aimed at improving conditions for those employed in Britain's factories, particularly the children. As such, he must surely be the only Old Etonian mentioned by Marx in "Das Kapital"; in Chapter 20 (Chapter 22 in the first English edition), the bearded revolutionary quotes Cowell as saying, in a report on the spinning industry, "In England wages are, in effect, lower for the manufacturer than on the Continent, even though they may be higher for the worker."[2] In this context, incidentally, it is interesting to note that the impulse for factory reform in England appears to have come mainly from Anglican Tories, while the largely Nonconformist factory owners, fervent abolitionists where America was concerned, seem to have been curiously reluctant to accept any suggestions for ameliorating the lot of their own workforce.

The Cambridge University lists describe Cowell simply as having been "in the Bank of England."[3] Curiously enough, the archive of the bank has no record of precisely when he joined and when he left its employ. We do know, however, that in November 1834 he was appointed agent at the bank's Gloucester branch, the previous agent having proved unsatisfactory. To obtain this position, Cowell was required to provide security to the value of £10,000, a considerable sum for those days.[4] So successful was he in this post, however, that in 1836 he was made responsible for the Bristol branch as well.[5] Then, in 1837, the bank sent him to America.

At this time, a number of British firms (the so-called "American houses") which had been doing business with companies in the United States found themselves in serious financial trouble as a result of the failure of their American business partners to settle their debts. In order to avoid a crisis, the bank agreed, in March 1837, to support these firms by taking over responsibility for the debts. Since the sums involved were large, the directors of the bank then decided to send a representative to America to collect the money due to them as backers and creditors of the British firms.

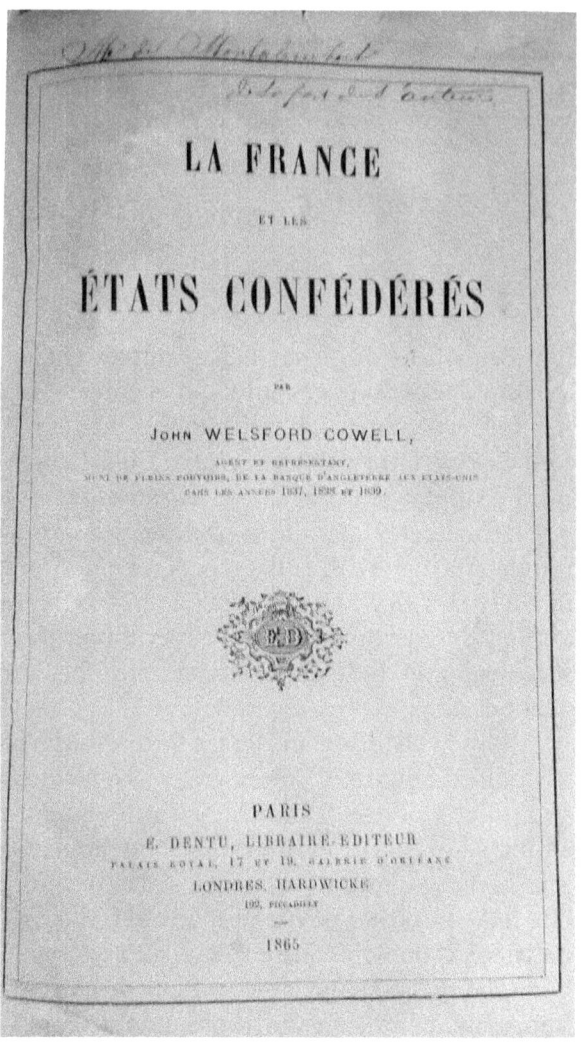

Front cover of *La France et Les États Confédérés* (author's collection).

The employee entrusted with this delicate task was Cowell, who was thereupon instructed to take the packet ship *Independence*, due "to sail from Liverpool on or about the 24th September to New York," in order "to recover from persons in the United States the amounts of unpaid Bills and Notes, drawn, endorsed or accepted by them."[6]

Cowell had married, on March 30 of that year, Frances Maberly, daughter of a former member of parliament for Abingdon; the marriage took place in the British Embassy in Paris. Leaving behind his pregnant wife (as mentioned earlier, their son, John Jermyn Cowell, was born on January 30, 1838, in London), Cowell now embarked for New York and took up residence in Philadelphia; this city was chosen probably because it was the seat of the United States Bank of Pennsylvania (formerly the Bank of the United States), with which the Bank of England had been in contact for a year or two past. Here he stayed until the spring of 1839, joined, at some point, by his new family. The Bank of England Archive contains a long and interesting letter to the then Governor of the Bank, T.A. Curtis, dated February 19, 1839, in which Cowell lists the sums of money successfully collected, complains of the "interference" and the "dilatory" attitude of various representatives of British companies on a similar mission to his own, states that he has achieved what he was sent out to do and, accordingly, asks to be allowed to return home in April because he wishes "to spend as much time as I can in Switzerland this year."[7]

In the first paragraph of this letter, Cowell tells his correspondent: "I go to Washington tomorrow where I have not yet been and where I wish to pass a few days before the breaking up of Congress on the 4th proxo. for the purpose of seeing some of [the] distinguished men of the States." Was one of these "distinguished men" John C. Calhoun? Certainly Cowell seems to have had a number of meetings with the Southern spokesman, whom he describes as an "eminent statesman" ("*homme d'État éminent*") and who had apparently informed him that the cotton-producing states had "taken the irrevocable decision to withdraw from the Union at the first favourable opportunity" ("*pris **irrévocablement** la résolution de se retirer de l'Union à la première occasion favorable*").[8] Cowell's stay in the United States and his position there as the representative of the Bank of England inevitably brought him into contact with many of the important men of the day, North and South, and gave him a chance to see at first hand the workings of American public life ("*tous les rouages de la vie agricole, industrielle, commerciale et financière de l'Union*"). In particular, his background in economics enabled him to understand what he described as "the most complete organisation of the protectionist system ever seen," which, he quickly decided, was "incompatible with the maintenance of the Union." He returned to England convinced, both from his own observations and from his conversations with Calhoun and others, that Southern secession was both inevitable and justified.

When the Civil War began more than 20 years later, Cowell lost no time in expressing his views, which remained unchanged. "For four years," he tells us, "I ... tried, on various occasions, to explain to my fellow-countrymen the vital duty which England had, in 1861, been called upon to fulfil towards herself, towards her race in the South and towards the whole of humanity." As a part of his efforts on behalf of the South during the first years of the war, he published two pamphlets: *Southern Secession: A Letter Addressed to Captain M.T. Maury, Confederate States Navy, on His Letter to Admiral Fitzroy* (1862) and *Lancashire's Wrongs and the Remedy* (1863). England having failed to listen, however, he had no option as "a devoted friend of the cause of the South" ("*un ami dévoué de la cause du Sud*") but to turn to France. "My only aim," he explains, "is to contribute to bringing about between France and the South an agreement which will spare the latter any further suffering and put her in a position to establish her independence."

La France et les États Confédérés was apparently published simultaneously in Paris and London. Its Paris publisher was E. Dentu of 17 and 19 Galerie d'Orléans in the Palais-Royal; in London, it was issued by Hardwicke of 192 Piccadilly. Both firms had already published a number of pro–Confederate pamphlets by various authors. It seems unlikely, however, that Cowell would have found many readers in England for his final literary effort on behalf of the Confederacy, since the pamphlet deliberately addresses, from the start, the interests of a patriotic French audience. He explains that if it had been a purely political question, he would have accepted England's lack of action as the decision of the majority of his countrymen. In this case, however, it is a question of principle involving "the highest and most sacred interests of human nature" ("*les intérêts les plus élevés et les plus sacrés de la nature humaine*"), and these must take precedence over the "narrow and purely material interests" of his own country. It is therefore "the French people, and the populations [*sic*] of the Confederate States, and not the English public, that I am addressing today."

He starts with an appeal to French national and commercial pride. The whole world knows that France has a natural and, indeed, legitimate desire to be as powerful on sea as she is on land. Furthermore, her manufacturers long to be free of their dependence on England for their supply of cotton. Napoleon III now has in his hands the means to achieve both of these objectives and to establish French naval and commercial supremacy for the future to an extent which he can never have imagined possible. However, France must act fast. England might yet decide to move, and tomorrow the opportunity could be gone forever.

Cowell then goes on to deal with the background to the war, emphasizing, in passing, his qualifications, in terms of both his profession and his experience, for speaking as he does. Calhoun had shown him, he says, that the apparent power of the Yankees (Cowell uses this term throughout the pamphlet) depended entirely upon the South. First, the protective tariff of 1816 had given Yankee shipowners a monopoly to transport Southern products, principally cotton. In 1860, "the last year of the Union," the value of American exports, excluding gold from California, amounted to 1,750,000,000 francs (£70,000,000) in round figures; of this, cotton and other Southern crops accounted for 1,250,000,000 francs (£50,000,000), or more than 70 percent. Secondly, Northern industry relied entirely upon a system of protectionism; this had led to a form of capitalism which had eventually involved, directly or indirectly, the entire population of the North in an "artificial system of exploitation" of the country's resources. The South was "the victim whose blood fed this system." Secession, however, had ended at last Northern exploitation of the South. The Yankees thus now had a desperate need to regain both their sole right to transport Southern products and their monopoly of the Southern market. Otherwise, they were doomed to lose all political, commercial and naval power. As a result, in order to recover their privileges they were now "massacring men, women and children throughout the South" and showing "a degree of ferocity which surpasses the cruelties practiced in the Wars of Religion."

This leads Cowell into a brief sketch of the Yankee character. The narrow, fanatical puritanism of their ancestors, which was at least sincere, has now, he tells us, "degenerated into a mixture of hypocrisy, cruelty, falsity, total lack of self-respect, gross presumption, indifference to the opinions of others, absolute ignorance of good, savage delight in doing evil and total moral depravity." These, he says, are now revealed to the entire world as the characteristics of the Yankee, female as well as male, and he follows this up by listing a selection of contemporary villains conforming to the type of the "pure-blooded Yankee," including Butler, Seward and Sheridan but also (rather unfortunately for his argument) the Russian-born Turchin.

The South, however, was a different matter entirely. The natural riches of "these privileged regions" had inevitably impelled the first colonists there to adopt the agricultural way of life, "which men have everywhere found the most agreeable and which has always contributed most powerfully to forming a national character of the noblest stamp." Cowell shared the view, common among the more upper-class sympathizers with the Confederacy in Britain (and not uncommon in the South itself, of course), that the Virginians, Carolinians and Georgians, at least, were of the stock of the old English country gentry. This race, "generous of old, noble alike in the men and the women it produced," had "in no way degenerated on Southern soil." Secure on their plantations, which provided all their needs, confident in their ability to supply the world's ever-increasing demand for their wonderful crop, the Southerners were not tempted to indulge in commercial or maritime ventures. They "never had nor ever could have the slightest interest in common with the Yankees"; their temporary alliance during the revolution had ceased in 1783, and since then they had gained nothing but harm from the association. The South's one aim was to cultivate its cotton and other crops to meet European demand; the "natural rôle of the European nations" was thus to send their ships to fetch these products and to bring in manufactured goods in return. The two sides had "no more need of the intervention of Yankee shipowners and financiers" than they had of that of "Eskimos and Patagonians."

Clearly, the South would never submit again to the "commercial and financial yoke of the Yankees." Equally, the Yankees could not give up their attempt to impose it once more; if they did, their "artificial system of production" and their maritime power would be finished forever. The South's problem was that she had allowed the Yankees "to organise a powerful navy at her expense." As a result, her coast was blockaded, and her attempts to build a navy herself having failed totally (one wonders how Raphael Semmes, for example, would have received this statement), her only hope was to form an alliance with a power strong enough to break the blockade—and France was more than strong enough for that. However, the South must make sure that any such alliance was both commercially and politically in France's interest. Cowell's suggestion, therefore, would be that the South impose immediately a double import duty and a 3 percent export duty on all goods carried on ships other than those belonging to citizens of France or of the Confederacy. This would have the effect (as he shows by means of specific examples) of immediately giving France's merchants a huge advantage over their English rivals and, within quite a short time, of shifting the main European entrepôt for cotton from Liverpool to Le Havre. An alliance with the South would make the Second Empire more glorious and more powerful than the first, and France would never need any other alliance either in Europe or in America. "A nation as intelligent, active and ambitious as the French" surely would not hesitate for a second!

But what must France do in return for this extraordinary opportunity? Nothing that will cause her the slightest inconvenience. She is already on the point of modifying and relaxing her maritime laws; all that she needs to do is to accelerate this process. In particular, French merchants must be permitted to buy the best ships at the best price wherever they may happen to find them. By Cowell's calculations, two-thirds of the merchant marine in the United States in 1860 had been dedicated to the transport of Southern products. Since the secession of the South, these ships must therefore have been lying idle and would be available cheaply. Why, then, should French shipping companies not be permitted to buy them up, and with their crews too? After all, most sailors on Northern ships were not native-born; in 1839 (according to Cowell's figures), 40,000 to 50,000 English sailors were employed on American vessels, and that number would certainly have increased since then. The only stipulation would have to be that on each vessel the captain, the officers and a quarter of the crew should be French by birth.

Naturally, there would be objections to this plan on the part of certain French politicians, and Cowell shows that he has anticipated these. For a start, France had been conditioned for years to think of the United States as "a strong naval power, essentially hostile to England," whose friendship she could always count upon. The Yankees, well aware of this, had taken care always to proclaim their natural alliance with France against the common enemy. In normal circumstances, of course, France would be sorry to see a state which she considered her ally lose its power at sea. If, on the other hand, all of this power was to come by default to her, surely she should rejoice rather than lament, and that was precisely what would happen if she was prepared to ally herself with the South.

A more serious objection was that France might thus find herself at war with the United States. Any such war, however, could only be a minor one ("*mesquine*"). If the Yankees really wished to damage France, they could do so only by means of a war of aggression. Now they were able to carry out a war of aggression against the South because they had command of the sea and because England had recognized the blockade and allowed the North to buy arms and to recruit soldiers and sailors from Britain; she could hardly permit this in the event of a Union war against France. Certainly, Union privateers would be able to cause a certain amount of harm at the outset, but they would hardly be able to keep it up for very long. After four years of war, the Union treasury was almost bankrupt; annual production in the North could not possibly have replaced the capital expended so unproductively. Furthermore, their navy today consisted of a few undoubtedly formidable ships and a large number of aged and unserviceable vessels. While these might possibly be enough to defend the coast of the United States against a French blockade, they could only do so at the expense of raising the blockade of the South.

The Yankees would thus be unlikely, in Cowell's opinion, to declare war on France. Yet, so blind are they to the realities of their situation that they might think it worth risking such a war. "Vain, bombastic, rash, audacious," they try always to push things as far as they possibly can and as their own ignorance and their opponents' fears allow them. On the other hand, they lack moral fiber. "They have no dignity, no human respect, they are totally lacking in pride, in greatness both of spirit and of character." If France were to declare herself openly in favor of the South, supporting this with the necessary military and naval preparations, there was little doubt, in Cowell's experience, that the Yankees would quickly yield.

Blair's recent mission to Richmond could be a simple "Yankee trick." In Cowell's opinion, however, this was evidence of the "desperate condition" to which the Yankees realized that they had been reduced. "All the world" could see that they were on the edge of bankruptcy. Their credit had dried up, and for some months now they had been forced to re-export "entire cargoes of goods" without unloading them, since they were unable to pay for them either in specie or in products of an equal value from their own territories. Recruitment, too, had ceased, even with the incentive of a bounty of $1,000 per man. There was thus no solid basis to their much-vaunted power. From Cowell's observations during his stay among them, and from his experience of their "vacillating and presumptuous character," he was convinced "the moment France raised her voice above the clamor of this contemptible boasting ('*cette misérable jactance*'), the empty shadow of their short-lived greatness would be seen to vanish."

However, it is essential for France to show herself firm and resolute. If she does so, she will be amply repaid for the costs of any war which she might possibly find herself forced to undertake against the North. Aligning herself with the South, in short, will give France a faithful ally in permanence and will make her the greatest power in the world. Moreover, thanks to France's presence in Mexico and to what Napoleon III has already achieved there, this result can be obtained even more quickly.

Furthermore, France would have justice on her side. By virtue of previous treaties, she has as much right to trade with Charleston, New Orleans and Mobile as she has with New York and Boston. For four years she has been prevented from exercising this right. Now, either these ports are integral parts of the Union or they are not. If they are, then the Yankees have no right to deprive France of the freedom to trade with them. Should France demand compensation for the harm done her, as she would be perfectly entitled to do, the Yankees could hardly object that an external force hindered them from protecting her in her enjoyment of her rights, since the whole world knows that the cities in question would be only too happy to trade with France and that they are only prevented from doing so by the Yankees themselves. If, on the other hand, the Southern States are no longer *de jure*, as they are no longer *de facto*, members of the old Union, then what possible right can the Yankees of a new Union claim in order to justify impeding France in the exercise of a right given her by treaty and upheld by the states directly concerned themselves? Finally, Cowell reminds his readers that the people of Louisiana are French. France ceded Louisiana to the former United States under certain conditions; these conditions are now being flagrantly violated by the Yankee government, and France owes it to her old subjects to demand that they be fulfilled.

Cowell ends by restating his conviction that by following the course outlined by him in the previous pages of the pamphlet, France is now in a position to effect the transfer of the main European cotton entrepôt from Liverpool to Le Havre. The choice before her is between becoming completely independent of England for her supply of cotton, on the one hand, and, on the other, seeing her commerce subordinated to England's within a very short period. Already, England is making enormous, and largely successful, efforts to increase the cultivation of cotton in India. Unless France's manufacturers and merchants are prepared to abandon all hope of ever competing with England in the international market, there is no time to lose.

Cowell's approach is thus very different from that of other British sympathizers with the Confederacy. Although he admits, at one point, that his one aim is to help the South to establish its independence, his appeal throughout is to French self-interest and to France's envy of England as a commercial and maritime power. Furthermore, he ignores completely the question of slavery. Whereas men like Spence and Beresford Hope, writing for a British audience, had felt compelled to bring this awkward issue out into the open in order to anticipate and deal with the most obvious objection to what they were proposing, there is not a single reference to slavery in the whole of Cowell's pamphlet. Presumably he either considered it irrelevant to his argument or felt that it would be unwise to remind his French readers of its existence.

One final point of interest is that the copy of the pamphlet in the possession of this writer is inscribed on the front cover, in Cowell's hand, "*M. de Montalembert de la part de l'auteur*" ("Monsieur de Montalembert from the author"). Charles de Montalembert was a Liberal Catholic writer, a champion of the cause of Polish independence and well known in French literary and political circles. His father had been a minister under Charles X, the last reigning Bourbon king of France, together with the father of the Confederate General Camille de Polignac. Unlike Polignac, however, Montalembert was a firm supporter of the Union. He was a friend of John Bigelow, the energetic U.S. Consul in Paris, and he wrote a lengthy article in the *Correspondant* hailing the victory of the North.[9] Cowell must have been well aware of Montalembert's views. Why, then, did he present him with a copy of the pamphlet? Can he seriously have expected to convert the Frenchman, or was this merely the literary equivalent of scrawling a moustache and a pair of spectacles on a political poster?

Cowell did not long survive the fall of the Confederacy. He died on February 9, 1867, in St. Leonards-on-Sea, at a boarding-house run by a Frenchman.[10] Since the cause of death was given as "chronic bronchitis," we can presume that Cowell had gone to the Sussex coast for the sake of his lungs. His son, Jermyn, who, as we have seen, fully shared his father's views on the war, died unmarried in December of the same year. Cowell's house, however, at 41 Gloucester Terrace, London, is still standing, although as a result of renumbering it is now 126 Gloucester Terrace. A modest, bow-fronted Victorian building, it is thus one of the few remaining relics of an elderly Englishman whose devotion to the ideal of Southern independence was such that he was prepared to appeal to England's hereditary rival in a final, desperate attempt to bring it about, even at the possible expense of his own country's commercial interests.

John Welsford Cowell's grave, Hastings (author's photograph).

8

Death in Paris

"The Civil War was fought in ten thousand places," intones the narrator, David McCullough, at the start of Ken Burns's television documentary *The Civil War*, "from Valverde, New Mexico, and Tullahoma, Tennessee, to St. Albans, Vermont, and Fernandina on the Florida coast." And, he might have added, in London, England, and Paris, France. Scholars will continue to argue over whether the South could actually have won.[1] There can be few serious students of the war, however, who would disagree with the premise that some form of European intervention—which, in effect, means intervention by Britain or France or both—would undoubtedly have influenced the course of the war and would very possibly have decided the eventual outcome. It has been aptly stated that, in order to win, the South had merely not to lose. Had Britain and France agreed to break the blockade, for example, as they were urged to do by both Confederate agents and local sympathizers, it seems probable that, in the end, the United States would have had little option but to accept the fact of Southern independence. It is true that the Union could reasonably have expected the sympathy and moral support of Russia, her chief friend in Europe, but she could not have hoped for very much more; for Russia, while well able to defend herself on land (as she had shown less than ten years previously in the Crimean War), would hardly have wished to risk her fleet against the Royal Navy. British and French support for, or at least recognition of, the Confederacy could thus have been crucial, and both sides showed themselves well aware of this from the start.

The war was therefore fought no less fiercely in Britain and France than it was across the Atlantic. There was no actual bloodshed, of course, in this particular theater, no Sharpsburg or Gettysburg. Nor was there any real physical violence, if one excepts the attempt by a group of Yankee students from the famous Lycée Condorcet, armed with peashooters, to ambush Slidell on the Champs-Élysées on New Year's Day, 1864—a skirmish, incidentally, from which the veteran Confederate emerged victorious, bearing away, as a trophy, the coat of one of his assailants.[2] Nevertheless, there were casualties here, too, among them a 57-year-old lawyer from New Jersey hailed, by the attorney general of that state, as having "died in the service of his country" and "joined that heroic band of younger members" of the state bar who had "freely given their lives for the same great cause."

This was the United States Minister to France, William Lewis Dayton, who died in mysterious circumstances on December 1, 1864.[3]

Dayton was born in Basking Ridge, New Jersey, on February 17, 1807. He graduated from the College of New Jersey (now Princeton University) in 1825 and then studied law, being admitted to the bar in 1830. Seven years later, the people of Monmouth elected him to a seat in the New Jersey legislature as a Whig, a position which he held for only a few weeks before being appointed an associate justice of the state's supreme court. A judge's salary, however, proved inadequate for the demands of his growing family, and he therefore resigned after three years and set up in private practice. In 1842, he was appointed by Governor William S. Pennington to the seat in the U.S. Senate left vacant by the death of Dayton's cousin, Samuel Lewis Southard, being reelected in 1845 for the full six-year term.

William Lewis Dayton, U.S. Minister to France (from Bigelow, *Retrospections of an Active Life***).**

Dayton was not a particularly prominent or active member of the Senate, being noted only for his determined opposition to any measure which might be construed as increasing the power of the slave states. This position, however principled, cannot have been a popular one in the New Jersey of those days, and in March 1851, Dayton duly lost his seat and returned to the law. Five years later, he joined the newly formed Republican Party, which promptly nominated him, at its first National Convention, as its vice presidential candidate. Taking up his private law practice once again after the Republican defeat in November 1856, he was almost immediately appointed attorney general of New Jersey. Then in April 1861, Abraham Lincoln, the newly elected Republican president, named him United States Minister to France.[4]

The infant Confederacy, meanwhile, was also engaged in selecting its representatives to the various European nations and especially to the two key countries: Britain and France. It might be supposed, at first sight, that Britain would have been a more fruitful field for Confederate endeavors than France. For a start, sympathy for the South in Britain was widespread and grew as the war continued; it cut across party lines, could be found at all levels of society and was particularly strong in the established church, the Church of England. Furthermore, Britain, more even than France, needed Southern cotton; it has been estimated that between 4,000,000 and 5,000,000 people, or something like one in seven of the population, depended directly or indirectly for their livelihood on the cotton trade.[5] The problem, however, was that the British government proved strangely reluctant to commit itself, preferring to pursue a policy of, in Calhoun's phrase, "wise and masterly inactivity."[6] We know now that British recognition of the Confederacy was only briefly a serious possibility in September 1862, and the failure of Lee's invasion of Maryland ended even that possibility. In short, Palmerston and his cabinet, like the House of Peers in the Gilbert and Sullivan opera *Iolanthe*,

> throughout the war
> Did nothing in particular
> And did it very well[7]

at least in their own estimation, although they managed thereby successfully to antagonize both sides in the conflict. British sympathizers with the South, certainly, never entirely gave up hope of persuading their government to intervene, but it is not surprising that the Confederates themselves tended increasingly to concentrate their efforts upon France.

Southern diplomats and officials recognized, as did everyone else, that while British foreign policy was discussed in cabinet and debated in Parliament, French foreign policy was the result of the decisions of one man—the Emperor, Napoleon III. All written pleas for recognition or any other form of intervention were thus addressed to him, either directly, as in Paul Pecquet du Bellet's *Lettre à l'Empereur*,[8] or indirectly. Napoleon was generally supposed to favor the South, if only because it was clear from early 1862 that he had plans for Mexico, and it was therefore obviously in his interests to have a friendly power across the Rio Grande. What the more optimistic advocates of recognition had failed to grasp, however, was that Napoleon's long years in exile had left him, like Charles II of England before him, determined never "to go again to his travels," and this basic fact informed all his actions. Certainly he had come to power in 1852 through the popular vote, expressed in a plebiscite. Opposition to his regime, however, while not always overt, came from all parts of the French political spectrum, from the Legitimists, who still hoped for the return of the Bourbon monarchy, through the Orleanists to the Republicans. He had therefore to tread carefully. The experiences of his first 40 years had taught him to dissemble, and he had developed a facility for leaving all who had dealings with him convinced that he agreed wholeheartedly with them—without once ever actually saying so. (This, incidentally, almost certainly explains the later disagreement over what precisely he had said in his meeting with the British Members of Parliament John Arthur Roebuck and William Schaw Lindsay in June 1863 and the consequent failure of Roebuck's motion for recognition in the House of Commons). The truth, in fact, is that there was never any possibility of the emperor's acting independently of Great Britain where intervention was concerned. Slidell, the Confederate Commissioner to France, was indeed frequently depressed by or impatient at what could be seen as French prevarication and procrastination.[9] Nevertheless, long after Benjamin had withdrawn Mason from London and dismissed the British consuls in the

Confederacy, Slidell and others, both native and foreign, continued to place their hopes in France. As we have already seen, the British economist John Welsford Cowell was still urging French intervention in February 1865, his main argument being that this would enable France to steal a march over her old rival, England.[10]

In its relations with France, in fact, the Confederacy had one distinct advantage—the strong links between the Creoles of Louisiana and the mother country. A recent article by Professor Salwa Nacouzi of the University of Poitiers[11] makes the point that in 1860 those citizens of Louisiana of French origin who could afford to do so continued to send their children to study in Paris, first at one of the great lycées and then at law school or medical school. France, too, was where the Creole aristocracy still tended to go on vacation, to attend performances at the Paris Opera or to take the waters at Vichy. The outbreak of the Civil War found many of these Creoles in France, and determined to defend there the cause of the South, *"prenant la plume ne pouvant prendre l'épée"* ("taking up the pen, not being able to take up the sword"), in the words of Paul Pecquet du Bellet.

Confederate propaganda in Britain, whether produced by Southerners or by local sympathizers, tended to stress the South's essentially Anglo-Saxon nature and to compare it favorably with the "scum and refuse of Europe"[12] which was supposed to compose the population of the North. The Louisiana Creoles in Paris, however, not surprisingly adopted a rather different argument. By focusing on the writings of three Louisianians—Paul Pecquet du Bellet, Charles Deléry and Alfred Mercier—Professor Nacouzi shows how these Creoles chose rather to emphasize a common Latin heritage. She points out that they see themselves as "Français d'Amérique" rather than as Americans. In their writings, the Yankees are depicted as hypocritical, intolerant Anglo-Saxon Puritans, in contrast to the generous, openhearted Latin and Catholic South.

But the Confederate government did not, of course, leave the defense of the South in Paris entirely in the hands of exiled Creoles, however prolific their written efforts. The original Confederate mission to Europe, in the spring of 1861, had included Judge Pierre A. Rost, who, although brought up in Louisiana, had actually been born in France. The final choice for Confederate Commissioner, however, was John Slidell, who, despite his New York origins, had been living in Louisiana since 1819, spoke good French and was an astute and experienced politician. Finally, the journalist and sometime diplomat Edwin De Leon, who had been dispatched to Europe with a "secret-service fund" of $25,000 "for the special purpose of enlightening public opinion" and had arrived in London in June 1862, decided soon afterwards to base himself in France, as offering better opportunities for influencing the press; after first publishing a pamphlet, *La Vérité sur les États Confédérés* ("The Truth about the Confederate States"), he worked diligently and with some success to persuade the French journals to accept articles favorable to the South—largely, it must be said, through judicious application of his State Department funds.[13]

To counter all of this effort, the Union had William Lewis Dayton. At first sight, Dayton would appear an odd choice for the post. He had no diplomatic experience, does not appear to have been in very good health and could neither speak nor read French. His photograph shows a stout, florid, middle-aged man with a determined but somewhat dyspeptic look. In fact, Lincoln, who had been greatly impressed by Dayton's stand against slavery ten years earlier, had wanted to make him Minister to Great Britain. Seward, however, convinced the president to appoint to London Charles Francis Adams (almost certainly to the eventual advantage of the United States), and Dayton was sent instead to Paris.[14] Here he set up the United States legation with William S. Pennington, of the well-known New Jersey family, as his first secretary and his own son, William L. Dayton, Junior, as his second secretary, and for over three years labored to block any French move towards recognition of or assistance to the South. It is only fair to say, though, that much of the credit for the success of Union diplomacy in Paris must go to the younger and more energetic John Bigelow, who had travelled widely in Europe before the war, had good contacts in both France and England and could speak French. Bigelow was sent out to Paris in August 1861, officially as consul but in practice "to look after the press."[15] He remained in close contact with Seward throughout and appears to have carried out his task with little reference to Dayton; indeed, one has the impression that he became somewhat impatient at times with the minister's slower and more cautious style of diplomacy.

At any rate, by the end of 1864, Dayton's honest and straightforward manner had gained him the respect of his French hosts, and he could justifiably feel that he had handled a difficult mission with skill and success. The strains of his position, however, had inevitably affected his health. He was ill more and more frequently, and "an increasing addiction to the pleasures of the table" did little to help. On the evening of December 1, 1864, he died of a brain hemorrhage while visiting the apartment of "a notorious courtesan" in the Hôtel du Louvre.[16] The funeral service was held the following Tuesday, December 6, at the American Church in the Rue de Berri. Members of the French government and the diplomatic corps attended, and Bigelow gave the main address before introducing Professor Laboulaye of the Institute of France, a staunch and influential friend of the Union.[17] The body was then sent back to the United States and buried in the Riverview Cemetery in Trenton, New Jersey. So much for the basic facts of the minister's death; there is rather less agreement as to the details.

Who was this "notorious courtesan," and what was the United States Minister to France doing in her apartment that December night? The fullest, as well as the most sensational, account of the death appears in a book published in 1932 by a Canadian author, Beckles Willson, and titled *John Slidell and the Confederates in Paris (1862–65)*. Henry Beckles Willson was born in Montreal in 1869. After a successful career as a journalist and newspaper editor in the United States and Britain, he became a freelance writer, producing a number of books. He served with the Canadian Expeditionary Force in France during the First World War and then settled in Paris. He died in Beaulieu-sur-Mer in the South of France in 1942, Paris being then occupied by the Germans.[18]

Willson's book on Slidell has a number of failings for what purports to be a serious work of history. To begin with, it has no index and no bibliography, a curious omission. It is clear, however, that the author has consulted many of the

The original Hôtel du Louvre (author's photograph).

surviving documents of the period, as well as the memoirs of such key figures as Bigelow and James Dunwoody Bulloch. He tells us, in his foreword, that he had also had access to various letters and documents belonging to the family of George Eustis, Slidell's secretary, as well as to material collected by the historian Henry Vignaud,[19] another member of the Confederate mission. Finally, his long residence in Paris had given him an opportunity to meet many who, while not personally involved, had known the participants in the events he describes.

It is thus unfortunate that the book is, in many matters of detail, highly inaccurate. Where Willson quotes directly from a reliable source, such as the various papers in the Library of Congress, he can, of course, be trusted. In all other cases, he has to be treated with caution. In his two final pages, for example, he manages to give both the wrong dates for the deaths of Slidell and Judah P. Benjamin and the wrong number for Benjamin's house on the Avenue d'Iéna.[20]

Willson's account of Dayton's death was taken, he tells us, from a pamphlet published in 1869 titled *The True Account of the Death of Minister Dayton*, described, apparently, by Henry Vignaud as "exaggerated, but not improbable." The main character is a certain Sophie Bricard, a young singer from New Orleans who had been studying at the Conservatoire in Paris. Like the other Louisiana Creoles in Paris, she was a fervent Confederate, and her rendition at various concerts and fund-raising evenings of such pieces as *La Bannière Bleue* (presumably a French version of *The Bonnie Blue Flag*) and *Aide-Nous, Ô France Aimée* had made her the toast of the exiled Southern community—or at least, it appears, of the male portion of it. Shortly after Slidell's arrival in Paris in February 1862, she was lucky enough to be given a part in *Florian*, a new operetta by Jacques Offenbach which was due to open at the Bouffes-Parisiens Theatre. Slidell was, of course, encouraged to attend, as did both Dayton and the emperor. Invited backstage after the second act, Slidell found Offenbach presenting the company to the emperor. On catching sight of the Confederate Commissioner, Sophie Bricard fell to her knees and, with an impassioned gesture, begged Napoleon to aid her "suffering country" (*"mon pays souffrant"*). Appalled by this breach of protocol and deeply embarrassed, Napoleon left the room at once, but the story circulated rapidly and caused great affront to the Unionists in Paris, which was exacerbated by Mademoiselle Bricard's insistence in the following performances on wearing a Confederate flag on her bosom and deliberately emphasizing "certain ambiguous lines in her part" until ordered to desist by the Prefect of Police.

The operetta soon ended its run, and Sophie, who, whatever her other gifts, does not appear to have been a particularly talented singer, had no further engagements on the Paris stage. Shortly after this she married a man named Eccles, who later conveniently disappeared—to join the Confederate Army, some said. The new Mrs. Eccles now rented an apartment in the Hôtel du Louvre, where she gave regular parties for her various admirers, including a number of Confederate naval officers, in a large room decorated with framed portraits of Confederate notables and with a Confederate flag draped over the piano. During this period, she was memorably described by an unimpressed visitor of Unionist sympathies as "a shameless Jezebel of Secession."

The story then moves on to the evening of December 1, 1864. Dayton was just finishing his dinner when he was handed an anonymous letter informing him that his First Secretary, Pennington, had for some time been conducting a "scandalous liaison" with "the former Sophie Bricard, now known as Mrs. Eccles, and a rebel spy" and that Pennington would be at her apartment that very night. (The U.S. Legation at that time was in Dayton's apartments, which were in the street which forms an outer circle around the Étoile at the upper end of the Champs-Élysées. Originally known, for convenience, simply as the Rue Circulaire, this street had, by a decree of March 2, 1864, finally received a name, or rather two names, the northern half becoming the Rue de Tilsit and the southern the Rue de Presbourg; Dayton's apartments were in what today is 6 Rue de Presbourg).

Since his son, William L. Dayton, Junior, was about to leave for the Palais-Royal Theatre, a short distance across the square from the Hôtel du Louvre, Dayton decided to accompany him. The carriage dropped them off at the Palais-Royal, and the minister then went on alone to the hotel. (The Hôtel du Louvre was not then in its current position on the west side of the Place du Palais-Royal but in the similar building on the east of the square now occupied by the antique shops of the Louvre des Antiquaires; its owners moved it in 1875 to create more space for their retail business. The side of the building facing the square, however, is unchanged, and the words "Grand Hôtel du Louvre," although faded, can still be seen across the center of the façade).

Mrs. Eccles's apartment was on the third floor, and the minister was breathing heavily from the climb when he reached her door. Here he was greeted by the lady herself, who informed him, once she had recovered from her surprise at this unexpected visit, that his secretary was not there. Confused and embarrassed, Dayton suddenly swayed and seemed about to fall. A glass of brandy revived him, and his hostess then proceeded to explain that, so far from being a "rebel spy," she had for the past year been working for the Union. Confederate representatives in Paris had, apparently, been expressly forbidden by Benjamin to have anything further to do with her, on the grounds that she was "a young woman of dubious morals, whose championship would compromise the Cause." Disgusted at this ingratitude, after all that she had done for the South, she had decided, she said, to transfer her allegiance and had been in contact with both Pennington and Bigelow. Already half convinced, the susceptible Dayton was completely won over when she produced letters bearing the address and seal of the U.S. Consulate.

6 Rue Presbourg, Paris, which housed Dayton's apartments (author's photograph).

She then persuaded the minister to share a bottle of champagne with her, and a friendly conversation ensued. Finally, Dayton begged Sophie to sing for him. Going over to her piano, she smilingly complied, choosing a piece from *Florian*. All was going well when she suddenly heard a groan, followed by a dull thud. Turning round, she saw her visitor lying on the floor, apparently in some kind of fit. The doctor was summoned, but, before he could arrive, Pennington entered the apartment. It was now apparent that Dayton was dead. Clearly, the body could not be left where it was. Enlisting the help of Sophie's black servant and of the doctor, who had now appeared, Pennington succeeded in getting the body down the stairs and persuading a reluctant cabdriver to drive it to the legation. There was then a delay, for at this point Mrs. Eccles emerged, dressed to go out and determined to accompany them to the legation in order to explain everything to Mrs. Dayton. Managing, at last, to convince her that, in the circumstances, this was perhaps not a particularly good idea, Pennington thrust a gold piece into the coachman's hand, and the cab set off at a trot. The following morning, it was announced that the United States Minister to France had died at the legation of an apoplectic stroke.

Such is Willson's version of events, and it has been accepted without question by a number of other authors. An article on Dayton's death by Serge Noirsain of the Confederate Historical Association of Belgium, for example, repeats Willson's story almost word for word, with the addition of a few descriptive details presumably from the author's imagination, such as that the minister was "on the verge of sipping a good Old French Cognac" when the letter arrived.[21] Monsieur Noirsain does, however, allow himself to speculate that Dayton's reason for going to the apartment may have been rather different and that his death may have occurred in somewhat more compromising circumstances; here he cites the cases of Mata Hari and Christine Keeler.[22] Professor Nacouzi, too, although her article on the Creoles in Paris does not mention Dayton, accepts at face value Willson's account of Sophie Bricard's choral activities on behalf of the South in the early days of the war.

It is certainly a good story, but how accurate is it? Preliminary investigations are not encouraging. In the whole of Offenbach's enormous body of work, for example, there is not one piece called *Florian*, nor anything with a similar title. Nor is there a character of that name in any of his operettas.[23] Furthermore, inquiries to the relevant university and other libraries in New Orleans have produced no trace of a Sophie Bricard.

At this point, then, it is time to look at what we have in the way of real evidence. Almost certainly only one person actually witnessed the death, but we do have a number of more or less contemporary accounts which, when taken together, allow us to draw certain conclusions.

First, there are the press reports. Typical of these is that by the Paris correspondent of *The Times* of London. Written on Monday, December 5, four days after the death, his account reads as follows:

> It appears that [Mr. Dayton] left home about 9 o'clock in the evening of Thursday to pay a visit to an American family residing at the Hôtel du Louvre. He had been only a few minutes there when he felt a dizziness in the head, accompanied by a violent pain. His friend gave him some vinegar to bathe his temples and a bottle of salts, which seemed to revive him. He lay down on the sofa for some time, and appeared to slumber. After some time his friend, not hearing him breathe, took him by the hand and found it quite cold. A doctor was sent for, but when, after the lapse of an hour or so, he came, he found it was too late; he had been dead some time.

Apart from the confusion over precisely who it was that Dayton was visiting, this account is interesting in that it contradicts Willson's statement that it was given out that the minister had died at the legation, rather than in the Hôtel du Louvre.

The Trenton, New Jersey, *Daily True American* for March 3, 1865, quoting the attorney general's[24] eulogy on his departed colleague, gives additional, and rather touching, detail:

> On the evening of his death, he called on an acquaintance from New Jersey at his hotel. Not finding him in, and wearied with the ascent of the stairs, he called on a lady friend to rest a little while. He conversed pleasantly for a few minutes, and then asked her to play for him the "Star Spangled Banner," which she did. He then requested her to sing "Home, Sweet Home," and she complied. He said, "I wish I was there," and, apologizing, he cast himself on a sofa and gave a slight groan. The family physician was sent for—an hour elapsed before his arrival—and he said he then had been an hour dead. So that the banner

of his country, and his home were the last objects present to his mind before he went home forever. [This version of the death, incidentally, is the only one apart from Willson's which mentions any singing.]

Secondly, both William L. Dayton, Junior, and the doctor in question made statements immediately after the event, these statements being among the Dayton Papers at Princeton. According to the younger Dayton,

> After dinner on the 1st of December, 1864, about 7 o'clock my father and I got into a cab near the Arc de Triomphe and rode to the corner of the street nearest the Palais Royal theatre. We then entered the Palais Royal Arcade and walked slowly together around looking into the different windows along the western gallery. I walked with him perhaps one third the length of that Arcade. At that time he seemed in his ordinary health. I remarked nothing which indicated special weakness or failing. I then said I thought I would go into the Palais Royal theatre awhile. "Well," he replied, "go on," and he walked on as if with the intention of sauntering along and looking into the windows. That was the last I saw of him until I was sent for towards midnight when I found him lying in Mrs. Eckel's apartment on a sofa dead.
>
> He dined with his usual appetite and seemed if anything in somewhat better spirits than usual that day.
>
> He did not say where he was going when he left me; he had previously said that he felt as if he ought to take a little air and exercise, not having been out much the previous few days.

The doctor involved, Dr. Edward John Beylard, had previously treated Dayton. His statement, signed and dated December 9, 1864, runs:

> At half past ten on Thursday evening the 1st of Dec., a german woman speaking bad french [sic][25] called at my apartment, No. 7 Rue d'Anjou St. Honoré, and said that she wanted me to go to the Hotel du Louvre where Mr. Dayton, the American Minister, had suddenly been taken quite ill. I went in a carriage which was waiting immediately, and reached the hotel about a quarter before eleven. I was taken to Mrs. Eckel's apartment and on opening the door found Mr. Dayton lying on the sofa as if asleep. Mrs. Eckel said immediately "Mr. Dayton is very dangerously ill and has had an attack of some sort." Fearing that she might say something that might alarm him I proposed to her to pass into the adjoining room and tell me what had occurred. She replied that it was useless to leave the room for she thought he was dead; he was perfectly insensible. I looked for his pulse without finding it and applied my ear to his heart, but found no sign of life. His hands were quite cold and my impression at once was that he had been dead for some little time. He was lying on his right side upon the sofa in an easy position as if he had just come in from the street and had laid himself down to take a little sleep. Mrs. Eckel then went on to say that Mr. Dayton had called about 8 o'clock to see Mr. Vanderpool at the Hotel; not being able to see him, he had come into her room; that he complained of head-ache, but however had talked some little time with her still complaining of head-ache, dizziness and not being able to see well. He then sat down on the sofa and she offered him various restoratives, which appeared to have no effect. He suddenly began to snore and to make quite a noisy expiration from the mouth which, she said, had lasted ten minutes or a quarter of an hour, at the end of which time she thought he had ceased to breathe. It was evident that he had died of a rupture of a blood vessel in the brain. I at once proposed to have the body taken home. Mrs. Eckel preferred that some members of the family should be sent for to come and see the condition in which the body was found, before it was removed from the apartment. That course was taken. Mr. Dayton's sons were sent for, arrived in due time, returned to the Legation to prepare the rest of the family for what had occurred while I took charge of the remains and had them taken to the Legation.

As an afterthought, the doctor added:

> I omitted to state that shortly after I entered, Mrs. Eckel drew from her pocket a sheet of foolscap with writing on both sides and mentioned that Mr. Dayton had called to see her on some important business and that the paper was a brouillon [draft] of something that was to be written out for Drouyn de Lhuys [the French Minister of Foreign Affairs]; that he had called the evening previous and not finding her at home had left his card.[26]

Finally, we have Bigelow's version of events, as recorded in his autobiography. Although written more than 40 years after the Civil War, this work consists, in the main, of letters and other documents with a linking commentary. It is clear, then, that Bigelow had preserved an enormous number of papers from the period and was not relying on his memory alone. He repeats the story told him, he says, by Dr. Beylard on the morning of December 2, 1864. Bigelow's account thus follows the general outline of the doctor's statement, with, however, a number of additional details and some omissions.

First, Bigelow says that Dayton and his son had decided to take a walk after dinner and had "strolled down to the Palais Royal." Given the distance from the Arc de Triomphe to the Palais-Royal and Dayton's age and physical condition, this seems highly unlikely, and it is in any case contradicted by the son's account. He then says that, while the son went into the theater, the father went off "to make a call or two. He appears to have gone first to his friends the Vanderpoels." As they were at dinner, however, Dayton did not stop but "was next heard of at the apartment of a Mrs. Eckels [sic]." Bigelow goes on to say that, according to the doctor, Dayton "called upon his hostess to give three cheers for Abraham Lincoln, the news of whose reëlection had recently reached Paris." Shortly after this the minister complained of feeling unwell and died in a few minutes. Bigelow then describes the doctor's efforts, with the help of William L. Dayton, Junior, who had been sent for, to get the body into the younger Dayton's carriage and back to the legation "before the police could interfere." The proprietor of the hotel was most unhappy about this and only agreed when Dr. Beylard promised to take full responsibility. Bigelow also says that, despite their protests, "Mrs. Eckels insisted upon riding up to the legation with the body to explain how it happened," on the grounds that her reputation was involved. Finally, he adds the homely detail, relayed to his wife later that day by Mrs. Dayton, that the minister "had eaten very freely of pumpkin pie" the previous evening.[27]

While it would be natural enough for Bigelow, writing for a general readership, to leave out the medical details, it will be seen that there is one rather more significant omission in his account; there is no mention whatsoever of the mysterious draft document for the French Foreign Minister mentioned in the doctor's statement.

But there was, after all, probably only one witness to the actual death, and perhaps we should now see what she has to say. Her real name was Lizzie St. John Eckel, and her evidence of what happened that night is included in the autobiography which she published in 1874, ten years later.

Her story of her life, if true, is an extraordinary one. First, she was, or at least claimed to be, the daughter of Maria Monk, a poor Canadian alcoholic and part-time prostitute who achieved fame in 1836 with the publication of *The Awful Disclosures of Maria Monk*, a lurid exposé of scandalous goings-on at the Hôtel Dieu Nunnery in Montreal.[28] Maria Monk's claims were denied by her mother, who stated on oath that her daughter had never been in a nunnery, and refuted by the impeccably Protestant Colonel William L. Stone, editor of the *New York Commercial Advertiser*, who investigated them thoroughly. That the book had, in fact, been written by a group of unscrupulous Protestant ministers, one of whom had been living with Maria Monk at the time, came out when they started to sue each other for a share of the profits.[29]

Lizzie St. John was born in 1837 in New York and spent her early years in poverty. Tiring, finally, of his wife's drunken rages, Mr. St. John left in 1843, taking with him the three children, whom he placed with various female relatives in and around Amenia, Dutchess County, New York State. Lizzie appears to have been highly attractive to men from a very young age. Determined to better herself, she moved to New York City and took various menial jobs until she was taken up and more or less adopted by a kindly judge, a friend of her relatives, and his wife, who paid for her to attend Madame Martinet's Academy. Here, at the age of 19, she attracted the attention of the rather older Samuel Eckel, of Tennessee, a former United States Consul in Talcahuana, Chile. They were married a few months later and shortly afterwards moved to Washington.

Here the former Lizzie St. John was able to mix with a number of prominent people and "first learned the magical power of woman over man, and even over the destinies of a state." Continuing her intrigues after she and her husband had returned to New York, she found that she was able to use her charms to gain influence and her influence to gain money, obtaining government contracts and appointments for various interested parties and receiving a percentage in return. But her husband became too jealous, and in 1861 she left him and moved to Brooklyn. The outbreak of the Civil War gave her further opportunities to employ her wiles to her financial advantage; making use of the contacts made earlier in Washington, she provided a service for those New Yorkers who had friends or relatives in the South or who simply wished to ship goods across the lines.

In July 1863, for reasons which are not entirely clear but which may well have been

Lizzie St. John Eckel (from *Maria Monk's Daughter*).

connected with her recent activities, she sailed for Paris, taking her young daughter with her—as well as a number of introductions from her contacts in New York. Here she swiftly blossomed into a full-blown "adventuress," to use the Victorian term. She soon gathered around her a group of young men-about-town, chiefly American, including, apparently, Pennington, Dayton's first secretary. Through his influence, she was able to obtain an invitation to the first ball of the 1864 season at the Tuileries Palace, where she seems to have succeeded in bewitching the honest Dayton. This gave her an entrée into the upper levels of both French and American society in Paris, one of her conquests being the Duc de Morny, the emperor's half brother and one of the most influential men in France, who was actually introduced to her by the U.S. minister.[30]

Although her life continued much as before after Dayton's death, with her circle of powerful admirers growing ever larger, she tells us that she found herself becoming increasingly disenchanted with it. Gradually she started, despite herself, to turn to religion, until finally she was received into the Roman Catholic Church. She left France in 1870, just before the outbreak of the Franco-Prussian War, and returned to the hills of Dutchess County where she had spent so much of her childhood. Settling just across the state line in Sharon, Connecticut, she built a church in honor of St. Genevieve and became a familiar figure in the community until her death in 1916 or 1917.[31]

On that fateful evening in 1864, she tells us, she dressed herself with even more than her usual care, for she was expecting the United States Minister to "come and pass the evening" with her. She had written to him the previous week, explaining that she wished to see him "on a matter of importance"; in fact, an American entrepreneur who had set up a business in France wished to be made a Chevalier of the Légion d'Honneur and had promised her $5,000 if she could obtain the coveted red ribbon for him, and she wanted to enlist Dayton's help. He had apparently called the previous evening, when she was out, and had left word that he would call again that evening.

As soon as the minister arrived, she handed him the application, which he promised to have drawn up properly at the legation and presented to the Minister of Foreign Affairs as soon as possible. He would do his best, he said, to make sure that it was dealt with promptly because he was planning shortly to return to the United States; he had had enough of his post and would be writing to Seward to tender his resignation. Horrified at this news, and at the consequent threat to her $5,000, Mrs. Eckel turned all her charms upon the minister. First fascinating him with amusing stories, she then assumed "a dreamy sadness" and exclaimed: "How sorry I am, that you are going away! For you alone can protect me against the envy and jealousy of the Americans." The conversation continued for some 20 minutes, until suddenly Dayton complained of a headache. Fetching some bay rum, she began to bathe his head, while he begged her not to leave him. At last she asked if he would like to lie down and went off to get a pillow. On her return, she found that he had fallen sideways onto the sofa and was breathing heavily, apparently asleep. She placed the pillow under his head and covered him with her opera cloak. Some 40 minutes later, at about 10 o'clock, she felt his hand, which was cold. Failing to rouse him, she summoned her German maid, and both realized that he was dead.

Her account now descends into melodrama, but she does tell us that she sent her maid for the doctor, who finally arrived shortly before midnight, and that she also sent word to Dayton's family. When Willie Dayton arrived and asked her what his father had been doing there, she replied that he had come to call on Mr. Vanderpoel but finding him out had decided to visit her. The youngest Dayton son now appeared, and she drove back with the brothers to the legation to break the news to Mrs. Dayton and her daughter while the doctor arranged for the body to be sent home separately. The family kindly tried to insist that she spend the rest of the night with them, but she was unable to sleep, "so poignant were my sufferings," and finally drove home in the doctor's carriage through the fog. Once back in her apartment, she threw herself on the floor and "gave vent to the torrent of grief, that was raging within me." Seeing this, her servant, too, began to weep "for all that I must have suffered." The reader can decide how much of this was genuine sorrow at the untimely death of a good man and how much sheer frustration at the unexpected loss of a powerful protector.

The death of the U.S. Minister in Mrs. Eckel's apartment caused great excitement in Paris, and a few days later "an American official" who, she had been advised, was her "worst enemy" in Paris, called on her and "requested me to state to him the circumstances of Mr. Dayton's death, in order that he might inform Mr. Seward." This can only have been Bigelow, the U.S. Consul.[32] It is curious that he makes no mention of the interview in his memoirs. At any rate, she gave him, she says, a long and largely imaginary account, carefully concealing the real reason for Dayton's visit.[33]

Having heard all the evidence, we can now attempt a summing-up. First, it seems probable that Dayton went to Mrs. Eckel's apartment that evening because she had summoned him and that she had summoned him for the reason which she gives; the last part of Dr. Beylard's statement appears to bear this out. Second, the story of his attempt to visit the Vanderpoels is almost certainly a fabrication of Mrs. Eckel's, invented on the spur of the moment in order to hide the truth behind his appearance in the Hôtel du Louvre. Third, for some reason Dayton did not wish to tell his son Willie where he was going but preferred to pretend that he merely wanted some fresh air. Fourth, we know from Willie Dayton's statement that father and son left the Arc de Triomphe in a cab at about 7 o'clock. The distance to the Palais-Royal Theatre is a little under two and a half miles, and they then spent some minutes walking around together before Willie entered the theater, and his father went off to the Hôtel du Louvre, some 400 yards away. Dayton would therefore have arrived at Lizzie Eckel's apartment at about 8 o'clock, just as she told Dr. Beylard. Fifth, we can say that death probably occurred shortly after 9 o'clock, although the minister was not certified dead until the doctor's arrival a little before 11, the cause of death being, as Dr. Beylard says, "a rupture of a blood vessel in the brain." Finally, contrary both to French law and to the wishes of the hotel proprietor, the body was hurriedly removed from the hotel before the police could intervene.

Unfortunately, a number of questions remain. Who, for example, was Sophie Bricard? Did she actually exist? It would be easy, and tempting, to dismiss her as a creation of Beckles Willson's imagination, were it not for one curious piece of evidence. As has already been mentioned, while Willson is not a very reliable authority, he can at least be trusted when he quotes from others. Although, as so often, he fails to give the source, he does reproduce in his book part of a letter from "a youthful American visitor to Paris, written early in 1864," which reads as follows:

> P. took me on Sunday night to one of Mrs. Eccles' receptions, formerly the notorious Sophie Bricard of New Orleans. Her apartment is fairly large and gaudily furnished. It is in a hotel close to the Théâtre Français. She is very petite, looks about twenty-five [Lizzie St. John Eckel was 26 or 27 at this time] and has beautiful hair and eyes, but I don't care much for her expression. Learning from P. that I was from Missouri she was pleased to show me flattering attention; but as she is a rabid Secessionist I guess it would have disgusted her to know my real sentiments and that my two brothers are just now fighting in Grant's army. There were several queer-looking customers about, said to be naval men, but I suppose these regard Sophie's place a convenient rebel rendezvous. I must not forget to mention that there are large framed portraits of Jeff Davis, Lee, Beauregard, Benjamin and the rest about the place, and that the end of a big piano is draped with a rebel flag.[34]

Assuming that it is not a complete invention on Willson's part, what can this mean? We know from her own account that Lizzie St. John Eckel preferred to keep her origins a mystery during her time in Paris; might the character of Sophie Bricard then have been a creation of her own? She had been married to a Southerner, and her activities while living in Brooklyn during the early part of the Civil War could certainly be considered as having aided the South. Did she, initially at least, continue the same sort of activity in Paris? Furthermore, there is a possible New Orleans connection. In March 1862 (the year before Mrs. Eckel arrived in Paris), Jacques Offenbach had handed over the direction of the Bouffes-Parisiens Theatre to Alphonse Varney, father of the very much better-known Louis Varney. Alphonse Varney was born in the Crescent City and had been director of the French opera there until 1851; he might well have been amenable to giving a pretty Southern sympathizer a part in one of his short-lived (and now forgotten) pieces.

Secondly, did Bigelow ever make use of Lizzie/Sophie, as Willson claims, to gain information? Much of what she learned from her highly placed contacts might potentially have been very valuable to him, and it would have been unlike him not to attempt to get his hands on it. He tells us, perhaps a little too glibly: "I never had a spy in my employ during my official residence in France, nor did I ever pay anyone nor authorize anyone to be paid a penny for any secret information, procured at my instance for a mercenary consideration."[35] What, however, if it was not "procured at his instance" but merely passed on to him spontaneously as a result of a preliminary agreement?[36] Again, why does Bigelow in his memoirs refer to "a Mrs. Eckels"? He had a highly efficient intelligence network and must have known very well who she was. Why, too, does he not mention the interview which she says that he had with her after Dayton's death and which, given his position as U.S. Consul, he almost certainly must have had?

This, of course, brings us to the final question. We know that Dayton died of a brain hemorrhage, but what was the immediate cause of this? Was it simply the exertion involved in walking the 400 yards from the Palais-Royal Theatre and climbing the two flights of stairs to Mrs. Eckel's apartment? Or did the lady in question resort, as Serge Noirsain suggests, to some rather more active means of persuading the minister to help her to obtain her $5,000? After all, as she puts it herself: "I now felt, that the time was precious, and that I must do all I could to enlist his sympathies.... Mr. Dayton was an open-hearted, candid, pure-minded man; and one, who was totally off his guard against the seductions of a woman like myself." This would certainly explain Dr. Beylard's reaction when, on finding his friend and patient dead, he "came up to me, and stood in an attitude, as though he were going to strike me."[37] Could it also explain his eagerness to remove the body before the arrival of the police?

Why, too, did the minister not tell his son where he was going? It may well be, of course, that Dayton's interest in Mrs. Eckel was purely paternal, or at most that he was guilty of nothing more serious than a middle-aged man's foolishness when confronted with an extremely attractive (and highly unscrupulous) young woman. Certainly it can be argued that, if there had been anything improper in his relationship with Lizzie Eckel, either then or earlier, the family would hardly have continued to treat her as they did; even if we discount her evidence that she was invited to stay with them after the death (and there seems no real reason to do so), the Dayton Papers at Princeton contain two later letters from her to Willie Dayton which show that she was on friendly terms with them, one asking for an introduction to Drouyn de Lhuys and the other thanking Willie for having helped her obtain a ticket to a ball.[38] On the other hand, though, if they had immediately started to shun her, would that not have been taken as confirmation of what all the gossips and scandalmongers must have been saying?

There is a clue in a curious letter to Bigelow from Seward dated February 13, 1865, and reproduced in Bigelow's memoirs. In this, the U.S. Secretary of State says that he has "received, read, and burned your note of the 27th, as you suggested." A footnote explains that this refers to Bigelow's *official report* of the death of his predecessor.[39] If this is so, why did Seward have to burn it after reading it? Clearly, there was something in it which Bigelow wished hidden. Who was it, then, that he was trying to protect—himself, Mrs. Eckel or the late William L. Dayton?

I had long given up all hope of finding the answer to this question, when Professor Don H. Doyle of the University of South Carolina revealed in his book *The Cause of All Nations* (2015) that Bigelow's own copy of his letter to Seward was among the Bigelow Papers at New York Public Library. Although Bigelow had left clear instructions for it to be destroyed, these (fortunately for the historian) had been disregarded. Professor Doyle had discovered the letter just as his book was going to press. I immediately contacted Don Doyle, who very kindly sent me a copy of the letter. The letter makes it finally clear that it was indeed

Dayton's reputation that Bigelow was concerned to protect. Bigelow states, "From the appearance of Mr. Dayton's clothing," Dr. Beylard was "of the opinion that something had been going on to which neither party could afford to have witnesses" and refers to reports that the death was the consequence "*de faire amour* too soon after dinner."[40]

9

The Last Days of the *Alabama*

By June 1864, after nearly two years at sea and some 75,000 miles, the CSS *Alabama* was a tired ship. Her bottom was fouled, the copper sheathing peeling off her hull, her decks were leaking and there were holes in the tubing of her wheezing boilers. Officers and men were "pretty well fagged out," as her captain put it,[1] and he himself had a bad cold which turned into a fever. "Our bottom is in such a state that everything passes us," he had written in his journal on May 21. "We are like a crippled hunter limping home from a long chase."[2]

The night of June 10 found the ship in the Channel in thick fog, but she took aboard a Channel pilot off the *Lizard*, and the following morning, Saturday, June 11, 1864, she arrived safely off the long breakwater marking the entrance to the great harbor at Cherbourg. At about 12:30, she came through the West Pass and anchored just inside the harbor.[3]

On duty in Cherbourg harbor that day was the pride of the French Navy, the ironclad *Couronne*, under the command of a Breton officer called Jérôme Penhoat. Penhoat now sent off a boat to find out who the stranger was and what she wanted. The boat came back with an officer in a gray uniform who explained that the vessel was the CSS *Alabama* and that she wanted permission to land some 40 prisoners from the last two prizes she had captured. Penhoat replied that he was not authorized to give permission but would have to pass the request up to the Préfet Maritime. Meanwhile, however, the *Alabama* could come in and anchor in the inner part of the harbor, which she did.[4]

The title of Préfet Maritime is usually translated, by Semmes and others, as "Port Admiral." In reality, however, it is very much more than that. The Préfet Maritime is responsible not merely for the port but for the whole of that particular part of the coast and everything that happens there.

The Préfet Maritime at this time was Vice-Admiral Augustin Dupouy, a career naval officer of 56 who, as captain of the *Napoléon*, had taken part, with the Royal Navy, in the bombardment of Sebastopol during the Crimean War. He was very much a technical man; he had invented a new naval gun carriage,[5] for example, and when he was finally able to visit the *Kearsarge* after the battle of June 19 and to talk to her captain, John Ancrum Winslow, he was clearly disappointed

Cherbourg harbor (author's photograph).

that Winslow was unable to answer his questions about the precise method of casting used on the *Kearsarge*'s 11-inch guns.[6]

Dupouy had been appointed only three weeks earlier, and he was just beginning to get the measure of his new responsibilities when the arrival of the *Alabama* presented him with his first problem. He was, after all, a sailor, not a diplomat, and he had absolutely no idea what to do in a case like this; his previous career had not prepared him for it. The chain of command went from Penhoat to Dupouy to the Minister of the Navy, Count Prosper Chasseloup-Laubat, and from Chasseloup-Laubat direct to the Emperor, Napoleon III, who was conveniently on holiday in Fontainebleau at the time. At 2 o'clock, then, Dupouy sent off a hasty telegram to the minister, asking for instructions.[7]

While Dupouy was still waiting for an answer, Semmes compounded the problem by sending ashore his Executive Officer, John McIntosh Kell, with a letter for the admiral asking permission for the *Alabama* to enter the dock in order to carry out extensive but essential repairs. In desperation, Dupouy sent off a second telegram to the minister, asking what he should do now.[8]

Finally, shortly after 7 p.m. that evening, an answer came to the first telegram: the prisoners must be released immediately! There was no response as yet, however, to the question of repairs.[9]

Semmes, delighted to be rid of his reluctant guests, loaded them into two of the *Alabama*'s boats and landed them at the Vigie de l'Onglet,[10] a former battery near the quay which was now a signal station and acted as a kind of control tower, as it were, regulating traffic in the harbor. Here they were discharged into the care of the U.S. Consul, Édouard Liais, a naval provisioning merchant from a prominent local family.[11]

Préfecture Maritime, Cherbourg (author's photograph).

The night before arriving in Cherbourg, Semmes had written in his journal these curiously final and prophetic words: "And thus, thanks to an all-wise Providence, we have brought our cruise of the *Alabama* to a successful termination."[12] He expected the repairs to take a couple of months. His plan, as we know from a letter which he wrote two days later to the senior Confederate Navy officer in Europe, Flag-Officer Samuel Barron, was to pay off his officers and crew and give them an extended run on shore, as he put it, and for himself to ask to be relieved of his command.[13] As we know, however, it was not to be.

The next day was Sunday and a quiet day aboard the *Alabama*, with only a few curious visitors. Semmes reported in his journal that the weather continued cloudy and cool and that he was still suffering from his cold and fever. Nevertheless, he mustered and inspected the crew. There was still no answer from Paris, but at least officers and men could enjoy fresh food for the first time since they had left the Cape. It was the start of the strawberry season, and Semmes wrote appreciatively in his journal of the "very large and fine" berries, as well as of the good beef and mutton and the excellent Normandy milk and butter.[14]

Back on shore, meanwhile, the admiral received a telegram from Paris. Was he certain that the mysterious vessel was indeed the *Alabama*? Might she not be the *Florida*, which had been in Brest for repairs from August 1863 until January 1864, when she evaded the *Kearsarge* and made for the open sea? After questioning the *Alabama*'s newly released prisoners and the pilot who had brought her in, Dupouy sent off a telegram to Paris confirming that the vessel was indeed the

The Vigie de l'Onglet, Cherbourg (author's photograph).

Alabama and then a further one confirming that Semmes was her captain, following both telegrams with a letter the next day.[15]

The next day was Monday, June 13, and Semmes went ashore in the morning to see the admiral and to explain what exactly he needed. He met Dupouy in his office in the Préfecture Maritime, a few minutes' walk from the landing stage. The admiral gave him a courteous welcome and was very friendly—until it came to the question of the repairs. What a pity, he said, that Semmes had not gone to a commercial port like Le Havre or Bordeaux, where he could easily have been accommodated. The problem was that Cherbourg was a naval base, and the docks were naval docks. However, he had of course referred Semmes's request to Paris and was waiting for a response. How unfortunate that the emperor was away at the moment!

A rather frustrated Semmes took his leave, writing later to Barron about the need for patience "as all the Latin races are proverbially slow in their movements."[16]

It seems probable that he also took the opportunity that morning to visit the Confederate consular agent, Adolphe Bonfils,[17] another naval provisioning merchant and a neighbor of Liais. Bonfils was also the consul of Brazil, but it is clear both from his actions and from the evidence of John Slidell, the Confederate Commissioner to France, that he and his sons took their responsibility to the Confederacy extremely seriously.[18] Indeed, Bonfils had written of his own volition

Naval Arsenal Gate, 1862, Cherbourg (author's photograph).

to Slidell, on the very day that the *Alabama* arrived, asking him to apply direct to the government for permission for her to go into dock.[19]

If Semmes did visit Bonfils that morning, though, it would have been of necessity a fairly short meeting, since the Imperial Brazilian Navy training ship *Bahiana* was arriving that day on a courtesy visit, and Bonfils would have had to be on hand to welcome her.[20]

That afternoon, rumors began to circulate in Cherbourg that the USS *Kearsarge* was on her way from Flushing, so Semmes continued to keep the crew on board.[21]

The following day, Tuesday, June 14, these rumors turned out to be true. At about 12:30, the dark shape of the *Kearsarge* appeared off the breakwater. She made no attempt to enter the harbor but anchored just outside the East Pass.[22] A boat then came out to the *Couronne* carrying her surgeon, Dr. John M. Browne, who asked permission for her to enter the harbor. Penhoat, having signaled the admiral, gave permission, but the *Kearsarge* made no move to come in. Instead, her captain, John Ancrum Winslow, came ashore at about 3:30 to speak to the U.S. Consul, Bonfils's neighbor Édouard Liais. Liais then informed the admiral that the *Kearsarge* had come to pick up the *Alabama*'s former prisoners, whereupon the admiral sent another telegram to the minister, asking for instructions.[23]

At this point Dupouy's worst fears were realized, as Semmes decided to fight the *Kearsarge*.

It seems that he had come to this decision virtually as soon as he saw the *Kearsarge*. He called Kell into his cabin and discussed the situation with him, but his opening words were: "Kell, I am going out to fight the *Kearsarge*. What do you think of it?" The meeting was thus similar to a certain type of business meeting, called simply to approve a decision already made. Kell could never have dissuaded Semmes, even if he had wanted to. He could, and did, point out the *Alabama*'s weak points, but, as he said, "I stated these facts simply for myself."[24]

Later that day, Semmes wrote to Samuel Barron in Paris. "As we are about equally matched," he said, "I shall go out to engage her."[25]

Why did Semmes fight? In reality, he had very little choice. The *Alabama* was far too slow now to make a run for it, and his only real alternative was thus to sit bottled up in Cherbourg until the end of the war. Since this was not Raphael Semmes's style, he decided to fight. In any case, as he said to Kell, "I am tired of running from that flaunting rag!"[26]

"As we are about equally matched." On the face of it, that was true. The two ships were of similar size. The *Kearsarge*'s crew was slightly larger than the *Alabama*'s, but the *Alabama* had one more gun. The *Kearsarge* had seven guns—four 32-pounders, a 28-pounder rifle and two huge Dahlgren 11-inch guns on pivots amidships. The *Alabama* carried eight—six 32-pounders, an 8-inch smoothbore pivot aft and a 7-inch, 110-lb. English Blakely rifle as a forward pivot.[27]

Kell reminded his commander, though, of the *Alabama*'s disadvantages. It was not merely the state of her hull and her boilers. In the course of her long cruise, both fuses and powder had deteriorated. When Semmes had used one of his last two prizes, the *Rockingham*, for target practice in April, only a third of the shells had exploded.[28] Trying a few shots in open sea three weeks later, Semmes found that not one of them burst. "Bad fuses," he scribbled in the margin of his journal.[29] The powder, too, was affected by dampness, probably because the magazine was located next door to the freshwater condenser. Some of it had to be thrown overboard.[30]

The *Kearsarge* had one advantage, however, which was not mentioned. Some months before, Winslow had had 1.7-inch iron chains slung along her sides to protect her vulnerable machinery. The chains were then boxed over with deal boards, which were painted black.

Historians have argued ever since over whether Semmes knew about these chains. Semmes himself, and Kell, always denied that he could have known. Three of his officers, however, said much later that he did. Lieutenant Arthur Sinclair first said so in *Two Years on the Alabama*, published more than 30 years after the event. The *Alabama*'s surgeon and paymaster, Dr. Galt, said so in 1900 in a letter to Mrs. Kell, and Semmes's clerk, W. Breedlove Smith, apparently repeated the claim in an interview with the New Orleans *Daily Picayune* in 1912—48 years after the battle.[31]

If Semmes did know about the chains, though, how did he find out? Sinclair says that Dupouy told him.[32] Dupouy's reports to the minister, however, make no mention of the chains until June 21, by which time he had had a chance to go on board the *Kearsarge* and examine her. In any case, one consistent element in the story of the *Alabama*'s last days is that Dupouy was desperate throughout to be seen as absolutely impartial; he would hardly have compromised his position by tipping Semmes off. It is also claimed that everyone in Cherbourg knew about the chains; the local fishermen had apparently seen them. On May 20, however, less than a month before, when the *Kearsarge* was at Calais, five officers from the CSS *Rappahannock* had put on civilian clothes and rowed around her; they reported only that she was "very dirty," making no mention of any chains.[33] On balance, then, it seems highly unlikely that Semmes knew about them.

At all events, Semmes decided to fight, and that evening he delivered an extraordinary challenge to Winslow. He wrote to the Confederate consular agent, Adolphe Bonfils, as follows:

> SIR: I hear that you were informed by the U.S. Consul that the Kearsarge was to come to this port solely for the prisoners landed by me, and that he was to depart in twenty-four hours. I desire to say to the U.S. Consul that my intention is to fight the *Kearsarge* as soon as I can make the necessary arrangements. I hope these will not detain me more than until to-morrow evening, or after the morrow morning at furthest. I beg she will not depart before I am ready to go out.[34]

Bonfils then took this letter down the rue du Val de Saire to the house of his neighbor Liais, the U.S. Consul, and delivered it to him.[35]

Semmes and Dr. Galt, his paymaster, then took ashore, according to Semmes, four and a half sacks of sovereigns, containing about 4,700 in all, the ship's payroll and a package of ransom bonds, which they deposited with Bonfils.[36] It will be noticed that Semmes makes no mention of his collection of chronometers. One account says that he had hoped to sell them in Cherbourg but was forbidden to do so by the French authorities and had therefore had to deposit these, too, with Bonfils.[37] It is known that they were eventually brought to England on the British yacht *Hornet*, but they may possibly have been held by Bonfils in the meantime.

Meanwhile, the French authorities had noticed unusual activity aboard the *Alabama*. The admiral sent his aide-de-camp, who came back with the news that Semmes had determined to go out and attack the *Kearsarge*. The admiral replied that Semmes could not go out until 24 hours after the *Kearsarge* had left. Semmes, however, having practiced law, was ready with his answer. The 24-hour rule *would* apply, he said, if the *Kearsarge* had come into the harbor and anchored, but she had not; she was cruising up and down outside the breakwater, so he was free to attack her when he wished. The admiral retorted that in his opinion the 24-hour rule applied as long as the *Kearsarge* was in French waters and that if necessary he would use force to stop Semmes from going out. Semmes then changed tack and protested that allowing the *Kearsarge* to take his former prisoners on board would amount to giving her reinforcements. This does not appear to have occurred to the admiral, but he decided to hold back the embarkation until he had received instructions from Paris.[38]

Early the next morning, June 15, Semmes temporarily withdrew his request to be allowed to go into dock and asked instead to be permitted to take on coal.[39] At about 10 o'clock, the admiral received a visit from Winslow and Liais. Dupouy says that it was immediately clear to him that the *Kearsarge* had not come to Cherbourg simply to pick up the prisoners. Her aim was obviously to cruise up and down until the *Alabama* came out. He therefore asked Winslow either to come into port and anchor, as he had been authorized to do, or to go further out. Winslow agreed to wait for the *Alabama* in the open sea.[40]

Shortly after noon, a telegram arrived from Paris finally giving a ruling on the two questions perplexing the admiral: the *Alabama* could not be permitted to go into dock, but equally the *Kearsarge* could not be permitted to embark the prisoners.[41] As Semmes had by now withdrawn his request, though, Dupouy decided not to tell him about the telegram.[42] Coaling started that afternoon.

That day, however, Dupouy had something to take his mind briefly off his American problem, because June 15 saw the official inauguration of Cherbourg's new Casino des Bains de Mer. Sea bathing had apparently been brought to France by Royalist émigrés who had been in exile in England during the Napoleonic Wars, and it had become very fashionable. Cherbourg had in fact had a sea-bathing establishment as long ago as 1829, but unfortunately it had gone bankrupt. Now a new company, with extensive capital, had been formed by Count Hippolyte de Tocqueville (brother of the writer Alexis de Tocqueville), and this week marked the opening of the new establishment. The plan, apparently, was to make Cherbourg into the French Brighton.

The new Casino des Bains de Mer was an enormous complex. Apart from sea bathing, it offered hydrotherapy, gaming rooms, billiard rooms, lecture rooms, a restaurant, a ballroom, luxurious apartments with sea views and a garden modeled on Versailles. The administrator was the British Consul, Horace Hamond, and the director was another Englishman called Alwood, who had done his best to make the opening a success by inviting to it a number of his richer friends and acquaintances from England, including a certain coal-mining magnate named John Lancaster. Invitations had also been sent, of course, to everyone of importance, whether military, religious or civilian, in Cherbourg and the surrounding area, including Normandy's most famous author, the novelist Octave Feuillet, and his beautiful wife. Finally, Alwood had made an arrangement with the directors of France's Western Railway, who had agreed to lay on a special train leaving Paris at 8:20 on the Saturday night, arriving in Cherbourg early on the Sunday morning, June 19, and returning to Paris at 8:45 that evening—the only possible problem here being that Cherbourg time was 20 minutes behind Paris time.[43]

The day of the inauguration began early with a religious ceremony to bless the new enterprise. Dupouy was unable to attend, however, since he had received an overnight telegram from Paris asking for a full report on the situation, and he had been working on that when Winslow and Liais appeared in his office.

Finishing the draft of his report and leaving it to one of his staff to check, he hurried off to the casino, arriving just in time for the banquet for the 70 most distinguished locals, at which he was one of the speakers. He was unable, though, to enjoy the food, the wine and the conversation, nor the music by the band of the 18th Regiment of the Line, for worrying about what was going on outside. Once the speeches and the loyal toast were over, he was able at last to return to his office, where he was updated by his staff. He then read through his report for the minister, signed it and went off to change for the ball which was to close the day's festivities.[44]

Here the admiral could finally forget his worries over the contending Americans. The evening started at 9:30 with a massive public display of fireworks from the terrace of the casino. Then the whole of Cherbourg society gathered in the great hall of the casino for the ball. Everyone was there—government officials, military and naval officers, political figures, the local business community, the Brazilian officer cadets from the *Bahiana* and, inevitably, beautiful women. This was clearly the biggest event on the Cherbourg calendar for 1864, and the local press published ecstatic descriptions of the lights and flowers, the uniforms, evening dress and decorations, the bare shoulders and the jewels. The "sumptuous buffet," too, received appreciative mentions. More column inches, however, were devoted to the beautiful Madame Feuillet, the star of the evening, who was generally described as "éblouissante," "dazzling." The admiral seems to have been particularly taken with her and was quick to promise her a pleasure trip around the harbor in his barge,[45] as a result of which we have a description from her pen of both the *Alabama* and the battle.

Only one group was absent. To the disappointment of the revelers, there were no officers, as they had been hoping, from the *Alabama*. Retiring to his room with a glass of champagne in order to write up his copy, one of the journalists wrote poetically of the dark shape of the Confederate vessel sitting silent out there in the darkness across the water, a single lantern burning in her rigging.[46]

The dancing went on until dawn, but the admiral was back in his office as usual the next morning, Thursday, June 16, in time to send off another of his anxious telegrams to Paris, following it up with a letter. The *Kearsarge* was continuing to cruise up and down outside the harbor, further out than before, although still in view of the port. The admiral felt that this was acceptable. Did the minister agree? Meanwhile, the *Alabama* had finished taking on coal and was probably preparing to go out, though he did not know when. He would do his best to make sure that the fight took place outside French territorial waters. Finally, he begged the minister once more to let him know if he was not happy with how Dupouy was handling the situation.[47]

Friday, June 17, started off peacefully enough for the admiral, with the *Alabama* still at anchor and the *Kearsarge* still cruising around outside the breakwater. At 10:30, however, Liais, the U.S. Consul, suddenly appeared in his office. He had learned that reinforcements were on their way for the *Alabama*; what did Dupouy propose to do about it? Dupouy thought this highly unlikely, but just in case he sent off a telegram to the ministry asking for instructions. A reply came back four hours later saying that in no circumstances could the *Alabama* be allowed to take on any reinforcements. By this time, however, the admiral was out in the harbor on the promised boat trip with Madame Feuillet.[48] He had done some advance planning for this, sending an aristocratic young officer who spoke good English to the *Alabama* to ask permission to visit the ship. Given his official position, Dupouy felt that he could not go on board himself, so he sent Madame

Feuillet and her husband in the care of the young officer. In her memoirs, she describes Semmes as "a lean little man, slightly stooped, having something of the bearing of the first Emperor."[49] He offered them Cape wine and cakes, and she reports seeing him "surrounded by his collection of chronometers." If correct, this means that Semmes still had his chronometers on board two days before the battle.

Madame Feuillet was not the only visitor that day, however. The last entry in Semmes's shipboard journal is dated June 16, for on June 17 he also received a visit from Warren Adams, an enterprising publisher from the house of Saunders, Otley, which had published a number of pro–Confederate works. Adams had hurried over from England to see if Semmes would allow him to take back the two volumes for publication. Semmes was delighted to do so, and the manuscript was handed over for editing to the novelist and poet George Meredith, who supplemented his income by moonlighting as a publisher's reader and who, like many of what today might be called the liberal intelligentsia, was a fervent Confederate.[50]

June 17 was also the day on which John Lancaster's yacht *Deerhound* arrived, anchoring near another English yacht called the *Hornet*.[51]

At about 8 o'clock the next morning, Saturday, June 18, the people of Cherbourg were startled by a tremendous cannonade. Naturally assuming that the long-awaited battle had begun, they rushed down to the port, where they were amazed to see the *Alabama* still peacefully at anchor, although there was a thick pall of gray smoke on the horizon. A naval officer on the quay reassured them. It was the Brazilian training ship *Bahiana*, he explained, firing a salute at the end of her courtesy visit and being saluted in turn by the guns on the Fort de Chavagnac[52] at the West Pass of the harbor.[53]

By now, police and gendarmes had been posted at the railway station and the harbor to prevent any potential reinforcements reaching either ship. William Lewis Dayton, Junior, second secretary at the U.S. Legation and son of the U.S. Minister to France, had arrived at the admiral's office late the night before but had been told to come back in the morning. He had come down from Paris with a dispatch from his father for Winslow. He now returned at 7:30 a.m. and was told that he could go out to the *Kearsarge*, but he must make his own arrangements to get there and must give his word to return as soon as he had delivered the dispatch. As he was waiting at the Vigie de l'Onglet while the gendarmes examined his pass, he noticed two young men who had been stopped by the police while attempting to go out to the *Alabama*.[54] These were in fact the two German master's mates, Maximilian Mulnier and Julius Schrader,[55] and they were finally allowed to go because they had been a part of the *Alabama*'s crew when she arrived at Cherbourg. They had been on their way home on leave and had just reached Paris when they heard the news and came rushing back. Several other Confederate naval officers who had hoped to be allowed to join the *Alabama* were disappointed, even Midshipman William Sinclair, who had been on the ship from the start before transferring to the *Tuscaloosa*.[56]

On board the *Alabama* there was much to be done, and civilian visitors were probably not welcome at this late stage. Exceptions could always be made, however, one of them for Alicia Maria Hamond, the daughter of the British Consul. She was invited to go out to visit the *Alabama* by the owner of an English yacht, an old friend of the family. She tells us firmly, incidentally, that this yacht was not the *Deerhound*. She describes Semmes as "a very quiet, silent man, with a face full of determination.... He talked with a strong American accent, and seemed to be incessantly receiving reports from his officers." "They say I am afraid to fight the *Kearsarge*," he said. "Do I look afraid?"[57]

That afternoon, Semmes went ashore to take his leave of the admiral and to deliver a letter telling him that he planned to go out the following morning between 9 and 10 a.m.[58] The news soon became known. While the admiral himself had to be seen to be studiously neutral, his officers clearly did not feel any such restrictions, and Semmes received many expressions of support from them. Indeed, Cherbourg in general seems to have been strongly on the side of the *Alabama*; when the victorious *Kearsarge* arrived in the harbor the following evening, she was met with absolute silence from the crowds on the quay.[59]

In the evening, Alicia Hamond and her father were among the crowd of people promenading in the Place Napoléon, listening to the military band. Her father was talking to the admiral when Semmes suddenly passed them and, recognizing her from the morning's visit, came and sat by her. They walked up and down together. "Have you heard that all is settled?" he said. "Tomorrow we fight." He was, she said, very quiet and very grave. She was a typically romantic Victorian girl, and the morning's visit to the *Alabama* had reinforced her view of Semmes as a knightly hero. Now she was thinking of the next day's battle. "Little girl," he said (though she was nearly 25 years old), "little girl, you are crying," and she was.[60]

They parted, and Semmes went off to see Adolphe Bonfils, the Confederate agent, and to thank him for all his efforts on the *Alabama*'s behalf.[61] In a final, extraordinary display of loyalty earlier that day, Bonfils, without telling Semmes, had written to Slidell, the Confederate Commissioner, begging him to stop the fight, but Slidell had refused.[62] Semmes now went for a final prayer to Bonfils's parish church, St.-Clément, some 200 yards up the street from the agent's house. As the next day was Sunday, Semmes begged his friend to attend mass in his place and to offer prayers for the officers and men of the *Alabama*. The two men said goodbye for the last time, and Semmes was rowed back to his ship.[63]

That night the admiral gave a party in his quarters for some of the more important visitors—among them, inevitably, the beautiful Madame Feuillet. Perhaps Madame might care to come out the next day and view the projected battle from the breakwater, the admiral suggested. If so, his barge would be beneath her windows at 5 o'clock.[64]

Meanwhile, in another part of town, a number of the *Alabama*'s officers attended a banquet given by local sympathizers. After a series of toasts, they parted, promising to meet again the next evening to celebrate their victory.[65]

The weather had been unseasonably cold and drizzly more or less since the *Alabama*'s arrival, but at 3:30 a.m. on Sunday, June 19, the officer of the watch noted in the log of the *Couronne*: "Weather fine, slight north-westerly breeze."[66]

Shortly after 6, the *Alabama* lit her fires, although Semmes gave most of the crew a bit of a rest, not turning them to till about 9. At around 6:15, a boat came out to the *Alabama* from the *Couronne*. Semmes was still in his cot at this time, so the officer on board the boat explained the procedure to Kell: the French warship would escort the *Alabama* out to the limits of French territorial waters, after which she would turn back.[67]

At about 8 o'clock, Commander George Terry Sinclair, CSN, Arthur Sinclair's uncle, was inexplicably allowed to go on board the *Alabama*. He had come down the day before with his son William, the former midshipman on the *Alabama*, who had been prevented by the French authorities from joining his old ship. Now, for some unknown reason, the father was permitted to visit her and to view her preparations. He offered his services to Semmes, but Semmes declared himself honor bound not to accept them, so Sinclair had to content himself with advising Semmes to keep Winslow at a distance so as not to let him have the advantage of his powerful 11-inch guns. Semmes's response was: "I shall feel him first, and it will all depend on that." Sinclair stayed on board until the *Alabama* was underway and then took a boat back to the town to view the battle—giving us, as a result, one of the very few contemporary eyewitness accounts of the fight by someone not directly involved.[68]

By now the sun had broken through a light early fog, and it was a beautiful day; as Dupouy put it in his report, it was "superb weather, with scarcely a ripple,"[69] ideal for a naval battle. From early that morning, people had been staking out their vantage points all along the coast, from Cap Lévi on the East to Querqueville on the West. In Cherbourg itself, they crowded on to the roofs of houses and church towers, while in the harbor the sailors climbed the rigging.[70] The town's photographer, François Rondin, positioned himself with his camera in the tower of Ste-Trinité, just round the corner from his studio.[71] Numbers of people took the steep path up to the fort at the top of the Montagne du Roule, which dominates both town and harbor.[72] Young William Dayton hired a carriage with Liais and positioned himself with a powerful telescope in front of the tenth-century Chapel of St.-Germain at Querqueville, some five miles to the West.[73] He was responsible for another of the few contemporary eyewitness accounts. Almost certainly there, too, was a young American art student studying in Paris, Alfred Howland, who painted the scene.[74]

Spectators were forbidden to go out to the breakwater for fear that they might signal to one or the other of the contestants, but watching from there that morning were both Madame Feuillet and Alicia Hamond. Madame Feuillet, of course, was with the admiral in his barge. Alicia Hamond had a friend who was married to a French naval officer, so she, too, saw the battle from the breakwater. Both women left highly colored accounts written some 30 years later.[75]

In all, about 15,000 people are thought to have witnessed the fight. Adolphe Bonfils, though, was not one of them. As he had promised, when the *Alabama* went out to fight, he was in his seat in the church of St.-Clément, listening to the prayers for the *Alabama* and her crew.[76]

Soon after 9, the *Alabama* was ready. Her decks had been sanded, tubs of water placed at intervals. The officers were in their best uniforms, the crew in their white ducks. At about 9:30, her boilers wheezed into life, and she began to move slowly out towards the West Pass, followed by the *Couronne* and, at a distance, by John Lancaster's *Deerhound*, which was coming out to view the battle apparently as the result of a family vote. On her way through the harbor, the *Alabama* passed Dupouy's old ship, the *Napoléon*. Her crew manned the rigging and cheered the *Alabama* as she went by, while her band played what Arthur Sinclair described as "a Confederate national air"—presumably "Dixie."[77]

At 10 o'clock, the *Alabama* reached the West Pass of Cherbourg Harbour, the *Couronne* still following.[78] Back in the town, the great bell of Ste.-Trinité was just striking the hour when the *Alabama* went out to her doom.[79]

According to the prophet Isaiah, "Every battle of the warrior is with confused noise, and garments rolled in blood."[80] Although now dismissed by many as an inaccurate translation of the original Hebrew, this would serve as a good description of most battles, including this one. Both Dupouy and Sinclair separately interviewed the survivors after the battle, and both reported that they had had great difficulty in obtaining any sort of clear and coherent account of what had happened. As Dupouy put it, "All the facts are so distorted and interpreted so differently by the only people who could enlighten me, that it is extremely difficult to establish the truth with any degree of certainty."[81]

Nevertheless, the basic facts of the battle are clear. When the *Alabama* came out of the West Pass, she could see the *Kearsarge* out to the northeast. Winslow initially moved further out, presumably to avoid any difficulty with the French, and stopped when about 7 miles from the shore.[82] It took the *Alabama* about 45 minutes to come up with him, and Semmes took the opportunity to address his men. Standing on a gun carriage, he reminded them of all that they had achieved so far, of their victory over the USS *Hatteras*, of the countless prizes taken, the cargoes burned. Now they were in the Channel, "the theatre," as he put it, "of so much of the naval glory of our race." Would they allow the name of their ship to be tarnished by defeat? There was a shout of "Never!" and Semmes ordered the men to their quarters.[83]

When within range, about 1,200 yards away, probably just after 11 o'clock, Semmes opened fire. He had decided to fight the *Kearsarge* with his starboard battery and had therefore transferred one of his 32-pounders from port to starboard. This had the effect of making the *Alabama* lower in the water on that side and thus presenting slightly less of a target. As the range closed, the *Kearsarge* presented her starboard battery and opened fire herself, and the battle became general. In order to maintain their respective positions, the two ships were then forced to steam in a series of seven concentric circles,[84] reminding one Yankee sailor of two flies crawling around the rim of a saucer.[85]

It seems to have been generally believed in the North that the "British pirate" was crewed entirely by trained gunners from HMS *Excellent*. This, it need hardly be said, is untrue. The *Alabama* fired probably three shots to every two from the *Kearsarge*. "Her fire," Dupouy said in his report to the minister, "was extremely rapid, perhaps too much so."[86] Certainly that was one of her problems, since she actually had very few trained gunners. Powder and ammunition were far too valuable to waste, and her crew had in fact had very little practice. Their shooting, initially at least, was very inaccurate, much of it simply too high, although Winslow said in his report that it became better later.[87]

That, however, was not the only problem. Eyewitnesses reported that while there was a sharp crack, a flash and a fine blue vapor from the *Kearsarge*'s guns, the *Alabama*'s produced a dull, muffled sound and a mass of heavy gray smoke.[88] Clearly, the ship's powder had seriously deteriorated.

Seeing that his shots were having little effect, Semmes switched from solid shot to shell and back again, with no better result. Early in the battle, a shell from the *Alabama*'s Blakely rifle hit the *Kearsarge*'s sternpost. Had it exploded, of course, it might well have changed the course of the battle, but it did not. The only real damage was caused by a shell from her aft pivot, which exploded near the *Kearsarge*'s aft pivot, wounding three men, the *Kearsarge*'s only casualties, one of whom later died.[89]

Meanwhile, the *Kearsarge*'s heavy 11-inch Dahlgrens were causing terrible execution. A single shell killed or wounded the entire crew of the *Alabama*'s aft pivot, and the brawny Irishman Michael Mars had to sweep the mangled remains overboard so that men from one of the 32-pounder crews could take over.[90] David Llewellyn, the ship's British assistant surgeon, was operating on a wounded man below decks when a shot from the *Kearsarge* swept his patient from the table.[91] Finally, about 45 minutes into the fight, another shell holed the *Alabama*'s hull near the waterline; water poured in, extinguishing the fires. Setting sail, Semmes turned his ship's head to shore in a last desperate attempt to reach the safety of French waters, but the *Kearsarge* cut him off. At this point he gave the order to cease firing, shorten sail and haul down the colors.

He then had one of the *Alabama*'s two undamaged boats launched and hastily sent Master's Mate George Townley Fullam, another Englishman, off in it to tell the *Kearsarge* to stop firing. Fullam shouted up that the *Alabama* had surrendered, asked Winslow to lower his boats and then received permission to go back himself in order to help rescue the crew. The *Alabama* was now settling by the stern, and Semmes had given the order to abandon ship. The wounded and some of the nonswimmers were placed in the other undamaged boat with Dr. Galt and Lieutenant Joseph Wilson and sent off to the *Kearsarge*, while the majority, including Semmes, who had been wounded in the hand, and Kell, jumped into the water.

The *Deerhound* now steamed up, and Winslow shouted out to her: "For God's sake, do what you can to save them!"[92] He seemed unaccountably slow, though, to lower his own boats. The *Deerhound*, however, went briskly to work, pulling 41 officers and men, including Semmes and Kell, from the water and then, at Semmes's request, steaming off in the direction of England. Meanwhile, as the *Alabama*'s stern continued to fill with water, her shattered mainmast crashed into the sea, her prow gradually pointed to the sky, and somewhere around 12:30 or 12:45 she slid stern first below the waters of the Channel, some five miles off the French coast.[93] Her losses were nine killed, 21 wounded and 18 drowned,[94] including Bartelli, Semmes's steward, and little David White, the former slave from Delaware emancipated by Semmes.[95] Drowned, too, was David Llewellyn, who had told no one that he could not swim. He had refused to leave the ship in one of the boats but had tied two empty wooden shell boxes around himself in a vain attempt to keep afloat.[96]

The *Deerhound* had saved a total of 41.[97] The *Kearsarge* had now finally launched her two undamaged boats, and these started pulling in more of the survivors, though they seemed in no great hurry to do so. Three French pilot boats were rather more active. Antoine Mauger in the *Deux Soeurs* rescued ten, including Lieutenant Richard Armstrong, wounded in the side, and the irrepressible Michael Mars, who, picked up by one of the *Kearsarge*'s boats, leaped over the side and swam out to the Frenchman.[98] Constant Gosselin in the *Lutin* saved one or two more, and Auguste Doucet of the *Alphonsine Marie* picked up two men whom he was forced to hand over to one of the *Kearsarge*'s boats; once back on shore, he protested against this "act of piracy" in his official report.[99]

There is no real disagreement, then, over the main facts of the battle.[100] There are, however, a number of areas of controversy which have been argued over for 150 years, the main ones being these:

> Did the *Kearsarge* deliberately continue firing after the *Alabama* had struck her colors?
> Did the *Alabama* deliberately continue firing after surrendering?
> Did Fullam break his word by not returning to the *Kearsarge* with the men whom he had rescued?
> Did the *Deerhound* break international law by not handing over to the *Kearsarge* the men whom she had saved?
> Did the *Deerhound* actually collude with the *Alabama*?
> Did Winslow deliberately delay launching his two undamaged boats?

First, it seems unlikely that anyone *deliberately* continued firing after the *Alabama* had surrendered. Certainly, it does appear that the *Kearsarge* fired into the *Alabama* (Semmes says five times) after she had struck her colors, but this was probably in the inevitable confusion of the battle. Winslow seems to have thought that the *Alabama*'s flag had been brought down by his fire, rather than struck, but he does also say that he was "uncertain whether Captain Semmes was not using some ruse." He also says that the *Alabama* "opened on us with the two guns on the port side." This seems improbable but could possibly have happened in the confusion.[101]

As for Fullam, we know that he was permitted to go back and rescue men from the water, but there is no actual evidence that he gave his word to return with them to the *Kearsarge*. There is nothing in any of Winslow's reports, for example, which is surely significant. It is true that Frederick Milnes Edge, an Englishman who came over to Cherbourg immediately after the battle, interviewed many of the participants and wrote a useful but very one-sided account, claimed that Fullam had given his word.[102] Edge, however, was a fanatical Unionist so might be expected to say so. Dr. John M. Browne, the *Kearsarge*'s surgeon, repeated the claim, in remarkably similar language, in his article for the editors of *The Century Magazine*,[103] but Browne was writing 20 years after the event. On balance, then, it seems reasonable to give Fullam the benefit of the doubt.

Next, there is the question of whether the *Deerhound* had any right to take the men whom she had rescued to England rather than surrendering them to the *Kearsarge*. Semmes, of course, mounts a long defense of her right to do so, complete with various historical examples.[104] In 1886, however, the editors of *The Century Magazine* sought a legal opinion from James Russell Soley, a professor at the U.S. Naval War College and later assistant secretary of the navy. The professor was absolutely clear on the issue. A neutral ship, he said, in general had no right to play any part in a battle, even to the extent of rescuing survivors from one of the contestants. In this case, however, Winslow had actually *requested* the *Deerhound* to rescue the men in the water. Once they were on board, then, not only was the *Deerhound* under no obligation to surrender them, but it would have been a gross breach of neutrality to do so.[105]

Perhaps the key question, though, is whether the *Deerhound* had made some kind of arrangement with the *Alabama* before the battle, as was claimed afterwards by a number of Unionist partisans. If she had, that would imply that Semmes expected to lose, but that in itself does not necessarily rule out collusion. Semmes, of course, denied that there was any collusion. So does Kell, so does Arthur Sinclair and so does any other officer of the *Alabama* who pronounced on the subject; so do John Lancaster and his Captain, Evan Parry Jones; so does Alicia Hamond, who was not exactly unbiased but who, as the British Consul's daughter, had good local contacts. Admiral Dupouy, too, would most certainly have been very much on the alert for anything of that sort, yet his only mention of the *Deerhound* is in his long report to the minister on June 22, where he simply says "an English steam yacht" had rescued a part of the crew.[106]

The only evidence, in fact, if it can be called such, appears in affidavits sworn some time later by six members of the *Alabama*'s crew, four of them paroled prisoners from the *Kearsarge*, the other two among those rescued by the *Deerhound*.[107] It does not seem unreasonable to assume these to have been in response to some sort of financial inducement on the part of certain U.S. officials in England.

Nevertheless, it is possible that there was in fact collusion of a sort, albeit passive and not from the direction which one might expect. In this connection, the question of whether Winslow deliberately delayed sending his boats is relevant, because he may well have done just as Semmes accused him of doing, but for a very different reason.

What, then, do we know of John Winslow? He was a competent enough officer, probably, although his record so far in the war had not been particularly impressive; he was perhaps a little stolid and unimaginative but in general a decent, honest, straightforward man. Semmes, interestingly, remembered him from "the old service" as "a humane and Christian gentleman." "What the war may have made of him," he said, "it is impossible to say."[108] But what if Winslow behaved as he did precisely because he was *still* "a humane and Christian gentleman"? Winslow was well aware that there were some exceptionally bloodthirsty civilians back in the United States, particularly in Washington. When Lord Russell protested that the men rescued by the *Deerhound* would otherwise have drowned, for example, Seward replied, "It was the right of the *Kearsarge* that the pirates should drown,"[109] and Gideon Welles, if anything, outdid him in vindictiveness. Hearing that Winslow had paroled all his prisoners and sent them ashore, Welles was furious. The "foreign pirates," he said, should have been "held at every sacrifice" and transported back to the United States.[110] It seems highly probable, then, that, had Semmes been captured, Seward and Welles would have wanted him hanged, together, very possibly, with his officers, while the men could have expected, at best, a long term in a Yankee prison camp.

It therefore seems at least possible that Winslow deliberately delayed launching his boats in order to give the *Deerhound* and the French pilot boats time to pick up as many people as they could. In this context, there is an interesting passage in Lieutenant Richard Armstrong's report to Barron of his rescue by Antoine Mauger's pilot boat. Armstrong had been wounded in the side and was swimming with some difficulty towards the French boat when one of the *Kearsarge*'s two boats passed quite close to him but "laid on its oars and made no particular exertion that I could see to save me." Armstrong had on his officer's cap, which he says would have been quite visible from the boat. He says that the officer in charge appeared to be looking for someone.[111] Is it not equally possible that, following his captain's lead, he was deliberately looking the other way in order to allow Armstrong to reach the safety of the French boat?

Certainly Winslow protested furiously afterwards about the "disgraceful act" of the *Deerhound* in steaming off with his "prisoners,"[112] but then he could hardly have done otherwise. Welles's reaction to the news that Winslow had paroled his prisoners is indicative of what Winslow might have expected had there been any suspicion that he had condoned what had happened, let alone encouraged it.

That afternoon the *Kearsarge* came into port. The wounded men, three from the *Kearsarge* and 12 from the *Alabama*[113] were taken ashore in a boat from the *Couronne* in the charge of Dr. Galt and the chief French naval surgeon Dr. G.T. Dufour, landed at the Vigie de l'Onglet and were transported to the naval hospital.[114] The fine old Hôpital de la Marine just outside Cherbourg (now disused) had not yet been built,[115] so the provisional naval hospital of the time was split between a building in the former Abbaye du Voeu and a wing of the old barracks built in 1784 to house workers on the breakwater. Unfortunately, it is not known today to which site the 15 wounded men were taken.[116] Since the abbey is twice as far from the Vigie de l'Onglet as the barracks are, though, it is at least possible that it was to the barracks.

Three of the *Alabama*'s crew, however, never reached the hospital. George Appleby and James King had been carried on board the *Kearsarge* dead, and the ship's carpenter, William Robinson, had died shortly after of his wounds. Early on June 21, George Sinclair presided over a simple funeral ceremony in Cherbourg's old cemetery, high above the town. The dead men's comrades had made a

Confederate flag for them the night before, and Sinclair reported "this morning every man was present & sober."[117]

Across the Channel, meanwhile, the *Deerhound* reached Southampton in the evening of June 19 and, coming up the estuary of the Itchen, landed her passengers on British soil.[118] The wounded were taken to the Sailors' Home on Canute Road,[119] while most of the officers and men scattered in search of lodging along the harbor.[120] Semmes and Kell, meanwhile, found refuge in Kelway's Hotel, in

Alabama and *Kearsarge* graves, Cherbourg Old Cemetery (author's photograph).

Queen's Terrace.[121] The next morning, they found themselves heroes. After being photographed in Samuel Wiseman's studio, together with the port surgeon, Dr. Wiblin, who was treating Semmes for the wound on his hand,[122] they went to buy new clothes at Samuel Emanuel's establishment on the High Street. The proprietor insisted that they come back to his house for a glass of wine but then found that such a large and enthusiastic crowd had gathered outside in the hope of seeing them that he had to call the police to escort them back to their hotel.[123]

That afternoon, James Dunwoody Bulloch, the Rev. Francis Tremlett, the staunchly pro–Southern vicar of St. Peter's, Belsize Park, and James Murray Mason, the Confederate Commissioner, all arrived from London at the LSWR terminus to visit them.[124] In the following days, letters of support came in from far and wide, together with requests from dozens of young men eager to serve with Semmes on his next ship. Letters offering financial assistance, too, poured in, one of them from Gladstone's sister.[125] Admiral Talavera Vernon Anson and Captain Bedford Pim, RN, announced a fund to raise money to buy Semmes a sword to replace the one which had gone down with his ship. Lady de Hoghton, wife of the Confederate sympathizer Sir Henry de Hoghton, presented Semmes with a beautiful second national flag which she had made herself.[126] In London, the writer George Meredith wrote to a friend, "The *Alabama*'s sunk, and my heart's down with her."[127]

Nor was poor Llewellyn forgotten. Money was raised to install a memorial plaque and a stained glass window in his memory in Holy Trinity, Easton Royal, his childhood home, where his father was the vicar, and former students and colleagues at Charing Cross Hospital collected money to erect another monument there.[128]

The Confederacy, of course, survived the *Alabama* by barely ten months, and at the end of it all, to adapt the late Frank Vandiver, the United States went on to world power, and the *Alabama*, like the Confederacy itself, went on to legend.[129] Perhaps we should leave her final epitaph, though, to *The Times* of June 21, 1864: "She was a good ship, well handled and well fought, and to a nation of sailors that means a great deal."

10

Three Accounts of the Battle Off Cherbourg

1. The U.S. Minister's Son

The William Lewis Dayton Papers at Princeton University contain a number of documents relating to the sinking of the CSS *Alabama* by the USS *Kearsarge* off Cherbourg on June 19, 1864. Among these are four letters to the U.S. Minister to France from his son, William L. Dayton, Junior, known to the family as Willie. The younger Dayton, who was second secretary at the U.S. Legation, had gone to Cherbourg with a dispatch for Captain Winslow of the *Kearsarge* but stayed to see the battle. While the three letters written from Cherbourg itself are relatively brief and informal, the fourth, written after Willie Dayton's return to Paris, is a detailed, 30-page account of the battle and its aftermath.[1] Although addressed, like the others, to the writer's father, it is much more formal in tone and was therefore presumably intended, despite its numerous abbreviations, as the basis for an official report. In transcribing it for publication, I have made no changes beyond the occasional adjustment, where the sense of the passage demanded it, to Willie Dayton's somewhat inconsistent system of punctuation. It will be noticed that the writer consistently misspells the name of the *Kearsarge* until near the end of his account.

Paris, June 22, 1864

Sir,

On Friday last June 17. A.M. I left Paris for Cherbourg with a dispatch for Capt Winslow of the U.S.S. Kearsage which was lying off that port.

Upon my arrival at 9½ PM the U.S. Vice Consul informed me that no one, not even he, was allowed to communicate with the K. I insisted upon seeing the Admiral-Prefect of the port. The Admiral had retired to his room when we arrived. I sent word by Vice Consul that I had been sent by U.S. Minister at Paris in consequence of a conversation had the day before with the French Minister of Foreign affairs, to communicate and bear a dispatch to Capt. Winslow of the Kearsage. The Admiral said to Consul that he would be glad to see me the next day. Consul said that I, as well as he, feared the Alabama might leave that night. The Admiral said I might go to my hotel and sleep that night, intimating that he knew the Alabama would not leave. At 7½ the next morning I called again at the Prefecture, when the Admiral gave me a written permit to leave the port, saying at the same time that he hoped what I was doing was all regular and that he supposed he would see me upon my return. I of course promised to report myself.

10. Three Accounts of the Battle Off Cherbourg

Chapel of St. Germain, Querqueville, where William L. Dayton Jr. watched the battle (author's photograph).

The permit I found was altogether necessary to leaving the port. I was called upon to show it several times and I saw two other young men who endeavored to go with Alabama stopped by the police.[2] The Kearsage was not in sight when I left the harbor. After sailing about 2 or 3 miles outside the breakwater, she hove in sight. We came up to her in about two hours and a half. She was about 8 or 9 miles out. I remained on board of her about one hour and a half, delivering my letters and consulting with Capt. Winslow. Capt. Winslow asked me to request Consul at Havre to send out to him off Cherbourg about 75 or 80 tons of coal and some machine oil—and a few men if he could send them.

I returned to Cherbourg and at once reported myself to the Prefect and told him I expected to leave Cherbourg early the next morning. He then informed me that the Alabama would leave Cherbourg in 24 hours. I decided therefore for many reasons to remain and see the result.

The next morning about 8 o'clock I went to Querqueville (?) a little village 2 or 3 miles from Cherbourg[3] and with the Consul took my position on an elevated spot of ground to await the result. We could see the harbor perfectly and had a fine view seaward. The spot was a little to the west of Cherbourg and we had a finer and more extensive view than from the city. We were of course provided with a telescope. About nine o'clock the English yacht Deerhound (carrying the flag of the Royal Yacht Club and owned by John Lancaster, Esq, near or of Liverpool) got up steam and ran a little out towards the breakwater. After apparently observing for a few minutes she returned and went alongside of the Alabama. She then stood out again straight through the western pass to sea, about two miles out she changed her course heading more towards the Kearsage. The Alabama then came out by the same pass and stood straight out to sea the yacht running up near and apparently communicating with her. About this time the Kearsage made her appearance to the ordinary naked eye. This must have been between ten and half after ten in the morning. The relative position of the vessels at this time and afterwards was as follows:

The Kearsage at first instead of running directly towards the Alabama headed out to sea and ran a few miles in a line parallel with the Alabama in order as the Capt said to get as far out of french [sic] waters as to prevent any chance to the Alabama of ever reaching them again. When about 9 miles from shore the K. turned and directed her course towards the A. each vessel coming up on the starboard. Capt. W. had ordered the two port guns over to the starboard where they remained during the entire engagement. It was found however that one of them could not be used to advantage.

While the K. was coming down on the A. having her starboard quarter exposed the Alabama fired 18 shot at her without receiving any answer. The guns of the K. were not in exact range. When at about 800 yards the K. veered a little to port and gave the A. a broadside. From that moment the fight continued incessantly until the surrender. The A. turned to starboard and commenced running in a circle, the K followed on the same circle. The A. was to the windward at the beginning but in this manoeuvre they each had the wind in turn.

They passed each other as seen from shore I should think about five or six times for about three quarters of an hour. The Alabama then made sail forward and soon left the circle and seemed to be disposed to take refuge in french [sic] waters but the Kearsage pursued her keeping on a line nearer shore. In about ten minutes she had gained up to her. By that time the firing had ceased, the Alabama having run up a white flag.

Both vessels stood still. A boat then came on board Kearsage containing as I was informed the Master's mate an officer from the Alabama. Capt. of K. asked if the Alabama had surrendered. He said they had, that the ship was in a sinking condition, and he asked Capt W. to send boats to rescue the men. Capt. W. ordered all boats fit for service (being two) to go to their aid. Before they reached the Alabama she went down straight while you could count three, settling first at the stern. The Capt. of K. seeing an English yacht

The West Pass, Cherbourg harbor, through which the *Alabama* steamed out on June 19, 1864 (author's photograph).

near and fearing a great loss of life asked it to go and pick up some of the men. They said they would. The officer who came on the K. and surrendered the A. asked permission to go with his boat to the rescue. He received the permission and after having picked up a number he went with them on board of the yacht, who had already picked up a number of men and officers among whom was Capt. Semmes and 1st lieut Kell. The English yacht then left the Kearsage and stood direct for England. When it was reported to Capt. W. that the yacht was standing off he says he supposed she was looking for floating men. He says he could not believe that an Englishman carrying the Royal Yacht club flag could be so dishonorable as to run away with the Kearsage's lawful prisoners whom he had picked up at the request of Capt W. who made it for the sake of humanity. About 9 men were rescued by a small french [sic] boat and taken to Cherbourg.

There were 147 men on board the Alabama. 63 men, 5 officers & one dead man and two wounded who died afterwards on board K. were picked up by K. It was supposed about 20 were saved by the yacht and 9 by a small french [sic] pilot boat (there may have been more saved by the yacht) which would leave about 45 men unaccounted for. Only three seamen were wounded on board the Kearsage, one man most severely with a compound fracture of the leg. Another had his arm so shattered as to make amputation necessary which was done during action, a third had his leg injured—broken I think. He had perhaps also his arm injured. All three I understood were wounded by the same shell which pierced the bulwarks near the large pivot gun and exploded on deck. The Kearsage was not seriously injured at all. 8 shots struck in her hull–4 of them lodged; 2 shot struck the aft port boat,1 went through the smoke stack, 1 tore through the engine sky light room, the halyards were cut away. All the rest struck in the rigging. 28 shot struck in all. One shell entered the rudder post without exploding and is there still. Two shot struck against a double row of chains which had been hung over the side of the vessel for a few yards in length in order to protect the machinery. These two shots fell harmlessly in the water. The K. is now perfectly ready for service.

62 minutes elapsed from the firing of the 1st gun of the K. until her last gun. She fired 173 shots. The A. fired much more quickly but her firing was very wild. The practice on board the K is said to have been very fine; their second shot I was afterwards informed killed and wounded 15 out of a gun crew of 19. 4 were killed immediately. The last two or three shots from the K. were I am informed very effective. One shot I am told carried away her rudder, another went into her coal bunker and let the coal down into her boilers.

About two hours after the end of the fight the K. came in and anchored in the harbor. Mr. Badlam, 2d. Assist. Engineer of K. came on shore. I met him at the stairway of the dock and went with him to see the Admiral Prefect of the port.

He asked in the name of the Captain of K. if they could send their wounded and prisoners on shore. He said as soon as they came on shore they would cease to be prisoners, said that the French Govt. had just obliged the Alabama to set free the Federal prisoners which she had taken from the ships Tycoon & Rockingham and had brought to Cherbourg. In this case the prisoners had been sent ashore voluntarily. Mr. Badlam said, suppose we go immediately out to sea. He said in that case he would do nothing and they might go if they wished. As to the case of the prisoners he said he would not in any event use force to set them free. Finally he said he could not give definite answers to the questions put, that if Capt. W. chose to remain in port, he would refer the question to the Govt. at Paris and inform Capt. W of the answer received. In the meantime he advised Capt. W. not to send either his wounded or prisoners on shore. Mr. Badlam asked if his remaining in port until the answer was given would affect the question. Admiral said he could not compromise the Govt. by giving any answer but advised Capt. W. to remain. He finally said he wished the condition of things to be considered as that of a question having been asked and no answer as yet given. Mr. Badlam returned on board ship and I accompanied him. He reported to Capt. W.

Capt. W. had already telegraphed to Paris, U.S. Minister, to know whether he should parole his prisoners. No answer had yet been received. About two hours afterwards I understood that the three federal wounded and also about 15 Confederate wounded as well as all the prisoners had been sent ashore after having been paroled.

The wounded were sent to the hospital. The 5 Alabama officers were kept to await the answer to the telegram sent to Paris.

About 11. o'clock an answer came and was received by Mr. Hartwell the Captain's Clerk who was then on shore. The telegram said No, by no means; to parole them would be to acknowledge the Alabama as a man of war &c &c. The next day Capt. Winslow said he wished me to explain to Mr Dayton at Paris that he was forced to parole the prisoners as he had not room enough to keep them aboard, that his vessel was small and scarcely accommodated his crew. I said to him that the St. Louis would be at Cherbourg soon. He said he had telegraphed her not to come. The necessity for her had disappeared with the sinking of the Alabama. The 5 officers he retained as prisoners, although he allowed them to go on shore upon their promise to return whenever he should demand them.

A Mr. Galt who reported himself as surgeon & late acting paymaster of the Alabama was paroled at once as being a non-combatant. 3d. Lieutenant Wilson was the highest officer of the Alabama on board the Kearsarge as a prisoner.

The A. officers as well as the crew were treated with greatest politeness & kindness on board the K. They evidently did not expect it. I heard Lieut. Wilson when on shore afterwards say that they expected to be treated like dogs, put in chains and sent forward. He said that on the Alabama they did not think they were gentlemen. But he now said they were all gentlemen, that the fight was an honorable one and the A. had been whipped. He bore no malice and only asked to meet them again on equal terms &c.

The day after the fight I went with Doctor Brown [Browne] of the K. and U.S. Vice Consul, Mr. Liais, to call upon the chief surgeon of the hospital at Cherbourg, Dr. Dufour. We then went to the hospital to see the wounded. The federals and Confederates were treated alike in the hospital. The federals seemed all three cheerful, still elated apparently with their victory.

The Doctor of the K. spoke very highly of the heroism of one of the wounded federals named Gowan. He was wounded at the large aft pivot gun, wounded very severely—a compound fracture of the leg. Instead of falling down and crying out to be carried below, he dragged himself forward to the companion way when he was so weak he was obliged to be carried down. As he was brought in he said to the doctor with a smile on his face—you see doctor I have come to you. The doctor spoke sympathisingly to him, when he said oh! I don't care, I am ready to lose my life if we can sink the Alabama. His mind seemed still with his comrades fighting on deck; he would raise his hand and cry out when a gun was fired—give it to them boys! The doctor wanted to go on deck to cheer before it was certain the fight was ended when Gowan caught hold of him and held him back, saying it was not his post and he might get hit and then what would they do. Finally when the victory was won and the Dr. started again for the deck he told him to go and cheer for him too. In the hospital the next day when I spoke to him sympathisingly he said oh! I don't mind it *now*, meaning since they had gained the victory.

The coolness of two old seamen, who had charge of a little 12 lbs boat howitzer during the fight, was particularly amusing, each one was swearing at the other because he could not get his gun's crew to work right. One of them was pulling a chest of something, ammunition I believe, along the deck tugging and perspiring under the weight when a shell from the Alabama burst near him, some of its small contents grazing his hands, when he inquired rubbing his hands, "what are these peas flying around here."

The general coolness of the men on board was said to have been remarkable. They seemed no more excited than if they were practising. This was particularly striking as I understood the majority of all hands had never before been under fire.

Grand Hôtel, Cherbourg (author's photograph).

The Captain is said to have been very cool, explaining to his men the object of his manoeuvres &c. Both officers and men are said to have behaved admirably.

When the Alabama arrived at Cherbourg about a week before she landed 37 individuals whom she had taken about 50 days previously from the federal merchant ships the Rockingham and the Tycoon, Capts. Garrish [Gerrish] and Ayres. Among them was the wife of Captain Garrish, her maid and a little girl of perhaps 4 years old. These prisoners had been thus far taken care of by the U S. Vice Consul at Cherbourg. He now wished to send them to Havre supposing that from thence transportation might be furnished them to America. He requested me to take charge of them to Havre which I agreed to do. I left Cherbourg with them by steamboat on Tuesday the 21st inst. Upon arriving at Havre I put them under the care of Mr Putnam U.S. Consul at that port.

I then returned immediately to Paris where I arrived about 11. o'clock that night, June 21. 1864.

William L Dayton Jr.
Assist. Secy. of Legation, Paris.

P.S.

The tonnage of the Kearsarge and Alabama was about the same (1100 tons). The Kearsarge carried 7 guns. Two large 11-inch Dalgreen [Dahlgren] pivot guns, 137 pounders, and five broadside battery guns of 32 lbs. The Alabama carried 8 guns. One Whitworth rifle 110 lbs. One 68 pounder and six broadside 32 pounders.

The crew of the Kearsarge consisted of 165 men, that of the Alabama of 147 men.

D jr.

To.
William L. Dayton
En. Ex. & Min. Plen. of the U.S.
at Paris, France.

2. The French Naval Officer

Volume XXIII (1917–1918) of *The American Historical Review* contains a report of the battle by Captain Jérôme Penhoat of the French ironclad *Couronne*. It was the *Couronne* which was given the task of escorting the *Alabama* out of French territorial waters on the morning of the battle. Penhoat's report was apparently found by Waldo G. Leyland in the Bibliothèque Nationale in Paris and appears in Volume XXIII in the original French. Whoever transcribed it from the manuscript (presumably Leland himself) clearly had a good knowledge of French; there are a few small spelling mistakes, one word (as he makes clear in the text) defeated him completely, one word he simply misunderstood and one word he was clearly unfamiliar with and transcribed wrongly, but otherwise he has done a pretty competent job. Although it is clear that Penhoat's report is not unknown to writers in English (it is cited, for example, by William Marvel in "The Alabama and the Kearsarge"), it does not appear ever to have been translated—at least, as far as I can establish. I have therefore attempted to translate it myself, hoping that the interest of the document will compensate for any errors or infelicities resulting from gaps in my knowledge of naval terminology in general and nineteenth-century French naval terminology in particular. In order to retain the flavor of the original, I have kept as closely as I can to the format and layout of the report and have not corrected Penhoat's consistent misspelling of "Kearsarge," "Winslow" and "Dahlgren."

I. ACCOUNT OF THE FIGHT BETWEEN THE *Kearseage* AND THE *Alabama*.

Ironclad Frigate *Couronne* CHERBOURG, 19 June 1864.

Admiral,

In accordance with your orders I lit my fires at the same time as the Confederate vessel *Alabama*. At 7.50 a.m. we had pressure. The Federal vessel *Kearseage* remained a considerable distance away to the N.E. At 9.45 the *Alabama* got under way and the *Couronne* cast off and followed her at the prescribed distance. As soon as she was out of territorial waters, I made my way immediately to the roadstead and took up the position where I had previously been anchored.

We followed the movements of the two vessels from the masthead. They were a long way off shore, and we were having difficulty in making out their movements, when suddenly I was advised that one of the vessels was thought to have been seen to sink; a large number of ships and harbor boats could be seen gathering around the site of the disaster. I made haste to forward this information to you, but because of the distance the combatants were from us and the hazy conditions it was difficult to be sure of what exactly had happened. The steamer *Var* was also making her way to the site.

>I am with respect
>Admiral
>Your most obedient servant
>Captain Commanding the *Couronne*
>PENHOAT

P. S. We have learnt that it was definitely the *Alabama* which succumbed in this heroic battle.

II. MOVEMENTS OF THE *COURONNE* AND THE TWO AMERICAN VESSELS.

- 3:30. The *Kerseage* sighted to the N. E.
- 5:45. *Alabama* starts to heave in.
- 6:10. *Alabama* lights her fires.
- 6:10. *Couronne* lights her fires.
- 6:55. *Couronne* communicates with *Alabama*.
- 7:25. *Kerseage* to the N.E. running W.
- 7:50. *Alabama* has pressure.
- 7:55. *Couronne* has pressure.
- 8:00. *Kerseage* some distance away to the E.N.E.
- 8:30. *Couronne* ready to move.
- 9:30. *Alabama* heaves short.
- 9:30. *Couronne* in position to cast off.
- 9:35. *Kerseage* to the E. ¼ N.E.
- 9:45. *Alabama* gets under way.
- 9:50. *Kerseage* no longer in sight.
- 9:54. *Alabama* passes in front of *Couronne*.
- 9:55. *Couronne* gets under way.
- 10:00. *Alabama* rounds the end of the pier-head.[4]
- 10:07. *Kerseage* to the N. E.
- 10:10. *Alabama* drops the pilot.
- 10:18. *Couronne* rounds the pier-head.
- 10:20. *Kerseage* to the N. 80° E.
- 10:22. *Couronne* steers to the E.N.E.
- 10:23. *Alabama* to the N.E. ½ N.
- 10:30. *Kerseage* changes course (turns to starboard).
- 10:50. *Couronne* turns to port, returns.
- 10:50. *Kerseage* hoists her jack.
- 11:03. The battle begins.
- 11:50. *Couronne* anchors.

The Confederate vessel *Alabama*, commanded by Capt. Semmes, anchored in the harbor of Cherbourg on 11 June 1864, coming from the Cape of Good Hope. She had reported a crew of 122; we learned afterwards that she had on board 21 Confederate officers. The *Alabama* was a pretty screw vessel of 13 to 1400 tons,[5] well masted, of light wooden construction, armed with six guns.[6] Two of these guns were on pivots. The first, between the foremast and the mainmast, was a 9-inch rifled piece, carrying a cylindro-spherical hollow ball. The second, positioned between the mainmast and the mizzen, was a smooth-bore of 48 to 50 caliber, solid shot (there may be some doubt as to the calibers, since we relied on the officers' statements which, for reasons of tact, we did not check). The other pieces were of 30 lbs., similar in appearance to our 30-lb. naval howitzers. The Captain said that his copper was in very poor state: he had received permission to coal at Cherbourg [word illegible], but not to make repairs, for he did not enter the port.

The *Kerseage*, commanded by Captain Vinslow, appeared in front of the breakwater on the 14th, coming from Dover. She reported a crew of 140.[7] She is a screw sloop of 14 to 1500,[8] armed with 6 guns of which two are 11-inch (27 cm.) Dahlgreens weighing 7700 kg. on pivots on the deck, one between the mainmast and the foremast, the other between the mainmast and the mizzenmast. These two guns threw shells and grapeshot composed of biscayens and 4lb balls; there was no solid shot on board for them. The other 4 guns were pieces of 32 corresponding to our 30-pounders, nos. 3 or 4.

The *Kerseage* is a wooden vessel of fairly strong construction, armored on the side with chain-ends consisting of iron links of 36 to 40 mm., positioned vertically from the rail to 1 meter below the waterline. These chain-ends are pressed tightly against each other in such a way that the flat links mesh with the projecting ones. The whole thing is tied together with rope. I do not know how this sort of coat of mail is attached to the vessel (probably by clamps). The whole thing is covered by a light wooden extension.

This armor is positioned along the vessel's sides so as to protect her machinery.

The *Kerseage* arrived in front of the East Pass without entering the harbor and came to ask permission to communicate with her consul, which was granted her after a few medical formalities. She then began to cruise off the breakwater, outside our territorial waters, so discreetly that most of the time she was out of sight.

It has been said that the two captains had challenged each other. Captain Vinslow rejects this. He never sent any challenge, but he had received a letter from Capt. Semmes announcing that he would come out to fight him. Capt. Semmes had announced his intention officially and had given notice that he would come out on Sunday 19th between 9 and 10 o'clock in the morning. On their arrival in the port, both vessels had been given an extract of the rules with which belligerents are expected to comply during their stay in French roadsteads.

On the Sunday morning the *Alabama* lit her fires at about 6 o'clock and the whole population gathered on the quays, the jetties, the towers, the Roule[9] and the breakwater to view the naval battle. There was an influx of Parisians, who had come on a special excursion train that morning.

The *Alabama* got under way at about 9:30 and when she was level with the *Couronne* the latter cast off and followed her at a sufficient distance not to impede her. She had orders to prevent any engagement in territorial waters and to return to her anchorage as soon as she was confident that the fight would take place outside French waters.

At the time that the vessels doubled the eastern pier-head, the *Kerseage* was still to E.N.E. heading N. E., distant 12 miles. Having reached the limit of territorial waters, the *Couronne* signaled her position to the breakwater, which signaled her to regain her mooring, which she did immediately. There were a number of boats from the port in the open sea, including three English yachts, one of which was a steamer. The *Var* had her pressure up ready to offer help if needed.

As soon as the *Alabama* was free to move, she made towards the *Kerseage*, which continued her course to the N.E. Shortly afterwards, however, she changed course and headed for the *Alabama*. The two vessels were both steaming at full speed and the distance separating them was soon reduced to cannon-range. Now the *Alabama* changed course and seemed to make a half-turn to port in order to present her starboard quarter to her opponent. She then opened fire with her aft pivot. The vessels were perhaps 8 or 9 cables from each other and 9 or 10 miles from land. The *Kerseage* did not respond, and started firing only after the third shot.

This oblique defensive position taken by the *Alabama* was certainly the safest for a lightly-built vessel like her to adopt; she was presenting her enemy with a limited target, she was protecting her engines as much as possible and, believing that she had superior speed, she was able to control the distance. She was attacking the enemy with her most powerful gun where he was not armored. Whether Capt. Semmes let himself be carried away by his ardor, however, or whether he did not know, as we are assured, that the *Kerseage* was armored, he remained a very short time in this position and, making a half-turn to starboard, went to cross his opponent's bows broadside on while bombarding him vigorously from his starboard side. From this moment on the two opponents turned around each other in circles varying between 4 and two cables in radius, cannonading each other broadside on from starboard. We counted up to 7 turns. But at this game the *Kerseage*, with her armored sides, had all the advantage. Moreover, she could use her two huge guns. Struck on the side by three shots, two of which were near the waterline, her chain armor stopped the projectiles, which would have disabled her engine if they had penetrated. Without the armor, the result of the fight could have been different. Be that as it may, the *Alabama* received some shells which weakened her planking to the point that she speedily took on water. An exploding shell or a shot probably hit a boiler, for a cloud of steam could suddenly be seen issuing from her sides. Some people have asserted that she was struck aft by a shell which, on exploding, disabled her screw and her steering. The fact remains that her engines stopped and she set sail in an attempt to reach land; but from this moment on she was at the mercy of her adversary, who took full advantage of it, for a moment later the *Alabama* surrendered and very quickly went to the bottom, sinking stern first.

All those on the surface were rescued by the pilot Mauger's boat, the boats of the *Kerseage*, and the English steam yacht which rescued Capt. Semmes and the officers and made for the coast of England, to the consternation of Capt. Vinslow. Considering this disastrous outcome, the loss of men was not enormous. The total was 2 drowned, 6 killed and 16 or 17 killed [wounded].

The *Kerseage* received three shot on her armor in the area below her funnel which had only a minor effect. One shot went through her funnel, two projectiles passed just over the deck. One of the latter on exploding wounded three men; these were the only casualties the *Kerseage* suffered. One shell lodged in the head of the sternpost, where it remained without exploding. The sternpost has some vertical cracks here, but the structure is sound.

Both sides fought well, the Confederate dashingly, the Yankee doggedly. The *Alabama*'s firing was very heavy. The *Kerseage* fired 130 shots, 52 of them from her Dahlgreens.[10]

The dimensions of the *Kerseage*'s guns are as follows:

Dahlgreen Guns

		English Measurements
Diameter of bore	27c.94	11 inches.
Total length	4.12 [m.]	13 ft. 6 inchs.
Weight of solid shot	86.97 [kilos.]	192 pounds English
" of shell	62.96	139 " "
Weight of gun	7701.00	17000 " "
Charge for shell	6.800	15 " "
" for ball	9.07	20 " "
Initial velocity (unconfirmed)	4267.	

The *Kerseage* did not have on board any solid shot for these guns, but I am assured that experience has recently led to the adoption of solid shot for this particular piece.

3. The French Novelist

Among the prominent people invited to attend the inauguration of the new Casino des Bains de Mer in Cherbourg in June, 1864, were the novelist and dramatist Octave Feuillet and his beautiful wife. Although less well known today, Octave Feuillet was at that time one of France's most celebrated literary figures. He was born in St.-Lô in 1821 and in 1851 married his cousin Valérie Marie Elvire Dubois, daughter of the Mayor of St.-Lô. Feuillet was greatly admired by

Napoleon III and the Empress Eugénie, and he and his wife enjoyed a close relationship with the imperial family. After his death in 1890, his widow, too, turned to writing, publishing several novels and two volumes of memoirs, always under the name "Madame Octave Feuillet." Chapter XXI of her first volume of reminiscences, *Quelques Années de Ma Vie* (1894), contains a brief description of a visit to the *Alabama* on June 17, 1864, and an eyewitness report of the battle with the *Kearsarge* two days later. As mentioned in the previous chapter, her description of the visit to the ship includes the significant detail that Semmes was "surrounded by his collection of chronometers"; if correct, this is evidence that, two days before the battle, they had not yet been handed over for safekeeping to the *Hornet*. Otherwise, her breathless account of the events of June 1864, written 30 years later, has to be said to be more imaginative and impressionistic than sober and factual; the description, in her final sentence, of Winslow's arrival on the quay seems particularly improbable. Nevertheless, as the reaction of a French writer, an eyewitness to the drama she describes, and as an addition to the voluminous literature on the *Alabama*, it is not without interest. (As far as I can establish, the passage has never before been translated into English. In attempting to translate it now, I have done my best to give the flavor of Madame Feuillet's literary style without being too high-flown.)

> On another occasion, my husband and I attended a grand evening-party given by Admiral Dupouy in the Admiralty. The previous day, the Admiral took us out in his barge across the harbor to where the American ship *Alabama* was anchored. As we were desirous of visiting the vessel, the Admiral sent his aide-de-camp to the *Alabama*, asking him to obtain permission for our visit. The request was met with cheers and ladders were thrown down to us. Our boat was pulled alongside and, whilst it was rocking in the current, we climbed aboard. Two gentle-eyed officers, who looked like two brothers, welcomed us on deck. They wore long gray overcoats the color of their eyes. They expressed a desire to introduce us to the Captain and we followed them to his cabin.
>
> Captain Sems [sic] received us surrounded by his collection of chronometers. He was a lean little man, slightly stooped, having something of the bearing of the first Emperor. He bade us be seated, treating us with the greatest courtesy and offering us cakes and Cape wine. We talked of the war in which the two Americas were at that moment engaged. He became animated, and told us that he had just been advised that an enemy ship, the *Kerseage* [sic], had stationed herself on the coast of La Hague, apparently waiting to intercept the *Alabama*. "We shall meet," said the Captain, "and it will be a duel to the death."
>
> The following day, while the dancing was in full swing in his suite, the Admiral informed my husband and me, in the strictest confidence, that there would be a naval battle at daybreak outside French waters between the *Kerseage* and the *Alabama*; the news had just reached the Admiralty. "It will be an extraordinary, terrible sight," he added. "Should you have the courage to witness it, Madame, I would be happy to take you in my barge to the breakwater, where you would be able to view the battle. If you agree, I shall be under your windows at 5 o'clock with my barge and my men." Our hotel was on the quay.[11] We thanked the Admiral and agreed, and prepared ourselves for this strange, thrilling expedition. My mind was in such a fever that I could not go to bed. I sat in an armchair and waited for the appointed hour. The clock struck, and at that very moment I heard the rhythmic noise of the oars and the voice of the Admiral, then the sound of his footsteps on the stones of the deserted quay. He had come personally to fetch us. We climbed down into the barge, where we found Admiral Roze and Admiral Ducrest de Villeneuve

accompanied by several staff officers. Admiral Dupouy wrapped me in furs, gave the order to cast off and directed our course through a thick fog.

We passed in front of the *Alabama*, which was lighting her fires. The two officers who had given us such a warm welcome two days before were once again on deck and saluted us as we passed. Poor *Alabama*! They were dressing her masts. They were polishing the copper of her gun-ports as if for a holiday. A few hours later, there was to be nothing left of her.

When we arrived at the great wall of the breakwater, the fog lifted and we saw on the horizon a motionless black dot; it was the *Kerseage*, lying in wait for her prey.

It was 10 o'clock when the first shot was fired. Up to that point, the two ships had been challenging each other, tacking round each other with fearsome grace. When they had narrowed the circle, they stopped, took the measure of each other like two wrestlers, then heading straight for each other both opened fire from their batteries at the same time. A black cloud enveloped them, spattering the sea, as still as a millpond, with dark patches. Columns of thick smoke drifted over to us and for a moment hid from us everything between. Once they had passed overhead, we saw the combatants once more. They were drawing breath! Soon flames running along the sides of the ships gave notice that the guns were beginning to thunder again. Sometimes we heard their mighty roar, sometimes the wind carried it away to other parts of the coast. Through the dim haze of powder-smoke, we could see balls fall into the sea, then, emerging from the chasm which they had opened up, showers of light foam rising above the billows.

It was impossible to predict how the fight would end. Neither one of the ships appeared to be suffering from this fearful struggle. Both still had their masts, their funnels, their flags. Suddenly the *Alabama* shuddered. It was as if some underwater eruption had shaken her to her very core. Giant waves enveloped her, then subsided around her, revealing a vast, gaping hole in her bows. The pitiless foe continued the fire from his batteries. The *Alabama* no longer replied. Soon her masts and her funnels flew up into the air in fragments. She tried to flee and gain the coast, but the water entering her boiler brought her to a halt. She hoisted her flag of distress. Shortly after this, we saw the unhappy ship tilt her bows to the sea and disappear into the depths. While we were wiping away our tears, the *Kerseage* returned to port in the place of the vanquished vessel.

A number of French and English craft came out under full sail to endeavor to save the crew. We went back to Cherbourg with the boats, which were carrying the wounded and the dead. The unhappy wounded were lying in the bottom of the boats, covered with a piece of sail. Their groans could be heard above the noise of the oars. Sometimes the canvas was lifted and an arm was stretched out to the heavens, seeming to reproach God for permitting the carnage.

We were about halfway there, when we perceived a sort of raft surmounted by a human head. It came towards us borne along on the tide with the debris from the ship. We soon realized that the raft was a chicken-coop to which a man, or rather part of a man, was attached; this living corpse was missing both its legs. It was a dreadful sight. The poor wretch was lifted up and laid down in one of the boats, but no sooner was he there than he uttered a loud cry and breathed his last.

We found it impossible any longer to endure such sights. We begged the Admiral to take us out to sea again, and we left those funerary boats behind us. An hour later, we were climbing the steps of the quay once more, together with the captain of the *Kerseage*, who entered the town in triumph, pistols at his belt and his face blackened with powder.

11

The Prince Offers His Services

A large white marble tombstone, fixed to the back wall of the covered gallery running along one side of the Hauptfriedhof, the main cemetery in Frankfurt, Germany, marks the last resting place of a French prince who was also a Confederate major general.

Camille Armand Jules Marie, Prince de Polignac, was born in 1832 into an old French Royalist family. His father, Jules de Polignac, had been President of the Council of Ministers under Charles X, having previously been Ambassador to Great Britain, and his mother was the Honourable Maria Charlotte Parkyns, daughter of Thomas Boothby Parkyns, first Baron Rancliffe, and widow of César, Baron de Choiseul-Beaupré.[1] After the revolution of July 1830, so memorably depicted in the Delacroix painting "Liberty Leading the People," Jules de Polignac was arrested and sentenced to life imprisonment in the fortress of Ham, where the future Napoleon III was also to be later imprisoned. Freed under the amnesty of 1836 and sent into exile, he spent the next nine years initially in England and then in Bavaria before finally being allowed to return to France.[2]

The young Camille de Polignac was educated at the elite Collège Stanislas in Paris, where he distinguished himself particularly in mathematics.[3] His plan was then to follow his two elder brothers into the École Polytechnique, which would have given him an automatic commission in the French Army on graduation. To the surprise of all, however, and to his own dismay, he failed the entrance examination. Polignac was initially despondent at this, but he finally rallied, refused to be daunted and determined to work his way up through the ranks instead. Accordingly, he and a classmate from the Collège Stanislas, a young Louisiana Creole called Armand Blanchard de la Bretesche, set off for Chartres in March 1853 to enlist in the 3rd Chasseurs. The following year, learning that the 4th Hussars was being sent to the Crimea, Polignac managed to get himself transferred to that regiment, distinguished himself in the fighting before Sebastopol and was finally commissioned second lieutenant in the Chasseurs d'Afrique in July 1855.[4] With the end of the Crimean War, however, life in a peacetime army proved far too tedious and frustrating for someone with his striving and ambitious personality. In early 1859, he was able finally to resign his commission and promptly took ship for Central America—to study the geography and political economy of the region, according to most accounts, although others also mention its plant life, which had apparently excited Polignac's scientific interest.⁵

After spending a few weeks in Costa Rica, where he seems to have been warmly received by the president, Polignac moved on to Nicaragua. He spent a few months in Nicaragua, where he appears to have found some sort of temporary employment with a company organizing a transit route across the country. As we shall see shortly, the precise reason for Polignac's visit to Central America and the precise nature of his work in Nicaragua remain unclear, but by looking at what evidence is available we can at least draw certain conclusions. At any rate, following a further stay in Costa Rica, Polignac finally took ship for New York in November 1859. Here he spent some weeks meeting and becoming friendly with a number of men who were later to play a prominent part in the Confederate war effort, including Senators John Slidell and Judah P. Benjamin of Louisiana and a certain Captain P.G.T. Beauregard. Polignac's experiences in Central America had given him an idea, which he now laid before the two Louisiana senators. In the end, as we shall see, nothing came of his proposal, but it can nevertheless be said to have led indirectly to Polignac's later distinguished career in the Confederate Army.

Camille de Polignac in the uniform of a French général de brigade (Picture File, David M. Rubenstein Rare Book and Manuscript Library, Duke University).

Polignac and Benjamin had become particularly friendly during Polignac's time in New York, and the two continued to be in correspondence after Polignac's return to Paris later that year. In March 1861, the infant Confederacy sent its first three Commissioners to Europe, William Lowndes Yancey, Ambrose Dudley Mann and the French-born Pierre A. Rost, and on March 9, in advance of their arrival, Benjamin wrote to Polignac about Rost as follows:

> I beg of you to extend to him all the aid in your power towards the accomplishment of the object we have in view—any hints, suggestions, or information that you can give will be valuable and will be highly appreciated, and all courtesies that you may be able to render him will be particularly acknowledged as a favor to myself.⁶

This, however, was unfortunately not the sort of assignment likely to appeal to an active, restless character like Polignac. He had been following closely what was happening in America, and on March 22 he sat down and wrote a letter to Beauregard. He wrote in French, which was Beauregard's first language;

according to his biographer T. Harry Williams, Beauregard "probably could not speak English until he was twelve years of age."[7]

Polignac's original copy of the letter, together with all his other papers, is in the Polignac family archives in France. In 1962, however, the late Professor Roy O. Hatton was able to obtain from Polignac's youngest daughter, Princess Agnès, the Marquise de Créqui-Montfort de Courtivron, copies of a huge variety of family papers, including Polignac's Civil War diary, numerous letters, photographs and so on. Professor Hatton had become interested in Polignac while a postgraduate student at Northwestern State University (then known as Northwestern State College) in Natchitoches, Louisiana, and from this time on he published articles on his hero in a number of magazines and journals, in addition to his lengthy and very useful 1970 doctoral thesis for Louisiana State University, "Prince Camille De Polignac: the Life of a Soldier." Much of the material collected by him is now in the Watson Memorial Library at Northwestern State University, but a photocopy of the letter to Beauregard is held in the Hill Library at Louisiana State University, and I was able to obtain a scanned version of this through the kind offices of Dr. Germain Bienvenu there. The letter was accompanied by an old typescript translation. This is in general reasonably accurate, but it does contain several errors which unfortunately have been repeated by writers in English on Polignac who have clearly relied on the typescript translation rather than going back to the French original. In translating the letter now myself, I have tried to be as faithful as I can to what Polignac actually wrote, while at the same time avoiding a too-literal translation which would inevitably sound unnatural in English; I have also inserted punctuation here and there where the sense demands it.

The letter is worth studying in its entirety, not merely for its significance as a historical document but also for the glimpse it gives us of Polignac's character and personality. In its somewhat naïve view of America and Americans, it forms an interesting contrast to a letter which Polignac wrote 35 years later to be read out before a reunion of the veterans of his old Texas brigade. This is what it says:

Paris, March 22, 1861
Sir,

> I do not know whether you will recall meeting me in New York, a little over a year ago, at the office of your friend and mine Major Barnard.[8] In expectation of my visiting New Orleans, you were good enough to invite me to tour the defenses which had been constructed through your efforts. Unfortunately, I was unable to take advantage of your kind invitation, being forced, to my great regret, to return at short notice to France. Since then, I have followed with great interest the momentous events which have been unfolding in your country, and all my sympathies have been with the Democratic Party, whose rights, it seems to me, are unquestionable. I was pleased to see that you had been appointed to the command of the military forces of South Carolina; please allow me to congratulate you. I regularly see over here compatriots of yours interested in the cause of the South, including your acquaintances Messrs. Michael Heine, Calhoun (of Louisiana) etc. All of these gentlemen have told me that, according to the reports they received, one of the objects of the new government was to form a regular army large enough at least to guard the frontiers. Since you may perhaps have some difficulty in raising a mobile body of troops,[9] given the lack of poor and unemployed men in your happy country, I felt

that I should let you know that I might be in a position, should you wish to have recourse to this, to supply you with some Irishmen, through one of my cousins who has estates in Ireland and who recently offered the French Government 10,000 peasants for Algeria. Enlisting is very much in fashion at the moment, thanks to Garibaldi, Türr and Klapka, although, because of the coming events in Italy and Hungary, these three absorb a large proportion of it in all countries. I would also be able to find a number of retired French non-commissioned officers who could be useful in specialist arms of service. I am well aware that, while you have no lack of quality over there, it may perhaps be otherwise where numbers are concerned, whereas in France we have, at least, no shortage of numbers.

I write to you about all this as a soldier. I was in the French Army. I served my apprenticeship in the trenches before Sebastopol, but I have always had a deep admiration for your country. I have always considered it my adopted country, a country where one day I should be happy to settle. Indeed, I left the French Army purely in order to start to put this plan into effect. When I was charged by a transit company in Nicaragua to which I belonged with organizing the defense of the works, the government of Nicaragua put all its forces at my disposal, with the power to modify them as I saw fit, in order to fortify the weak points on the coast and protect the country. As this was an international enterprise, my idea was to propose to the government of the United States that it put me in charge of protecting and guaranteeing the lives and goods of those of its subjects making use of the transit. It was to be a sort of military consulate, set up in that country by the government of the United States, and one which would have been helpful to them in counterbalancing the influence of England, which is both very harmful to them and disastrous to Central America. I will not bore you with the details of this plan, which I explained in its entirety, while in New York, to Messrs. Slidell and Benjamin, and which failed through lack of funds. I merely wanted to show you that I continue the traditions which make sisters of our two nations, and that I would be happy to offer your cause the gift of my person.

Forgive this long letter, and allow me to clasp your hand warmly and extend to you my very best wishes.

How much of what Polignac says in this letter should we take at face value? In reality, probably not very much, apart from his obvious desire to find a position of some sort in the Confederacy. Polignac's biographer Jeff Kinard has aptly pointed out that it reads like "any typical job application."[10] Polignac, like many another job applicant, is exaggerating his qualifications and experience, emphasizing his enthusiasm for the job in question and making extravagant claims in order to appeal to potential employers.

Let us start with his claim to be able to supply troops to the fledgling Confederate Army. It is perfectly possible that Polignac had a cousin, presumably on his mother's side of the family, with estates in Ireland; what is less easy to believe is that this cousin had offered the French government 10,000 Irish peasants for service in Algeria or that Polignac himself might be able to procure numbers of them for the Confederacy. (It would be interesting, too, to know what the reaction of the British authorities would have been). Equally, how could he, as a mere second lieutenant who had resigned his commission two years before, hope to be able to persuade all of these experienced French noncommissioned officers to join the Confederate service? It is not even clear what Polignac meant by "the coming events in Italy and Hungary." With the invasion and occupation of the old Bourbon Kingdom of the Two Sicilies, most of Italy was now forcibly unified under the

Piedmont monarchy.[11] Garibaldi had retired to the island of Caprera, although he did attempt an unsuccessful assault on Rome in the summer of 1862. István Türr was now a general in the Italian Army and was also being entrusted with certain delicate diplomatic missions by King Victor Emmanuel. György Klapka was in exile. It is true that Türr and Klapka planned another abortive Hungarian national uprising together, but that was not until 1866.

Then there is the question of what exactly Polignac was doing in Nicaragua. We know that he arrived in Costa Rica sometime in March 1859, spent a few weeks there and then went on to Nicaragua. He can have been in Nicaragua for no more than about three or four months, since after that he returned to Costa Rica and spent four months there before boarding a ship for New York in November 1859.[12] Writers in English have asserted that Polignac was working for the Nicaraguan government, yet he states clearly that he was employed by "a transit company." There was much international interest in Central America at this time for a number of reasons, but one reason for Nicaragua's importance was the discovery of gold in California in 1848; Nicaragua provided probably the shortest and most secure route between New York and San Francisco. There were a number of attempts to make use of this route, and Michael Schreiber's excellent article in *Nicarao, the Philatelic Journal of the Nicaragua Study Group* (Volume 25, Number 2) provides a clear summary of what is an extremely complicated story involving a large number of different companies and entrepreneurs.

The first passengers for California via Nicaragua left New York in February 1849. Shortly after this, Cornelius Vanderbilt inevitably became involved. His American Atlantic and Pacific Ship Canal Company was incorporated in Nicaragua in March 1850 and began operations in July the following year. In August of that year, Vanderbilt's partner, Joseph Livingston White, secured the agreement of the Nicaraguan authorities to the creation of a new company, the Accessory Transport Company, to operate the route. During Vanderbilt's absence in Europe in 1853, White and an accomplice were able to gain temporary control of this company, and two years later operations were interrupted by the invasion of Nicaragua by William Walker and his filibusters, who seized the company's assets and used its steamers to ferry in new recruits. Although Vanderbilt had by then regained control of his company and was able to use his money and influence to ensure that Walker was finally ousted, regular service on the Nicaraguan transit route ceased in early 1857, and Vanderbilt's interest increasingly shifted thereafter to Panama.

Though regular service on the transit route was not resumed until 1864, Vanderbilt's former partner Joseph L. White made two attempts, in 1858 and 1859, to reopen it. White was a former member of the House of Representatives from Indiana. Vanderbilt's most recent biographer, T.J. Stiles, describes him as "an astonishingly vain and treacherous man" who had "double-crossed Vanderbilt more than once."[13] White had a misplaced but unshakable belief in his own abilities and was somehow able to persuade others at times to share this belief. He had now formed a new company, the American Atlantic and Pacific Ship Canal Company, in early 1858, and in November of that year one of his steamers arrived at

Greytown, Nicaragua, from New York with passengers bound for the land route, by road and river, to the Pacific coast and then on by ship to California. White's contract had not been ratified, however, and the Nicaraguan authorities refused to let him land. Meanwhile, his steamer on the Pacific side had to be sold through lack of funds. Nothing daunted, White announced in September 1859, that a new company of his, the United States and Central America Transit Company, would begin operations on October 5. This scheme, too, fell through, this time from lack of river steamers.[14]

There was thus no transit company actually operating in Nicaragua during the three or four months which Polignac spent there in the spring and summer of 1859. Given that White was planning to start operations in October, however, either he himself or one of his agents must have been in Nicaragua for some months before this time in order to make all the necessary preparations. It was presumably the United States and Central America Transit Company, then, which employed Polignac during his time in Nicaragua. It is less easy to see why White and his partners would have put him in charge of organizing the various defenses which he mentions, since he was not an engineer but had served in a light cavalry regiment; possibly he was able to convince them that his military experience was wider than it really was, or perhaps they simply felt that a French aristocrat with some military experience would be a useful addition to the board. What appears highly unlikely is that the Nicaraguan government would have put "all its forces" at his disposal for the work of fortifying the route. Previous agreements between Nicaragua and individual transit companies had given the company the right to fortify, but it is clear that this work was intended to be the responsibility of the company, not of the Nicaraguan government.

In any case, Polignac cannot have spent very long in White's employ because he must have been back in Costa Rica by the end of July. Perhaps he and White had fallen out, or perhaps he had simply realized that there was no substance beneath White's bluster. Whatever the reason for his leaving Nicaragua, Polignac probably devoted much of the four months he now spent in Costa Rica to planning his next move. A draft treaty of 1857 signed by Buchanan's Secretary of State, Lewis Cass, and the Nicaraguan Minister to the United States had given the United States "rights to all transit routes, their security and protection, and the right to protect the lives and property of U.S. citizens."[15] It must have been this which inspired Polignac to formulate the plan which he was later to present to Slidell and Benjamin and to propose that he be appointed some sort of military representative of the United States with responsibility for protecting the transit route. It was, by any standards, an extraordinarily audacious proposal to be put forward by a young man of 27, and a foreigner at that, with little real military experience and no connection with the United States, but then Polignac was never lacking in confidence. Certainly he seems to have succeeded in convincing Alexander Dimitry of Louisiana, the U.S. Minister to Costa Rica and Nicaragua, since it was Dimitry who gave Polignac the letters of introduction to Slidell and Benjamin.

What, though, was his real reason for leaving France to travel to Central

America? Was it really, as he claims in his letter, both to help the United States to counter Britain's baleful influence in the region and to enable himself eventually to settle in the United States? Whatever he may have said, then or later, there is no real evidence that either of these considerations was in his mind when he crossed the Atlantic. Certainly Britain had an interest in Central America at this time; indeed, the Mosquito (Miskito) Coast of Nicaragua and Honduras was a British protectorate until 1860. There had been clashes in the past between British and Americans in Nicaragua, and, despite the 1850 Clayton-Bulwer Treaty between the two countries, many American politicians would still have been nervous of the British presence in the region. Polignac himself, however, had no particular reason to be anti–British. He was, after all, half English himself. Furthermore, Polignac's father had been French Ambassador to Britain during the reign of Charles X, had spent a number of years, as a Royalist exile, in London and had many English friends. As with Polignac's repeated protestations of love for the United States, the most likely conclusion is that he was once again playing the part of a candidate for a job, telling his interviewers what he thought that they would want to hear. From an early age, Polignac had shown himself almost obsessively determined to make a name for himself and to prove himself worthy of his ancestors. The simplest explanation, then, for his choosing to travel to Central America in 1859 may well be the correct one—that he saw the region as likely to provide the sort of opportunity to win fame which the peacetime French Army could not.

Whatever the case, Polignac's letter to Beauregard swiftly produced a positive response. Polignac disembarked at New York on June 12,[16] possibly having sailed on May 29 from Liverpool via Queenstown on the S.S. *Glasgow*.[17] He crossed without difficulty into the South and was in Richmond towards the end of the month. The Richmond *Enquirer* of June 29 reports his arrival in the city "to draw his sword in behalf of a brave and generous people, who have taken up arms to resist the attempt of a tyrant and despot to subjugate and enslave them" and records his having been received the previous day by Jefferson Davis at his office in the War Department.[18] We know that Polignac dined with Jefferson Davis and his wife on July 4, because the diarist Mary Chesnut and her husband were also there that evening and Mrs. Chesnut mentions Polignac's presence. She also makes it clear that he had already dined with the president once before, since she recalls, rather cruelly, that on that first occasion Polignac had mistaken the wife of the Irish-born newspaperman William M. "Constitution" Browne for his hostess. On this second occasion, Mrs. Chesnut describes Polignac as "*triste* and silent, his English not being too ready."[19] If Polignac was silent on that occasion, however, it cannot have been because of his English. English was, after all, his mother's native language, and he spoke it fluently (as he did German), albeit with a French accent. Both his Civil War diary and his letters to his mother were written in English.

Two days after this dinner, on July 6, Polignac was appointed lieutenant colonel in the service of the Confederate States. Presumably in an attempt to appear less foreign, he had now taken to styling himself Camillus Julius Polignac, and the appointment was in that name. The official record of the appointment shows him as having been appointed from France, while under the heading "Remarks" is the phrase "Thru. Courtesy."[20] It would be a great mistake, at this point, to see Polignac as nothing more than an adventurer or a mere soldier of fortune. Certainly he was determined to make his mark, but he also needed a cause in which he could believe. His family was a Royalist one. His grandfather had fought against the French Revolution in the émigré Army of Condé and had then joined the Russian service,[21] as had his father[22] and other members of the family, and his father had then continued the struggle against Napoleon.[23] Polignac would have seen himself as following in their footsteps. How much he was influenced in his choice by his earlier meetings in New York with Slidell, Benjamin and other Southerners it is difficult to know exactly, but all the evidence is that in the Confederacy he had found a cause to which he could devote himself wholeheartedly. From then on, he showed total and unconditional loyalty to the South.

His career as an officer in the Confederate Army can be followed in detail in Hatton and Kinard. What follows, then, is a brief summary. Polignac's first position was assistant inspector general on Beauregard's staff, although he did not in fact follow Beauregard to the West until April 10, 1862. He arrived in Corinth on April 17 and performed his duties ably, both under Beauregard and then, after his replacement, under Bragg. He clearly craved more active service, however, and therefore requested a transfer to Kirby Smith's Army of Kentucky. Here, after a short time on the staff, he was finally assigned to the 5th Tennessee Infantry, in Cleburne's division. His contribution to the Confederate victory on August 30 at Richmond, Kentucky, where he seized the regiment's flag and led it forward in a successful charge, greatly impressed his superiors. On October 21, Kirby Smith wrote to Jefferson Davis recommending Polignac's promotion to brigadier general, and at the end of that month Polignac left for the Confederate capital in order to add his voice to Kirby Smith's and to press for the desired promotion. This came through at last on January 10, 1863,[24] and in March of that year Polignac was transferred to the

Camille de Polignac in Confederate brigadier general's uniform (Alabama Department of Archives and History).

Trans-Mississippi Department, finally arriving at department headquarters in Shreveport on May 22 after the long journey from Virginia; he had left Richmond on April 2.

It seems probable that Richmond imagined, logically enough, that Polignac would be given command of a unit of French-speaking Louisiana Creoles. In the event, Kirby Smith, who had been appointed to command the department at the beginning of the year, put him in charge of a Texas brigade. The men had been recruited in North Texas and had a reputation for being ill-disciplined and prone to desertion. They had been forcibly dismounted more than a year earlier, which had done little to improve their mood, and they were most reluctant to accept the orders of a foreigner whose name they could not even pronounce, referring to him derisively as "Prince Polecat."[25] Polignac by this time, however, was beginning to understand the character and mentality of the Southern soldier rather better than when he had first arrived in the country. By his coolness and bravery, as well as by his care for his men, he eventually won the Texans over, and the nickname became thereafter a badge of affection. Polignac's performance on April 8, 1864, at the Battle of Mansfield, where he took over the division of General Alfred Mouton after the latter's death and led it to victory, gained him promotion to major general, to rank from that date.[26]

On January 10, 1865, Polignac was sent by Governor Henry Watkins Allen of Louisiana on a mission to Paris in a last, desperate attempt to persuade Napoleon III to intervene on the side of the Confederacy; Polignac himself had suggested the idea of the mission to Allen and Kirby Smith and convinced them of its potential value. Running the blockade to Cuba, he finally reached Cadiz on March 21, 1865, and Paris, via Madrid, several days later. He had a courteous reception from the emperor, who granted him two interviews and (while carefully avoiding any sort of political discussion) questioned him closely about the military situation, but he had arrived far too late to have any hope of achieving his objective.[27]

Polignac continued, however, to defend the South even after the war had ended. In 1866, he published a pamphlet titled "L'Union Américaine Après la Guerre" ("The American Union after the War"), explaining in his preface that his intention was not to produce a detailed study of the right of secession and the causes of the war but rather to draw attention to the current attacks upon the South and to show how little basis there was to them. His chief target was the Liberal Catholic writer Charles Forbes René, Comte de Montalembert. As we have already seen, Montalembert was a strong supporter of the Union and a friend of John Bigelow, U.S. Consul in Paris and then, after the death of William Lewis Dayton, U.S. Minister to France. Montalembert wrote a lengthy article in *Le Correspondant* on May 25, 1865, hailing the victory of the North, which he later published as a pamphlet, "La Victoire du Nord aux États-Unis."[28] Polignac was predictably scathing about it. "M. de Montalembert's writing," he wrote, "contains almost all the sorts of error which help to blacken the South, and can thus serve as representative of everything that has been published on the subject."[29] Nor had his views changed 30 years later. In 1896, he drafted an address to the surviving veterans of his old Texas brigade, sending it to a "Mr. Derden" with the request that it be read out "at the next Confederate meeting." This is a very different document from his 1861 letter to Beauregard. With the benefit now of four years' service in the Confederate Army and another 30 years of reflection, Polignac sets out, clearly and cogently, the reasons for the Civil War as he sees them, explaining why, in his opinion, the South had no option but to secede and why he himself was naturally drawn to volunteer for the Confederate cause. Addressing himself to "Honoured Confederate Soldiers & companions in arms," he refers to the South's struggle as part of "the universal & ever recurring fight of Liberty against Oppression" and expresses his pride in having participated in "the defense of everlasting Principles of justice & liberty."[30]

With the advent in 1870 of the Franco-Prussian War, Polignac returned to the French Army. The war resulted in disaster for France, but by virtue of his skill and courage Polignac himself came out of it with his reputation still further enhanced. He was initially given command of the 67th Regiment of the reservists of the Garde Mobile. After the Imperial Army's defeat at Sedan on September 1–2 and the fall of the empire, he was put in command of the 1st Brigade of the 1st Division of the 20th Corps in the newly formed Army of the Loire. In the reorganization which followed the German victory over the Army of the Loire at Loigny, the 20th Corps was one of those which became part of the new Armée de l'Est under General Bourbaki, formed from remnants of the Army of the Loire and other units with the objective of relieving Belfort. Polignac was made commander of the 1st Division, which, again, consisted largely of reservists.[31] The Civil War veteran and soldier of fortune Charles Carroll Tevis, who commanded a brigade in Crémer's division in the Armée de l'Est, reported later that Polignac "behaved well, as he always has done in the field"—which, coming from Tevis, was high praise.[32] When Bourbaki, in turn, was beaten at the Lisaine, it was Polignac's division which was ordered to cover the retreat. In this capacity, much like Cleburne's division after Missionary Ridge, it continued to fight the Germans for a full two weeks after the armistice of January 28, 1871, apparently forgotten by the Government of National Defense. According to a major serving under him, the division left neither "a single cannon nor a saber nor a rifle to the enemy."[33] Polignac was awarded the Légion d'Honneur on January 19, 1871.[34]

There was a possibility, shortly after this, that Polignac might become one of the 50 or so former Union and Confederate officers who served in the Egyptian Army. Beauregard, who had been seriously considering accepting a position there himself, had written to Polignac in 1870 asking if he would care to accompany him as his chief of staff. Beauregard repeated the invitation in 1873, but in the end nothing came of his Egyptian plan, and the Franco-Prussian War thus marked the end of Polignac's soldiering days.[35] For then on, he was, in theory, free to devote himself to the study of mathematics, to music and to family matters. The last of these, however, involved rather more complications than the first two.

As a young man, Polignac had fallen in love with Cécile Léda Blanchard de la Bretesche, the elder sister of Armand, his old Louisiana Creole classmate at the

Collège Stanislas. Her parents refused their consent, apparently on the grounds that Polignac had no money and that in any case they did not approve of him. Eventually, in 1856, the young couple decided to go ahead without permission. They managed to find a priest who took pity on them, and he agreed to marry them at night in the cathedral of Valenciennes. Over the next two years, Léda bore Polignac two sons, and when he embarked for America, she accompanied him with the two boys. After some months, however, he sent her back to France with the children, promising to join her there in due course.[36]

Those who appreciate national stereotypes will be pleased to learn that in certain respects Polignac conformed perfectly to the British or American idea of a Frenchman. Kinard describes him as "a connoisseur of fine wines, cuisine, and women."[37] With Léda safely back in France, the entries in Polignac's diary covering his months in Richmond while waiting for his promotion to come through mention a series of trysts and flirtations with various unnamed Richmond belles. Where he identifies them at all, he does so only by their initials, often resorting in addition to military metaphor ("a successful dash into the enemy's lines," "carry the position," "effect a lodgement" and so on).[38] Through the family of his friend John Pegram, who had served with him in Kentucky, Polignac met Jefferson Davis's steward, Edward (Gustav Eduard) Eggeling[39] and other members of Richmond's German community. From then on, he was a frequent visitor to Eggeling's house, taking an active part in the German musical evenings held there. He became particularly close to a young German singer, who appears regularly in the pages of the diary. He never gives her name but refers to her in the initial entries as "the German singer" or "my charming German artist" and then simply as "E." From an earlier entry in the diary, however, it seems almost certain that she was Edward Eggeling's 22-year-old niece, Eugenie Hammermeister. Eugenie gave singing lessons and was described by Pegram's sister as "an accomplished artist."[40] She and her uncle left Richmond on March 16, 1863, however, on a planned trip to Europe.[41]

According to Léda's own account, she heard nothing from Polignac for two years, during which the elder of their two sons died at the age of five. When she heard that Polignac was now finally back in France and wrote to him to remind him that he had a wife and son to support, he replied that since the marriage was a purely religious ceremony, with no legal validity, she could not count on him for anything and that, in any case, he did not have sufficient financial resources to help her. Since French law expressly stipulated that a religious marriage must be preceded by a civil ceremony, Polignac was absolutely within his rights, legally, in now claiming that his marriage to Léda in the cathedral at Valenciennes in 1856 was invalid. This was to have repercussions, however, some years later.[42]

By French law, then, Polignac was perfectly free to marry, in 1874, Marie Catharine Adolfine Langenberger, from a prosperous Frankfurt family. She was the niece of the Franco-German Baron Frédéric Émile d'Erlanger, who was responsible for issuing the 1863 Confederate "Cotton Loan" and who subsequently married Marguerite Mathilde, daughter of the Confederate Commissioner to France,

John Slidell. Polignac's marriage to Marie Catharine was short-lived, however. She died in 1876, shortly after giving birth to a daughter, Armande.[43]

Since she could expect nothing more from Polignac, Léda herself now had the religious ceremony annulled and in 1877 accepted the proposal of a diplomat at the Rumanian Embassy, whom she married in full accordance with French law. Unfortunately, he died a few weeks later, leaving her with a small pension from the Rumanian government as her only means of support. The surviving son, Camille Olivier Blanchard, continued to live with his mother. Since he suffered from a disease of the nervous system, contracted in childhood, which left him prone to fits, he was unable to find regular work. As a result, mother and son were living in conditions of increasing poverty. Finally, on November 7, 1882, having visited Polignac the previous day to ask him for money and been refused, the young Camille Olivier went to Polignac's Paris apartment in its owner's absence and attempted to set fire to it. He made no attempt to run away and offered no resistance when arrested. The trial was set for the following March.

This sensational case was naturally followed in detail by the French papers, and Léda had a ready audience for her story in the reporters who interviewed her—how Polignac had married her in the cathedral at Valenciennes, how she had borne him two sons, how he had taken her with him to America and how, on his return to France, he had abandoned her and the surviving son. She added that Polignac had started to mistreat her two years after the marriage, at one stage actually breaking her arm. Nevertheless, she had continued to consider herself his wife. The basic facts of Léda's story appear to be true. She was able to show the reporters, and to produce later for the court, Polignac's letter to her parents asking for her hand, a letter from the priest who had married them and Camille Olivier's birth certificate.[44] All the same, there is likely to have been rather more to the story than that. We know, for example, that both the Polignac family and Polignac himself had provided some support to the mother and son, even if this seems to have come to an end with Léda's marriage to the Rumanian diplomat.

It is unfortunate, then, that Polignac does not appear to have left any record of his side of the story. Possibly he considered it beneath his dignity to do so, or perhaps he simply felt that in situations like this it is usually best simply to keep silent. The issue of *The New York Times* for December 3, 1882, however, contained a full report on the case, dated November 20, from the paper's Paris correspondent—who happened to be the same Charles Carroll Tevis who had served with Polignac in the Franco-Prussian War. "Now, it is possible that this unhappy mother may tell the truth," he says, "and I do not pretend to palliate the heartlessness of this unnatural parent. But there are generally two sides to a story, and I think it well to reserve one's judgment until Prince Camille shall have spoken." Tevis had lived, for a time, in the same building in Paris as Léda and her son and had not formed a very favorable impression of the youth, who spent his time with low drinking companions who flattered him by calling him "Prince" and who was apparently "not only addicted to howling violently, but also to tormenting a cat." Indeed, this had eventually caused Tevis to have to look for other quarters. In summary, though, Tevis's prediction was "an acquittal on extenuating circumstances are [sic] sure things, as no jury would class the prisoner at the bar as responsible for his acts."[45]

The trial took place on March 7, 1883. The defendant gave his name as Camille Olivier de Polignac. Being questioned, he denied knowing that his mother had been fined 100 francs in 1873 for calling herself Princesse de Polignac. He agreed that Polignac had sent him to the Collège Chaptal, until his mental health forced his mother to withdraw him from the school. He admitted asking Polignac for money, in vain, between 1878 and 1882, but insisted that it was not simply a question of money. His aim in acting as he had, he said, was to try to force Polignac to recognize him as his son and to provide him and his mother with the means of subsistence.

Polignac, who had declined to prosecute, was called as a witness. He refused to admit that Camille Olivier could be his son. He had known the defendant, he said, when Camille Olivier was a child, and had done what he could for him over the years, although he had given him nothing since 1878. In any case, whatever relations he might have had in the past with Léda Blanchard had nothing to do with the case. Unfortunately, his rather haughty manner and his monosyllabic responses produced a most unfavorable impression on the court, especially given the apparent physical resemblance between Polignac and the defendant, both men being a little below medium height, with a long nose and sandy hair. Following Polignac's testimony, two witnesses testified that, on his instructions, they had paid Camille Olivier's fees at the Collège Chaptal for three semesters and had tried to find him a position in a trading company.

Léda Blanchard was not called upon to testify, but she had supplied the defense with the three documents which appeared to confirm her story and which were shown to the court. The defense now called Léda's brother, Armand Blanchard. He had been working in Valenciennes in 1856, had seen his sister arrive at the cathedral with Polignac and had been assured by Polignac that the marriage would be made official in due course. He was followed by a woman who had lived in the same building as Léda Blanchard in 1862. She testified that the Polignac family had always paid Léda's rent and that Léda had never been referred to as other than Madame de Polignac. Polignac's mother, she said, had come at least twice a week to take Camille Olivier out in her carriage.[46]

The prosecuting counsel had decided that the most effective means of disproving the son's claims was to attack the mother's morals, and he set about doing so with vigor. Léda Blanchard was a loose woman, he assured the court, who had already had an illegitimate child before she met Polignac. By publicly treating her as his wife for eight years, Polignac had done more than enough for her. He owed her and her son nothing whatsoever. He had given the boy money; he could hardly be expected to give this bastard his name as well. Despite his best rhetorical efforts, however, his argument was poorly received by the court. Having heard the defense summarize, once again, the key points, the jury deliberated for a mere ten minutes before (as Tevis had predicted) finding the defendant not guilty, to the cheers of the spectators.[47]

Polignac was now 51 years old. He had recently been spending an increasing amount of time in England with a relative by marriage and her 18-year-old daughter. The former Jessie Ramsay had been married to Count Alexandre de Polignac, Polignac's first cousin once removed. On his death, she had married Charles Allanson Knight of Wolverley in Worcestershire.[48] He died in 1879, whereupon she had reverted to styling herself Comtesse de Polignac and had settled in London with her daughter, Elizabeth Marguerite Knight, known to the family as Rita. On May 1, 1883, the Comtesse wrote to one of the girl's two guardians, W.D. Fane of Fulbeck Hall, Lincolnshire, to inform him of her daughter's "approaching marriage" to Polignac and asking for his consent.[49] Fane then received a furious letter dated May 4 from Rita's uncle, Colonel Sir Frederic Winn Knight, M.P., referring to Polignac as "an old dirty looking Frenchman," accusing him of being after Rita's money and begging Fane to use his influence to delay things at least until the girl came of age. He reminded Fane of the Blanchard scandal (the case had been widely reported outside France) and offered to solve the problem, if necessary, "by kicking the Frenchman down stairs & shooting him."[50] His efforts were in vain, however. The other guardian had already given his consent,[51] and Polignac and Rita Knight were duly married at St. George's, Hanover Square, on May 5.[52] A daughter, Mabel, was born on September 7.[53]

The remaining 30 years of Polignac's life passed peacefully and without incident. Despite the age difference and Colonel Knight's pessimistic prognostications, the marriage appears to have been a happy one. Mabel was followed in 1886 by Agnès and in 1899 by Victor Mansfield, named after the scene of Polignac's greatest triumph. There were visits, from time to time, to Paris, London and Cannes, but the family's main home was a castle which Polignac had bought in 1885 in what is today Slovenia. Here he was able to concentrate on his mathematical studies and to relax by playing his violin, while his young wife accompanied him on the piano. He died in Paris on November 15, 1913, apparently while working on a mathematical problem which had been preoccupying him for some years, and was laid to rest next to Marie Catharine in the Hauptfriedhof in Frankfurt.[54] He had been the last surviving Confederate major general.

His is not the only grave in the Hauptfriedhof with Civil War associations, however. Baron Émile d'Erlanger spent most of his working life in France, although he moved his family to London on the outbreak of the Franco-Prussian War. He continued to travel widely on business[55] but actually ended his days as a British citizen. In death, however, he chose to be returned to Frankfurt to be buried with the rest of the Erlangers. His tomb is a short distance further up the covered gallery (Gruftenhalle) from Polignac's,[56] and in the alcove next to him is his son, Dr. Raphael Slidell Erlanger, who predeceased his father by 14 years.

According to the cemetery information, Polignac's white marble tombstone originally covered a stone sarcophagus. Today, a plain stone covers the actual grave, while the tombstone is fastened to the rear wall of the alcove. Beneath the coat of arms of the Polignac family is the following inscription:

HIER RUHEN IN FRIEDEN
CAMILLE ARMAND JULES MARIE
G^AL. FÜRST VON POLIGNAC
MILLEMONT 16. FEB. 1832 PARIS 15. NOV. 1913

———

MARIE CATHARINE ADOLFINE
FÜRSTIN VON POLIGNAC
GEBORENE LANGENBERGER
FRANKFURT^A/M. 7. JUNI 1852-PARIS 16. JAN. 1876

("Here Rest in Peace
Camille Armand Jules Marie
General, Prince de Polignac

———

Marie Catharine Adolfine
Princesse de Polignac
Née Langenberger")

Camille de Polignac's grave, Frankfurt (author's photograph).

Below this again is an adaptation, in German, of a verse from Chapter 4 of the Book of Baruch. In the King James Bible, the original verse reads: "For I sent you out with mourning and weeping: but God will give you to me again, with joy and gladness for ever."[57]

12

From Calais to Cairo

The standard answer to the question of what was the last shot fired in the Civil War is that it was the shot which the CSS *Shenandoah* fired across the bows of a Yankee whaler in the Bering Sea on June 28, 1865. On the other hand, it could plausibly be argued that the last shot of the Civil War was actually the one which killed a certain former Confederate guerrilla calling himself Mr. Howard as he was dusting a picture in his house in St. Joseph, Missouri, on April 3, 1882. John Dunn of Valdosta State University, however, has suggested yet a third candidate for the title, the shot which the secretary to Benjamin Butler's nephew fired in the best hotel in Alexandria on July 11, 1872, at a former Confederate States Navy lieutenant named William Campbell, hitting him in the leg.[1] The Alexandria in question, however, was not Alexandria, Virginia, but Alexandria, Egypt, known to the locals as Al-Iskandariyyah.

So what were Campbell and some 44 other Civil War veterans, North and South, doing in Egypt in Egyptian Army uniform? To answer that, it is necessary to go back to the beginning of the nineteenth century, or rather slightly before, to Napoleon's invasion of Egypt in 1798. The French occupation of Egypt lasted for only three years, but it had an enormous impact on both Western Europe and Egypt. Its impact on Europe, of course, is reasonably well known. Travelling with Napoleon's invading army were 150 *savants*—scientists, archaeologists, historians—and these men opened the eyes of Europe to the glories of ancient Egyptian civilization; in fact, the science of Egyptology really starts here. But the invasion also had a huge impact on Egypt, because it opened the Egyptians' eyes to the immense technical and military superiority of the West; and no one learned this lesson better than a wily old Albanian mercenary named Mehmet Ali.

Mehmet Ali arrived in Egypt in 1801 as the commander of an Albanian unit in the Turkish army sent by the sultan to cooperate with the British in driving the French out of Egypt, Egypt being then a province of the Ottoman Empire. He was uneducated and illiterate, and the only language he really spoke fluently was Albanian, although he was competent in Turkish, but he was a natural soldier and a natural leader and had enormous natural intelligence. The French withdrawal created a vacuum in Egypt, and in the struggle for power that resulted, Mehmet Ali came out on top, largely by sitting on the sidelines and letting the others fight it out among themselves until they were exhausted. By 1805, he was the main power in Egypt and, at the request of a number of prominent Egyptians, the sultan recognized this by appointing him officially wali, or governor, of Egypt.

Like a number of other famous people, Mehmet Ali had a dream, and his dream was to found a dynasty in Egypt and to make Egypt into a powerful, modern, independent country, freed from what he considered the dead hand of the Ottoman Empire. He succeeded in the first objective, and he came very near to succeeding in the second. He nationalized the land in order to raise funds to pay for what he wanted to do, made agriculture a state monopoly and created an industrial base, the main aim here being to make Egypt self-sufficient in weaponry. As a result, arms factories and powder mills sprang up in the country. Like Jefferson Davis in Gladstone's famous (if rather unwise) phrase, Mehmet Ali made an army and a navy; rather than simply making a nation, however, he made an empire.[2] In 1815, he formed what he called Al-Nizam al-Jadid, which translates roughly into something like our New Model Army. This army was to be formed, trained, drilled, uniformed and armed along European lines, and Mehmet Ali now set about finding Europeans to help him do this.[3] In 1815, the obvious place to look for these was France. Napoleon's defeat had left France with a vast pool of disbanded veterans, so that was where Mehmet Ali mainly looked for his foreigners. He said at the time that, out of every 50 foreigners he employed, 49 would be what he called "false stones," but the 50th would be a genuine diamond.[4] Fortunately, he did find several diamonds, probably the best example of these being a hard-bitten veteran of Napoleon's armies called Joseph-Anthelme Sève.

Sève had served Napoleon on land and sea, and there was not very much that he could not handle. Shortly after his arrival in Egypt, he was attempting to instill the rudiments of French drill into a reluctant group of officer cadets when they took exception to his methods and fired a volley of musket balls at him. This was a mistake. They missed, and Sève drew his saber, unleashed a volley of French curses, rushed at them and threatened to kill them all, one by one. After that, he had no more trouble. He converted to Islam, changed his name to Suleiman Pasha, and by 1847 he was the sixth-highest-paid officer in the Egyptian Army. His descendants married into the Egyptian royal family, and certainly until recently they still had a palace in Cairo.[5]

With the help of men like Sève, then, and under the inspired leadership on the ground of Mehmet Ali's son Ibrahim, who was a younger version of his father, Mehmet Ali's armies expanded south into the Sudan, overran the Hejaz (the whole western part of modern Saudi Arabia) and Syria and threatened Constantinople itself. Alarmed at this, the European powers rallied round, and by the Convention of London of 1840 Mehmet Ali was forced to retire from Syria and the Hejaz. In return, however, the office of Wali of Egypt was made hereditary in his family.

Mehmet Ali died in 1849, having in fact been senile for his last few years. His son Ibrahim had predeceased him, so he was succeeded by his nephew Abbas. Abbas, however, was not totally convinced of the benefits of aping the Europeans. He was much more concerned about balancing the books, and he instituted cuts in the armed forces which even certain recent British governments would have considered a little severe.

Abbas was succeeded in turn, in 1854, by his uncle Said, who was in fact younger than he was, as can sometimes happen in families. Unlike Abbas, Said was very much in favor of the army, but not as an instrument of empire. To him, as to Tsar Paul of Russia earlier, it was a toy, a plaything. Accordingly, he designed ever more exotic, expensive, impractical and uncomfortable uniforms for his soldiers, and he liked to call the regiments out at all hours of the day or night to parade in front of his palace.[6]

Said died in 1863 and was succeeded by his nephew, Ibrahim's son, Ismail. Here the story of the Americans in Egypt really begins, because Ismail was the man who invited them in.

Ismail's father, Ibrahim, and his grandfather, Mehmet Ali, had been tough old Albanian warriors, not exactly civilized but highly effective. Ismail, however, was very different. He was not a soldier. He was a cultivated and cosmopolitan figure who had been educated partly in France, spoke French fluently and was a great friend and admirer of Napoleon III. Indeed, in many ways he was rather like Napoleon III, with Mehmet Ali playing the part of Napoleon I. He was a highly intelligent man, with a strange habit of closing his right eye and looking at you with his left when he talked to you. In fact the Egyptians said that he saw with his left eye and heard with his right, and when a British visitor reported this to him, Ismail laughed and replied, "Yes, and I think with both!"[7] In one way Ismail, however, did resemble his grandfather, because he too had a dream, and his dream was, if anything, bigger than Mehmet Ali's. Ismail visited Paris for the International Exposition of 1867 and came back convinced that this was the blueprint for Egypt. Indeed, he summed up his vision for his country a few years later, near the end of his reign, when he said, "My country is no longer African. We now form part of Europe."[8]

Thus he imported French and Italian architects to build a new, European city on the east bank of the Nile, just north of the old city. He increased the production of cotton, introduced new crops, imported agricultural machinery, built roads, railways and bridges, dug canals and irrigation channels, established a telegraph system and nationalized the post office. It was in his reign, in 1869, that the Suez Canal was inaugurated, with weeks of festivities and the presence of the beautiful Empress Eugénie of France. All of this work, too, was under his direct supervision; he oversaw everything. Finally, in return for a substantial annual payment, he persuaded the sultan to confer on him the title of khedive, or viceroy, and to make it hereditary from father to son.

Nevertheless, even with all of this work, he did not neglect the army. Indeed, he saw himself as continuing the work begun by his father and his grandfather. At this time, there was still a core of French advisers in the army. In 1869, however, Ismail had something of a disagreement with his old friend Napoleon III. He had rather unwisely asked Napoleon to adjudicate in his dispute with de Lesseps over who was to pay for the cost of labor on the Suez Canal, and inevitably Napoleon had ruled against him and in favor of the French company. In addition, the French

Khedive Ismail (author's collection).

officers in his army were constantly badgering him to give weapons contracts to French companies and were, he knew, reporting secretly to Paris. "These men," he complained, "were virtually under the orders of the French Minister of War. I need soldiers who only answer to me."[9] He therefore determined to dismiss them and to look elsewhere for foreign military expertise.

Where could he look? Several thousand miles away, across the Atlantic, there was a country which, unlike Britain and France, had no territorial interests whatsoever in Africa and where there was, once again, a huge pool of recently demobilized or disbanded officers with experience of fighting a four-year modern war with modern weapons. Ismail therefore talked to a man he had met at the sultan's court, a former battery commander in the Union Army named Thaddeus Mott.

Mott's father had been personal physician to Sultan Mahmud II, his sister was married to the Turkish Minister to Washington and Mott spoke fluent Turkish, which was the language of the Egyptian court and the Egyptian officer corps—indeed, commands in the Egyptian Army were given in Turkish right up to 1920.[10] He also had very good connections in U.S. military circles. Accordingly, Ismail made Mott a *ferik*, lieutenant general, in the Egyptian Army and appointed him his personal military adviser, and Mott contacted an old acquaintance who happened to be Commanding General of the U.S. Army, a certain William Tecumseh Sherman, and together they started looking for potential recruits.

The contract they were authorized to offer was a reasonably generous one. The pay level was roughly the same as in the U.S. Army, with an additional 20 percent for serving in any of the distant provinces. If a man died in service, his heirs would receive a full year's pay, and if he was killed in battle, his widow would receive benefits until her youngest child came of age. Finally, transport costs between the United States and Egypt were covered by the khedive.[11]

For most of the Union veterans who answered the call, the main motives were probably lack of opportunity in the now very much contracted U.S. Army, love of adventure or, in the case of the one or two serving soldiers who were given permission to go, a wish to gain some military experience elsewhere. For the Confederates, forbidden in any case to serve in the U.S. Army, the motive was often financial. As Samuel Lockett, the Confederate engineer who had designed the defenses of Vicksburg, put it: "It is awful to be poor." Lockett could not even afford the cost of a ten-cent boat trip to see the Brooklyn Bridge, then under construction. Others may well have agreed with Henry Derrick, a former captain in the Confederate Army from Virginia, who joined the Egyptian service in order to escape what he called "the cursed tyranny of the United States."[12]

In the old Royal Archives in the Abdin Palace, there is—or was—a letter in French from Beauregard, offering to take command of the Egyptian Army.[13] There were rumors that Joseph E. Johnston had been asked. That Beauregard, at least, seriously considered going to Egypt is clear from his letters to various former comrades in the Confederate Army suggesting that they join him. Copies of two of these letters, written in English to Beauregard's former AIG Camille de Polignac, are in the possession of Daniel Frankignoul, president of the CHAB. The second of these is particularly interesting. The original approach to Beauregard was apparently made in 1870, and most of his letters on the subject were therefore written then. The second letter to Polignac, however, is dated April 7, 1873; this shows that Beauregard was still hoping to go to Egypt at this late date, even though it appears that the khedive's invitation had by now been withdrawn.[14]

In the event, however, no fewer than five former Confederate generals took ship for Egypt—William Wing Loring, Henry H. Sibley, Charles W. Field, Raleigh Colston and Alexander Reynolds, whose son, Frank, a former Confederate lieutenant colonel, joined at the same time.

The only former Union general who joined Ismail was Charles Pomeroy Stone, who had been imprisoned without charge after being made the scapegoat for the Ball's Bluff disaster in October 1861. He was one of the earliest to arrive and came strongly recommended by Sherman. Egypt gave him a chance to redeem himself, and in this he succeeded triumphantly. Ismail made him Chief of the General Staff, but by the end of 1872 he had supplanted Mott, and he continued to serve the khedive and his successor right up to 1883.

At any rate, whatever their various motives, in 1870 the first American recruits for Ismail's general staff arrived.

The men who volunteered for Egyptian service over the next few years started by taking a ship from New York. Some decided to bring their families with them, and there would probably be several veterans from either side travelling on the same boat. On arriving at Liverpool, they took the train down to London, then on to the coast, where they would board a ferry for France. They then continued by train through France, hardly stopping even at Paris, and down through Italy to Brindisi, where they took a steamer for Alexandria. The whole journey took about three weeks.

Alexandria was thus their first sight of Egypt. With its forest of masts and gangs of sweating, bare-chested men loading and unloading the ships, it reminded at least one former Confederate of New Orleans,[15] but to most of the veterans it was strange, exotic and even perhaps slightly alarming. Arriving there, they would, if they were lucky, be met by Loring, who was stationed in Alexandria from 1871 and who would see that they got safely onto the train for Cairo. Here they would be met by a scene of chaos worse even than at Alexandria. Porters climbed over each other in an effort to carry their luggage, hotel touts tried desperately to drag them off to their various hostelries, the streets were jammed with a heaving, swelling mass of humans and animals, and everywhere was noise, smells and confusion. The modern visitor's first impressions of Cairo, of course, are not dissimilar, except that today the thousands of donkeys and camels have been replaced by thousands of cars.

Eventually someone would appear and take charge of them and bear them off to the Grand New Hotel overlooking the Ezbekiyah Gardens, where rooms had been reserved for them until they were able to find their own accommodation. (Although the shell of the hotel is still standing, it looks neither very grand nor very new today). The next morning, an Italian tailor would arrive at the hotel to measure them for their uniform: a plain black tunic, buttoned to the neck, and black trousers for the undress uniform ("an exact reproduction of the coat of a Presbyterian parson," according to James Morris Morgan),[16] a far more splendid blue tunic (white for summer) and blue trousers with braid down the seam for full dress—both, of course, topped by the red tarboosh.

Once suitably attired, then, it was time for their first audience with the khedive. For the earlier arrivals, this probably took place at the Gezira Palace, so they would cross the Qasr al-Nil Bridge (the original iron bridge was replaced in 1933, but the two large bronze lions guarding each end remain today) to the island in the middle of the Nile and then walk through the extensive gardens to the palace.[17] Later arrivals were escorted to the khedive's newer Abdin Palace.

The next day, they would travel up to the Citadel to begin work. It is a 45-minute walk from the Ezbekiyah Gardens to the Citadel, uphill, so the Americans quickly learned to hire a donkey for the journey. Arriving at the Citadel, they passed through the Bab al-Qullah gate into Mehmet Ali's old Harem palace, which now housed the offices of the general staff. Early arrivals found this very exciting, and some even swore they could smell the perfume of its previous inhabitants, but the gloomy halls where they worked soon put an end to any romantic or erotic dreams of bosomy beauties in veils and wisps of gauze.[18]

Here, they were first issued with an ivory seal bearing their name and rank in Arabic letters, with which they had to sign any documents for which they were responsible. Their actual duties varied enormously, Stone and the khedive

Gezira Palace (now Marriott Hotel), Cairo, where the Americans were introduced to the khedive (author's photograph).

Citadel, Cairo (author's photograph).

deciding which tasks each man would best be suited for. Thus a man might be responsible for training Egyptian officers, drilling their men, mapmaking, piloting steamers, coastal defenses, surveying, exploration and a range of other duties. Certainly for those based in Cairo, however, the working day was not particularly onerous; it ran from 9:30 a.m. to 12 noon and then from 1 p.m. until 5 p.m., after which they were free. Social life, for both Americans and Europeans, revolved around the magnificent Ezbekiyah Gardens, with their lakes and shaded walks, little restaurants and lanterns in the trees at night, and the bars and cafes in the arcades surrounding them (only a small part of the gardens remains today, and the arcades are empty and dilapidated).

Among the Civil War veterans, military and naval, who answered the khedive's call were three former officers in the Confederate Navy who had been forced during the Civil War to spend far too many frustrating months in a French harbor: William Campbell, Charles Iverson Graves and James Morris Morgan. The first two had been respectively the captain and the executive officer of the CSS *Rappahannock* as she lay at Calais, waiting for permission from the French to sail. The third had been a midshipman on the CSS *Georgia*, which was temporarily blockaded at Cherbourg, but he had friends among the midshipmen on the *Rappahannock* and took the opportunity of a week's leave to go over to Calais and spend a day with them. Their very different experiences in Egypt provide an example of the varied fortunes there of the American volunteers.

Old Harem Palace, Cairo, where the American staff worked (author's photograph).

William Campbell was a Tennessean, a graduate of the Naval Academy at Annapolis and a brave and resourceful man. On November 25, 1863, dressed in civilian clothes and aided by a Scotsman called John Ramsay, formerly an officer in the service of the East India Company, he had snatched the *Rappahannock* (formerly HMS *Victor*) out from under the noses of the British authorities and across to Calais. Unfortunately, however, having got her to Calais, he was unable to get her out again. He volunteered for Egypt in 1872 and was put in charge of the steamers running between Alexandria and Constantinople. He was thus based in Alexandria, and it was here that he came into conflict with George Butler.

George Butler, a nephew of General Benjamin Butler, was the U.S. Consul General. He was a journalist with no diplomatic or military experience, so those

Colonel Charles Iverson Graves in Egyptian uniform (Charles Iverson Graves, seated, image P-2606/2, Charles Iverson Graves Papers, no. 2606, Southern Historical Collection, The Wilson Library, University of North Carolina at Chapel Hill).

knowing little of the elder Butler might well wonder how his nephew had obtained this post. Those with any knowledge of Benjamin Butler, however, would be less surprised. To adapt the common British expression, it was a case not so much of "Bob's your uncle" as of "*Ben*'s your uncle!" Benjamin Butler was a man of some influence in Congress at this time, and he used this influence to wangle consular positions for a number of his relatives.

It is reassuring to learn that George Butler was exactly what one would expect of a nephew of "Spoons" Butler, a credit in every way to his Uncle Ben. He started his diplomatic career by selling vice-consular positions to various Levantine businessmen of doubtful character for large sums of money. It may be wondered why Levantine businessmen of doubtful character would be willing to pay Benjamin Butler's nephew large sums of money for a vice-consular post. The reason is simply that it gave them consular protection and put them out of reach of the Egyptian police; no matter what dubious financial transactions they were involved in, they could only be tried in a consular court, and this consular court was, of course, presided over by Butler. Butler's next step was to team up with Mott in an effort to persuade the khedive to award a large arms contract not to Remington, as Ismail wished, but to the Winchester Repeating Arms Company and the United States Cartridge Company, which latter company just happened to be owned by Benjamin Butler; the motive here, of course, was the large amount of baksheesh which this contract would generate if they obtained it. The khedive, however, wisely chose the Remington Rolling Block rifle, which had won a silver medal at the Paris Exhibition in 1867.

Butler had a particular dislike for two groups of Americans in Egypt: the ex–Confederates and the missionaries. He referred to the Southerners as "overpaid former rebels" and suggested that they be deprived of any diplomatic aid and treated as non-citizens. The missionaries he dismissed as "bilious book-peddlers." In the case of the missionaries, the dislike was mutual. When one of Butler's dubious hangers-on, an Italian named Strologo, had a dispute with one of the missionaries' employees and beat him unconscious with a leaded cane, stories, inspired by the missionaries, of consular "bunga bunga" parties involving naked dancing girls and drunken revels started appearing in the American press. (These stories, incidentally, were all completely true). This alarmed the Grant administration, which started an investigation. In response, Butler threatened to "shoot to death" anyone slandering his reputation.[19]

Things came to a head on July 11, 1872. Three former Confederates, Campbell, Loring and Frank Reynolds, were having dinner in the Hôtel d'Europe in Alexandria when Butler came in with two of his entourage, Strologo and a former Union major called Wadleigh. Butler had tried to obtain a commission for Wadleigh in the Egyptian Army, but the khedive, who was a shrewd judge of character, had vetoed this. Butler had then given Wadleigh a job as his secretary, although, according to Stone Wadleigh was really his pimp. The three of them deliberately took a seat near the Southerners, who were preparing to leave. As they passed Butler's table, the three ex-Confederates, who were all in uniform, reluctantly saluted Butler but refused to acknowledge Strologo or Wadleigh. Since Campbell had said publicly that Strologo should be horsewhipped for his attack on the missionary employee, he was particularly hated by the Butler clique. Butler shouted sarcastically, "Good evening, Major Campbell!" and, when Campbell failed to respond, called him a dog. Campbell turned round, raising his cane. Butler picked up a chair, Strologo, showing great presence of mind, jumped hastily under the table and everybody else pulled out revolvers. Wadleigh now shot Campbell in the leg, urged on by Butler's shouts of "Give it to him, Wadleigh!" Loring and Reynolds then picked Campbell up and carried him to safety, pursued by a volley of shots from Butler and Wadleigh.[20]

Butler now telegraphed his uncle in Washington, saying, "Ask Secretary to telegraph leave immediately. Important. Rebel officers attempted my assassination. One assassin shot." The khedive's investigation, however, found in favor of the ex-Confederates. Butler warned that this could lead to a rupture in Egyptian-American relations, but the khedive countered by accusing Butler, in a rather curiously-worded translation, of "inebriety, notoriously corrupt practices and a general and openly displayed blackguardism." At this point, Butler lost his nerve and fled Egypt on a postal steamer.[21]

His uncle expressed himself as surprised at the accusations against his nephew. "The only reason I ever had to think he lacked refinement," he said, "was he was a newspaper man."[22] He even tried—unsuccessfully—to persuade the Department of State to refund the $700 which it had cost his nephew to return home.[23] With Butler gone, Mott had to go too, since he had been too closely associated with him in a number of his schemes, and Stone now took over Mott's responsibilities and the leadership of the Americans.

Fortunately, Campbell's wound was not serious, and he was soon back on duty. In 1873, he was selected to accompany Colonel Raleigh Colston, formerly a Confederate brigadier general, on an expedition south. They were to go up the Nile to Kenneh and strike out across the desert to the old Greek city of Berenice, where they were to link up with another group which had travelled down the Red Sea by steamer; then both parties were to proceed to Berber. The main objective was to look for a possible route for a railway. Colston and Campbell got on well together, Colston describing Campbell as "a genial and sterling gentleman,"[24] and during the journey over the desert to Berenice, the two Southerners learned how to handle both their camels and the local Bedouin. They learned the hard way, for example, not to treat a camel like a horse and in particular not to try to ride a camel like a horse, and also not to expect the Bedouin to dig out the sand clogging an ancient reservoir; no matter what the financial incentive, that sort of work was beneath Bedouin dignity and fit only for the fellahin.

After some three and a half weeks, they arrived safely at Berenice to be met by the leader of the main group, a former Union soldier called Erastus Sparrow Purdy. Here, however, orders were waiting for Campbell to return immediately to Cairo to join an expedition under the command of the famous British General Gordon—"Chinese Gordon"—who had been in the service of the emperor of China and was now in the Egyptian service. This time, the plan was to sail down the Red Sea to Suakin, then to strike southwest across the desert to Berber and to carry on up the Nile to Khartoum. Also with the expedition was a former Union officer from Maryland called Charles Chaillé-Long, later famous for his explorations in Central Africa and as the discoverer of Lake Kioga. Both Campbell and Chaillé-Long suffered during the long ride down to Berber, and Gordon, who prided himself on his endurance, made no secret of his contempt, considering them a couple of weaklings. By the time they reached Khartoum, Campbell was seriously ill, but Gordon was convinced that he was shamming. "If *you* put your finger down *your* throat," he said, "*you* will be sick." Reasoning that Campbell was quite well enough to work, he left him in Khartoum in charge of the stores, while he and Chaillé-Long carried on south.[25]

Campbell, however, had contracted typhus. The nuns at the Catholic Mission in Khartoum did their best, but they could not save him. Although, like most Tennesseans, a Protestant, he was buried in the Catholic cemetery, the only Christian cemetery there, and his grave was destroyed with the rest when the Mahdi and his Dervishes occupied Khartoum in 1885.

Thus the former captain of the CSS *Rappahannock* died in the khedive's service in October 1874, and the following year, 1875, his old executive officer on the ship, Charles Iverson Graves, arrived in Egypt. Graves was a Georgian, and he had attended Annapolis as one of Alexander Stephens's appointees. After the war, he had tried farming, but a flash flood in 1874 finally wiped out his hopes just as cotton prices were beginning to rise. His farm was heavily mortgaged, he had a wife and five children, he had no income and no prospects—and then he heard of the khedive's offer. He therefore set out for Egypt, promising to send for his wife and children as soon as he could.

Like many Americans, especially Southerners, even today, Graves was steeped in the language of the King James Bible. He was like Abraham and Lot, he said, who "sojourned in Egypt when the famine was grievous in their own country," and he had gone to Egypt "for the same reason Joseph's brothers went—to get corn for my family." So he lived as frugally as possible. He found the cheapest lodgings he could, ate in what he called "the cheapest respectable restaurant in Cairo," breakfasted on hardboiled eggs and bread ("Eggs are small in Egypt," he reported gloomily), and had his dinner in the open air so that he could listen to the band.[26] Everything he could, he saved, and he sent money home every month in order to reduce his mortgage.

Graves was an Episcopalian, and he was distinctly more tolerant of the religion of the majority of Egyptians than his compatriots were. "They worship the Living God," he said of the Moslems, "and regard our Savior a great prophet, and in this respect are better than either the Jews or the Unitarians."[27] With the local Egyptians, he rushed up to the Citadel to visit the Mosque of Mehmet Ali, which he considered "the finest in Cairo," on the one night of the year when the great man's tomb was opened. There were limits to his tolerance, however; like others among the Americans, he loathed the Nubian eunuchs who had so much power and who he felt were holding Egypt back.

Graves was put immediately into the Third Section of the General Staff, which was responsible for handling the more technical tasks of mapmaking and surveying. On December 11, 1875, however, a large Egyptian force landed at Massawa[28] on the Red Sea and prepared to advance into Abyssinia and take Emperor John's capital of Adowa. Towards the end of the month, Graves was sent down from Cairo as port officer, responsible for unloading stores and sending on supplies to the army. His personal shopping list for his new posting provides an interesting example of an American officer's priorities. It reads:

> 1 Pr.White Shoes; 1 Helmet Hat; Matttress; Tin Wash Bowl; Sponge & Bag; Looking-glass; Scissors; Soap; Toothbrush; Writing paper; Blank Book; Envelopes; Ink; PO Stamps; Tape; needles, pins, pens; buttons; thread; Burning glass; Tinder-Box; Matches; Candles; Tobacco; 2 Bots. Brandy; Box Mustard; Quinine; Diarrhoea medicine; Dysentery ditto; Sugar; Tea; Coffee; Curl paper; Umbrella; Almanac 1876; Camphor; fishing Tackle; Gum Camphor; Alcohol; pepper.[29]

An earlier Egyptian expedition under an inexperienced former artillery lieutenant from Denmark named Søren Arrendrup had been wiped out at Gundet in November, but Graves, who had not been long in Egypt, was confident that this time there would be an easy victory for the Egyptians—"It would be like a body of regulars firing into a street mob," he said.[30] It was thus something of a shock for him some three and a half months later when the survivors of the disastrous battle of Gura stumbled into Massawa and poured onto the transports, amid scenes which reminded former Union officers of Washington after the First Battle of Bull Run.

The Americans naturally imagined that after this reverse, the khedive would react as Lincoln had, reinforce and reorganize the army and send it South again.[31] Indeed, for a time it looked as if he would. In May, Graves was sent back down to Massawa to improve the landing facilities there. Nothing further happened, however, and Graves was soon back in the Citadel in Cairo again, only now with very little work to do. It was therefore something of a relief when the following year, 1877, he was given a job surveying the Land of Goshen and running telegraph lines between villages. It gave him a break from his duties in the Citadel, he had no expenses, of course, while in the field, and the extra allowance for work in the field was always welcome.

Back in Cairo at the end of the year, however, Graves found himself saddled with an unexpected additional responsibility. Robert E. Lee's daughter Mary arrived in the city in late 1877 with her widowed friend Mrs. Porter, and Graves had somehow been unanimously elected her escort during her stay. (Mrs. Porter was said to be looking for a husband, and some attempt was made to fix her up with Loring, but the general was having none of it; he liked the company of women, but he had been a bachelor for too long to be caught now.) Miss Mary was an extremely strong character, with an excellent sense of humor ("Isn't she ugly," said one of the other Americans to Graves, "and isn't she smart?") and pretty well tireless, and Graves found himself expected to take her shopping, to carry her various purchases back to her hotel, to show her the Pyramids, to walk with her in the Ezbekiyah Gardens in the evening long after they were closed and generally to be at her disposal 24 hours a day. Miss Mary was also responsible for the only display of Blue-Gray animosity during the whole of the American presence in Egypt.

There were of course a number of disagreements and arguments, some of them quite bitter, among the Americans, but these were always the result of clashes of personality rather than based on what uniform a man had worn. After all, as Raleigh Colston said, "we are all Americans."[32] In January 1878, President and Mrs. Grant arrived in Egypt as part of their two-year world tour, and Stone arranged a big dinner for them to which all the Americans, military and civil, were naturally invited. Miss Mary refused. She was tired after all her sightseeing, she said, and had to pack for her trip up the Nile the next day. To Graves, however, she gave the real reason. "I wouldn't sit down at the same table with General Grant," she said, "to save his life!"[33]

Graves was a good officer and a conscientious soldier. He had the full confidence of the khedive, and it was probably because of this that he received his final assignment, the last one given to any of the Americans.

In the spring of 1878, he was sent down to Cape Guardafui, the easternmost point of the Horn of Africa. His instructions were to survey the area and to decide on a suitable location for a lighthouse. This area today is part of Somalia, and it is directly on the route from the Red Sea out into the Gulf of Aden and the Indian Ocean. Not unnaturally, all of this shipping provided a temptation, then as now, for some of the more impoverished and criminally inclined locals. Today, of course, they are rather more proactive. The locals in 1878, however, lacked the resources that today's pirates have. In 1878, they simply waited for vessels to wreck themselves on the rocks of the Cape, which happened fairly regularly. The last thing they wanted was thus for an Egyptian unit commanded by an American to come down and start putting an end to this very profitable source of income. Things could have become a little difficult, but Graves solved the problem by kidnapping the local prince, forcing him to serve as a guide and holding him hostage until he had finished his surveys.

If Graves was one of the American success stories, James Morris Morgan was a disaster for American-Egyptian relations. After serving as a midshipman on the *Georgia*, Morgan had been sent to the training ship *Patrick Henry* and had then served in a naval battery on the James River. The war over, he had tried studying law, then growing first cotton and later potatoes, none of it with much success, so he jumped at the chance of volunteering for Egypt.

He arrived in Egypt in 1870 on the same boat which brought Stone over. There was no one to meet them at Alexandria, but they finally received a message asking them to go to the house of an official called Ali Bey. Here they were kept waiting for some time. Finally, the Bey appeared and told them testily in French that there were too many of them and that some of them would have to go home. Turning to Morgan, he asked him what rank he thought he was getting. When Morgan replied that he had been promised a captaincy, the Bey laughed in his face. Morgan was a 24-year-old Southern gentleman with all a young man's sense of his own importance. Furious, he shouted in English that he would take the next train to Cairo, find the man who had brought him 7,000 miles in order to be insulted and horsewhip him. At this the Bey turned white. Speaking now in perfect English, he assured them that it was all a misunderstanding. It turned out later that he was simply a minor official whose instructions were to speed them on their way, which he now hastened to do.[34]

On arrival in Cairo, Morgan was assigned to Loring's staff. One morning, he was sent off to inspect a regiment in the suburbs of Cairo. Hardly had he arrived when a number of the soldiers fell out and started praying. As good Moslems, they were theoretically perfectly entitled to do this, but Morgan had a suspicion that they were really doing it because their rifles would not have passed inspection. He reported his suspicions to Loring, who took it up with the regimental commander, Arabi Bey, an extremely religious man known for his piety who was indignant at this presumed attack on his faith. Loring therefore sent Morgan off again the next day to inspect the same regiment, and exactly the same thing happened. This time, Morgan simply snatched up half a dozen of the men's rifles and bore them off to the Citadel, where he examined them and found them, as he had suspected, absolutely filthy. When Loring reported this to Arabi, Arabi was furious, not with his men but with Morgan, and the Minister of War, to whom they took the case, was equally shocked. There is an interesting postscript to this story. Arabi Bey, later Arabi Pasha, was the man who led the nativist revolt in 1882 which resulted in the British occupation of Egypt. Could it be, then, that Arabi's revolt was born here and that perhaps Morgan was ultimately responsible for the 70-year British presence in Egypt?[35]

Next, Morgan accompanied Loring to the Cairo Opera House. Waiting in the foyer, he was asked by the Prefect of Police, yet another Ali Bey, to fetch him a glass of water. Morgan objected to his tone, so he went off, got a glass of water, threw it in the prefect's face, grabbed Loring's cane with one hand and the prefect with the other and started belaboring him until he was finally pulled away. The khedive, who had seen the whole thing, laughed and laughed and told the prefect that he would have been disappointed if Morgan had not reacted as he had. "I did not bring Americans here," he said, "to wait on you!"[36]

Loring was then put in charge of coastal defenses, based in Alexandria. He and Morgan were one evening invited to a banquet given by a local Pasha. Loring was seated on his host's right, but there was no place laid for Morgan. At Morgan's insistence, Loring explained to the pasha that he needed Morgan beside him, first to interpret for him, since Morgan, having grown up in Louisiana, spoke fluent French and had by now picked up a smattering of Arabic, but also to cut up his food, since Loring had lost an arm in the Mexican War during the assault on the Belén Gate in Mexico City. The pasha replied that he did not see why Morgan could not carry out both functions if he simply stood behind his superior's chair. Morgan was speechless with rage, and a chair was eventually placed for him beside Loring.

The next morning, Morgan took the first train down to Cairo, saw Stone and offered his resignation.[37] Stone, who, in Morgan's words, handled the Americans "as though they were so many naughty children,"[38] calmed Morgan down and temporarily solved the problem by promoting him to *qaimaqam*, colonel, and assigning him to the staff of Ratib Pasha, the commander-in-chief.

Morgan had inherited from Loring a horse called Napoleon. Napoleon was one of the many presents which the khedive had given the Empress Eugénie when she came to Egypt for the inauguration of the Suez Canal. The empress did not want to take him back to France with her, so he ended up with Loring.

Napoleon was a bay, and he was a kind of equine jump jet—he could do a vertical takeoff. Thus he would take off vertically, land again, take off again and so on. The problem was that one never quite knew when he was going to do this. As Loring had only one arm, the only way that he could control Napoleon when Napoleon started to do this was by pulling on the reins with his teeth, and since he found this rather tough on the teeth, he passed the horse on to Morgan.

Morgan was an excellent horseman, and he soon had Napoleon under control. He adopted the habit of taking the horse out along the busy Shubra Road, which led to the khedive's summer palace, and putting him through his paces for the benefit of the fashionable passersby. One day there was a tremendous commotion, and the khedive's carriage and its various outriders appeared from the direction of the palace. All those in the street immediately dropped to their knees and salaamed, except for Morgan. Just as the coach was about to pass him, Morgan made Napoleon rear up and then remain motionless, while he himself executed a smart military salute. Delighted by this, Ismail clapped furiously and called Morgan to the coach to congratulate him personally. Shortly after this, there was a military exercise involving a mock battle. Morgan had been planning to ride a more docile horse, but the khedive announced that he would be particularly interested to see how Napoleon behaved under fire. Early in the battle, Morgan was sent with a message to the commander of the artillery, so he rode up and delivered his message, whereupon the guns opened up. To his horror and embarrassment, Napoleon immediately dropped to the ground and lay on his belly, quivering with fear, until the barrage stopped and Morgan was able to ride him away.

It was impossible to keep Morgan down for long, however, and he and Napoleon were soon back on the Shubra Road again. One day, a carriage bearing two ladies from the harem, with an escort of eunuchs, approached. All the other men hastily turned their backs, but Morgan and Napoleon carried on showing off. Impressed, one of the ladies tossed a rose out of the carriage. Riding up at a gallop, Morgan leaned down from the horse and picked up the flower in one fluid movement. Flower after flower followed. Finally, the unseen lady handed Morgan a flower wrapped in a handkerchief. This was too much for the eunuchs, who spurred their horses after this rash infidel. Napoleon was too fast for them, however, and Morgan was soon back at home with his trophy. Here he was visited by the Foreign Minister, Nubar Pasha. The handkerchief belonged to the khedive's 19-year-old daughter, Princess Fatma, and the khedive had demanded its return. In response, Morgan disposed of the evidence by throwing the handkerchief in the fire. He was now in serious trouble, and for some days no one dared speak to him, but eventually the affair blew over.[39]

However, Morgan had now definitely had enough of Egypt, and he went to the khedive to offer his resignation. The khedive, rather to his surprise, begged him to reconsider and finally told him to take six months' furlough and go back to America for a rest. On arriving in New York, Morgan went to visit a friend. Waiting for the friend to return, he picked up a Bible lying on the table and opened it at random. His eye fell on the first verse of the 31st chapter of Isaiah. "Woe to them that go down to Egypt for help," he read.[40] Hastily he shut the Bible, fearful of what he might see next, and sent in his resignation by post.

"Woe to them that go down to Egypt for help." A few years later, a number of other Americans must have agreed with Isaiah. Since his accession in 1863, Ismail had been spending enormous quantities of money. He received a substantial income from his vast estates, but this was nothing like enough to cover his expenses. The festivities for the opening of the Suez Canal alone must have cost him millions. He had inherited a significant foreign debt, and his solution was simply to extend this. While times were good, the European moneylenders, the Rothschilds and others, were happy to oblige. Egypt appeared to be a good investment. As time went on, however, they started to become rather nervous about their money. In 1875, pressure from his creditors forced Ismail to put up for sale his shares in the Suez Canal, which were snapped up by Disraeli on behalf of Britain. After the disastrous, and very costly, failure of his invasion of Abyssinia, the foreign bondholders and their governments had had enough. Two commissions in

1876 forced Ismail dramatically to reorganize his finances and to accept a representative each from Britain and France into his Ministry of Finance. A third commission, in 1878, was more specific. Ismail must now drastically reduce the size of his army and dismiss the American officers. "Dismissal Day," as it was called, was fixed for June 30, 1878. Each American was then to receive full pay due, six months' extra pay for early termination of the contract, plus an additional £75 towards the cost of the fare home.[41]

When Graves returned to Cairo from his final assignment at the end of July, then, he found most of his friends and colleagues already gone. One or two had taken civilian employment, Stone was still in his office in the Citadel, but most were now back in their own country. Thus Graves went alone to draw his final pay. Having learned, as a Southerner, the lesson of the Civil War, he insisted on taking it in gold and waited patiently while the Coptic clerks carefully counted out the money. In the end, it weighed 24 pounds, and slinging it over his shoulder he marched triumphantly off. He came back to Georgia with over $5,000, enough to pay off the mortgage on his farm, renovate his house and dig the necessary drainage ditches around his fields to protect him against any future flash floods or freshets.[42]

Few of the other Americans, however, can have felt about their Egyptian service as positively as Graves did. More of them must have agreed with Samuel Lockett, who summed up his experience thus: "It was my fortune, good or bad—it is hard to say which—to have been an officer in the Egyptian Army."[43] Furthermore, they left behind them half a dozen of their comrades, their bodies lying in Egyptian or Sudanese soil.

However, that is not quite the end of the story. In 1886, perhaps in belated recompense for his mistreatment 25 years before, Charles Pomeroy Stone was asked to design and construct the pedestal for the Statue of Liberty, which was to be set up in New York Harbor just across from the two forts where he had been unjustly imprisoned. To help him, Stone brought in two of his old comrades from Egypt, two former Confederates who once again had fallen upon hard times—the former Confederate Army engineer Samuel Lockett and the former Confederate Navy midshipman James Morris Morgan.[44] Thus the pedestal of the Statue of Liberty stands today as perhaps the only memorial, however unlikely, to the nearly 50 Civil War veterans, North and South, who served the Egyptian khedive some 150 years ago.

13

Three Union Veterans' Overseas Graves

A famous line in Homer's *Iliad* speaks of the many Greeks who fell before Troy, "far from their beloved country." At the end of the American Civil War, "three hundred thousand Yankees," in Innes Randolph's words, were "stiff in Southern dust."[1] Nevertheless, at the close of the conflict, the Union Army still contained over a million men. Less than seven months later, according to William B. Holberton, 801,000 of these had been successfully mustered out and discharged.[2] The vast majority of them simply returned to their homes and offices, their factories and farms. Their hearts had indeed been, in Oliver Wendell Holmes's arresting phrase, "touched with fire,"[3] but for the most part they lived thereafter lives of quiet regularity.

Some, however, after four years of war, found themselves for various reasons—a yearning for adventure, financial difficulties, sheer boredom or a combination of these and other factors—unable to settle down to civilian life. The shrunken postwar army being too small to accommodate most of them, they were forced to look further afield to the armies of various foreign countries. The largest group, some 20 in all, thus found themselves in Egypt, whose ruler, Khedive Ismail, was by a happy coincidence looking at precisely that time for experienced military men to help him reorganize his army. Here, like their former Confederate counterparts, they were employed on a variety of tasks—mapmaking, exploring, surveying, training, engineering and, in some cases, actual fighting. Their duty done, most of them eventually returned to the United States. A minority, however, whether from choice or not, found graves overseas. This is the story of three of them—Charles Carroll Tevis, Erastus Sparrow Purdy and Henry Anker Irgens.

The most intriguing of the three, without question, is the soldier, adventurer and British spy Charles Carroll Tevis, whose picaresque career is reminiscent of that of George MacDonald Fraser's antihero, Harry Flashman. In the favorite phrase of the British newspaper columnist Richard Littlejohn, "You couldn't make it up!" Anyone interested in following the course of Tevis's extraordinary life owes an immense debt to Dr. Will Kurtz of the John L. Nau III Center for Civil War History at the University of Virginia. While admitting "a complete understanding of Tevis's post-war career will require travel to numerous foreign

149

archives and the ability to read sources in French, Italian, Latin, Turkish, and Arabic," Dr. Kurtz has nevertheless done an excellent job of piecing together, from a number of sources, the basic facts about Tevis's various military escapades both before, during and after the Civil War and summarizing them on his blog in the form of a three-part biography. The following account of Tevis's life and career, then, will inevitably lean heavily on Dr. Kurtz's pioneering work.[4]

Tevis was born Washington Carroll Tevis in Philadelphia on February 28, 1828, son of the well-known Philadelphia auctioneer Benjamin Tevis and the former Mary Hunter. After attending the University of Pennsylvania, he was appointed to West Point, graduating in 1849 somewhere in the middle of his class. Posted to Carlisle Barracks as a second lieutenant of Mounted Rifles, he quickly grew tired of the monotony of life in a peacetime army and requested a more active assignment. Just as it came through, however, his wife was taken seriously ill, and he left the army without permission in order to be at her deathbed.[5] As a result, he was later unfairly accused of desertion.

At some point after this, for reasons which are not entirely clear, Tevis moved to Paris, since he is known to have been received into the Roman Catholic Church there in 1853, changing his first name that same year from Washington to Charles. With the outbreak of the Crimean War in 1854 (or possibly even before this, according to some accounts), he made his way to Turkey and offered his services to the Ottoman sultan. Taking the name Nessim Bey, he was appointed Bimbashi (from the Turkish *bin*, "a thousand," and *baş*, "head," this rank is equivalent to major in the modern Turkish army, but equated to lieutenant colonel in the Ottoman army) and put in command of a unit of bashi-bazouks, the irregular cavalry drawn from the further reaches of the Ottoman Empire and with a reputation, not entirely unjustified, for indiscipline. He seems to have found action very much more to his taste than mere garrison duty, ending his Crimean service with both Turkish and British decorations.

In 1855, however, apparently for reasons of health, he returned to Paris. Here he seems to have lived the life of a carefree pleasure-seeker, exciting the disapproval of, amongst others, Benjamin Moran, at that time assistant secretary at the U.S. Legation in London, who appears to have developed an unreasoning prejudice against Tevis, there being no actual evidence that they ever met. Moran refers to him waspishly in his diary as a "*mauvais sujet*" and repeats a secondhand account, almost certainly apocryphal, of Tevis's attempting to enlist in the Persian service and being turned back at the frontier on account of his bad character.[6] Tevis can hardly have devoted himself entirely to leisure, however, since he also found time to invent a self-loading percussion revolver, which he patented in Paris on May 16, 1856,[7] and to write a book in French on the duties of outposts and pickets which received a very favorable review in Charles Dickens's magazine "Household Words."[8]

The Civil War provided Tevis with an opportunity to resume military life. He returned to the United States in 1862 (one is tempted to wonder why no earlier than this) and was assigned to the 4th Delaware Infantry with the rank of lieutenant colonel. In this capacity, he commanded the land force on a combined naval and military operation to destroy a Confederate foundry near Walkerton, Virginia. The expedition set off from Yorktown on the evening of June 4, 1863, and achieved all its objectives, destroying the foundry, a nearby gristmill belonging to a Colonel Aylett of the Confederate Army, various other industrial buildings and a quantity of stores, the total value of all of this being estimated by Tevis in his report at $200,000. He and his men had also captured a number of horses, mules and cattle but were unable to embark them in time and had to leave them behind. In his report of the affair, Major General Erasmus D. Keyes, commanding the U.S. IV Corps, referred to Tevis's "great skill and spirit" and the "splendid daring" displayed by him and his men. He also noted, in a postscript, that the expedition had "brought in about 100 contrabands."[9]

Even before this, though, Tevis had become bored with life as an infantry officer and yearned for some assignment where he might be able to make more of a name for himself. Earlier that year, he had conceived the idea of recruiting a cavalry regiment of black Southerners under his command. He reasoned that black Southerners would be very much better able to handle horses than most white Northerners, and with his experience of commanding bashi-bazouks he was confident that he could transform them into an efficient fighting machine capable of whipping any Confederate force up to twice its size. To aid morale and add to the sense of a corps d'élite, he proposed to clothe his men in uniforms similar to those of the spahis, the irregular cavalry recruited by the French in Algeria. Unfortunately for Tevis, the Union authorities unaccountably failed to welcome this suggestion with the enthusiasm which he clearly felt it deserved. He was at least partially mollified, however, by being authorized in late 1863 by Major General Robert C. Schenck, then commanding in Maryland, to raise a regiment of local white cavalrymen.

This happened to coincide with the state elections in Maryland. Tevis had become friendly with a radical Republican named John Frazier, who was standing for the position of Kent County Clerk. On November 3, Tevis issued an order demanding "full and ardent support to the whole Government ticket upon the platform adopted by the Union League Convention." "None other," he added threateningly, "is recognized by the Federal authorities as loyal or worthy the support of any one who desires the peace and restoration of this Union." To make sure of achieving the desired end, he then arrested Frazier's opponent, as well as several other local politicians. This was too much even for Schenk, who had Tevis in turn arrested. *The Cincinnati Enquirer*, a newspaper of Copperhead sympathies, took great pleasure in reprinting the offending order with the headline "Louis Napoleon Outdone," and the Unconditional Unionist ticket predictably lost the election.[10]

Although Schenk released Tevis after three days, Maryland's Governor, Augustus W. Bradford, refused to commission him, and Stanton had to intervene personally to allow Tevis to continue recruitment. Not content with limiting himself to local Unionists, Tevis now decided to fill up the ranks with Confederate prisoners from Fort Delaware. Winter was coming on and, despite initial government disapproval, Tevis was eventually able to recruit four companies from the prison camp. The 3rd Maryland Cavalry was mustered into service in January 1864 and soon after assigned to the Department of the Gulf, where it took part in Banks's ill-fated Red River expedition.[11]

Most "Galvanized Yankees" were wisely sent west to serve against Indians rather than against their former comrades. Finding themselves in the South, many of Tevis's reluctant recruits now took the opportunity to desert. Morale among the remainder was low, and in an effort to counter this Tevis decided to take his men off to the New Orleans racetrack, where he allowed them to race their horses against each other and to bet on the result. This led to Tevis's being arrested for a second time, this time on the instructions of Major General Edward Canby. He remained under arrest from April 30, 1864, until July 20, when he was discharged "for the good of the service." Tevis seems to have had a number of influential friends, however. By some mysterious means, his dishonorable discharge was later changed to an honorable one, and on July 16, 1867, he was finally promoted, for his "gallant and meritorious services," to brevet brigadier general, backdated to March 13, 1865.

Presumably still smarting over the indignity of his dishonorable discharge, and with the Civil War over, Tevis now became involved in the ambitious Fenian plan for an invasion of Canada under the former Union Brigadier General Thomas W. Sweeny. Appointed adjutant general of the movement by Sweeny in October 1865, Tevis entered into his new role with enthusiasm. By the time of the planned invasion, he was based in Chicago and had responsibility for the left wing of the attack, which was due to start on June 1, 1866. When the day came, however, Tevis failed to move, on the grounds that he had been unable to find transport for his men. The much-trumpeted invasion was a fiasco, and Sweeny, furious, dismissed Tevis for disobeying orders. Tevis, now furious in turn, at once wrote to Sir Frederick Bruce, British minister in Washington, offering to betray his former associates.

That, at least, is the story, and certainly by 1867 Bruce was indeed paying Tevis for information on the Fenians. Is it perhaps, though, a little too neat? What was Tevis's real reason for not moving on June 1? Had he possibly approached the British authorities earlier—or even the U.S. authorities, who also had an interest in seeing the invasion fail? Whatever the case, his career as a British secret agent continued for some time to come, as we shall see.

Restless again, Tevis next sailed for Rome to offer his services to the Pope. Pius IX's kingdom was threatened by the supporters of a United Italy, from whom it was temporarily protected by the bayonets of Napoleon III's troops. Tevis immediately joined the Papal Zouaves (*Zuavi Pontifici*), an international force which had originally been formed to defend the Papal States against the brief invasion of 1860 and in which a number of Irish-born Union officers had served before the Civil War in a specifically Irish unit, the Battalion of St. Patrick. Tevis now came up with a plan to recruit Civil War veterans for an American regiment, in furtherance of which he travelled to New York. The Catholic hierarchy in the United States proved less than enthusiastic, however, and Tevis was reluctantly forced to concede defeat and return to Rome.[12]

The Franco-Prussian War provided him with his next opportunity. The outbreak of the war in July 1870 led to the immediate withdrawal of the French troops who had been protecting Rome, and it was not long before Tevis followed them to France. Here, in December of that year, he was given command of the 2nd Brigade in the independent division of the 30-year-old General Camille Crémer, part of the newly formed Armée de l'Est under General Charles-Denis Bourbaki. As mentioned earlier, the former Confederate Major General Prince Camille de Polignac commanded the 1st Division of the 20th Corps in the same army. The final, terrible three-day Battle of the Lisaine in January 1871 resulted in the total defeat of Bourbaki's army, its only success being the temporary victory at Chenebier on the second day, January 16, which was attributed largely to Tevis's efforts. After silencing the enemy guns with the fire of his muzzle-loading four-pounders in a two-hour artillery duel at the start of the engagement, Tevis noticed that the Prussian left flank was uncovered and ordered an immediate attack on it which, after much hard fighting, led to the enemy's retreat. For this, Tevis was commended in front of his troops and decorated on the field.[13] This minor success alone, though, could not affect the course of the battle. Retreating into neutral Switzerland with the broken remnants of Bourbaki's army, Tevis was eventually able to make his way back to France. The war over, he settled once again in Paris, where he was to spend most of the rest of his life, taking French nationality.

Tevis is next heard of in Egyptian uniform. Most accounts of this period in his life say simply that he arrived in Egypt in 1872 and left in 1873.[14] The former Union General Charles Pomeroy Stone, however, who was now Chief of Staff of the Egyptian Army and thus in a position to know, stated that Tevis entered the khedive's service on January 21, 1873, as a brigadier general and resigned in the summer of that year[15]—although this would not necessarily, of course, preclude his having actually arrived in the country before the end of 1872. At any rate, he was put in charge of the new military school at Abbasiya[16] but seems to have made little mark. Hesseltine and Wolf describe him as "an adventurer who ... passed quickly through Egypt" and "served most inconspicuously" there.[17]

Tevis had not yet quite tired of military life, however, for in 1874 he returned, after 20 years, to the Turkish army. Little is known about his service there, although he is said to have taken part in the Russo-Turkish War of 1877–78 in which the English former blockade-runner captain Augustus Charles Hobart commanded the Turkish Black Sea Fleet. We do know, though, that, apart from whatever military duties he may have had, Tevis served as the local correspondent for *The New York Times* during this period. By the end of 1877, however, he was back in Paris to stay, his soldiering days over at last.

Here he continued to write from time to time for *The New York Times*. It seems likely, however, that he found a great deal more fulfillment (as well as a useful source of additional income) in his renewed career as a British agent. The impetus for this was the now almost-forgotten Fenian dynamite campaign of 1881–1885, the inspiration and largely the work of Irish-Americans. Had the British authorities maintained contact with Tevis ever since the abortive Fenian invasion of Canada? It is at least possible. Certainly he was now in a position to be of great service to them. Unsuspected by the Fenian leaders, who seem to have borne him no grudge for his curious failure to move in 1866 and continued to accept him as one of their own, he mixed easily in Fenian circles in Paris, passing on to the British authorities all that he learned. It was shortly after this that he met and befriended Duleep Singh, the last Sikh Maharajah, who, thwarted in his attempt to return to the Punjab, had settled in Paris, refusing to go back to England. Rejecting all his former British connections, Duleep Singh made approaches to both local Fenian agents and, apparently, the Russian government, unaware that everything that he said or did was being reported back to London by the friendly Tevis.

With Duleep Singh's death, Tevis's intelligence work may be presumed to have come to an end, and he spent the rest of his life living quietly at his home in Paris. His first wife had died, he had divorced his second wife in 1885, and his only daughter had married an officer in the French Army, but his widowed mother had moved to Paris in order to be near him. She died in 1893 at the age of 94 and was buried in Montparnasse Cemetery, and when Tevis himself died, on September 29, 1900, he was laid to rest in the same tomb. Their joint grave is in Division 10, Line 7 North, 6 East. Approached from the north, it is about 70 yards down the avenue de l'Est, some way in behind the tall sepulcher of the Famille Dandrieux and next to the Famille Durandeau grave; the soft white stone, although retaining its color, has crumbled badly, and the inscription, while still legible, is no longer very clear.[18]

Charles C. Tevis's grave, Paris (author's photograph).

The careers of our other two veterans, while interesting, are rather less dramatic than that of Tevis, and their ends rather sadder. Erastus Sparrow Purdy, whom we met briefly in the previous chapter, was born in New York on May 25, 1839. His father, Samuel Purdy, moved in 1849 to California, serving as the state's third lieutenant governor from 1852 to 1856. Once he had finished his schooling, Erastus Sparrow followed, arriving in San Francisco via Nicaragua on June 6, 1855. He worked first in various banking jobs, but in November 1857 he joined the Sonora Surveying Expedition led by the then Captain Charles Pomeroy Stone, who had been contracted, by agreement with the Mexican government, to survey the states of Sonora, Sinaloa and Baja California. Stone was expelled after three years by the Juarista governor of Sonora, Ignacio Pesqueira, but Purdy carried on making a survey of the northern border of the state before reporting back to Stone in Washington.[19]

Not long after this, of course, the Civil War broke out. According to Hesseltine and Wolf, the young Purdy "fought the Civil War valiantly at a desk in the Military Department of the Pacific."[20] This is not entirely fair. In June 1861, he assisted in organizing the 1st California Regiment (32nd New York Infantry) which the Scots-born Californian Roderick Matheson was forming in New York. He was appointed adjutant of the regiment, with the rank of first lieutenant, in which capacity he served at First Manassas. Posted to the staff of the division of Brigadier General William B. Franklin, he was promoted to captain on September 19, 1861, and appointed assistant adjutant general of the division.[21] He continued with Franklin when the latter received command of the VI Corps in March 1862 and by the end of August that year was a major and one of Franklin's aides-de-camp; a well-known photograph of Franklin and his staff from this period shows Purdy standing in the back row under a large slouch hat. Having served with the Army of the Potomac right through to Antietam, however, Purdy sent in his resignation in November 1862—on the grounds of ill health, according to his 1881 obituary[22]—and returned to California.

Again, according to his obituary, the government refused to accept his resignation, considering him too valuable to lose. Accordingly, we find Brigadier General George Wright, commanding the Department of the Pacific, reporting from San Francisco to Washington on June 16, 1863: "Captain E.S. Purdy, assistant adjutant-general of volunteers, has reported at my department for duty. I have placed him temporarily under instruction of my chief, Lieutenant-Colonel Drum."[23] Reading between the lines, one has the impression that General Wright was, initially at least, not particularly impressed with his new assistant adjutant general—who, it will be noticed, had now reverted to the rank of captain. Nevertheless, Purdy continued to serve in the Department of the Pacific, first under Wright and then, from July 1864, under Irvin McDowell, until the end of the war. On March 13, 1865, he was made brevet lieutenant colonel of volunteers for "gallant and meritorious service."

Then came Egypt. As we saw, one of the first of Khedive Ismail's American recruits was Purdy's old commander on the Sonora survey a dozen years earlier, Charles Pomeroy Stone, who had been a Union brigadier general in the early months of the Civil War but had been made the scapegoat for the Ball's Bluff disaster and imprisoned without charge for six months. He came strongly recommended by William T. Sherman, who was now Commanding General of the U.S. Army. Whether or not Stone had foreseen that much of the Americans' work in Egypt was likely to involve exploring and mapping, it seems probable that it was he who was responsible for recruiting Purdy for Egyptian service. Certainly they travelled out to Egypt together on the same ship from New York in a group of Civil War veterans which also included the former C.S. Navy midshipman James Morris Morgan.[24] Purdy was officially appointed *qaimaqam* (colonel) in the Egyptian Army on April 21, 1870.

Once he had been measured for his uniform and had met the khedive, Purdy was quickly put to work. In the autumn of 1870, he was sent off, with some junior Egyptian officers, to map the country between Cairo and Suez and to examine the route from Kenneh on the Nile to Kosseir on the Red Sea. In a later report to the Khedival Geographical Society, Stone said of Purdy and his force that they "carried out minute reconnaissance in the region between the Nile and the Red Sea, conducting their survey from the line between the Mokattam hills and Suez to that between Kenneh and Kosseir" and "mapped out routes for the passage of troops across this country."[25]

Stone was appointed chief of staff in 1871 and immediately set about organizing a proper general staff to consist eventually of seven sections. The main duties of the Third Section—based, like the other sections, in the Citadel in Cairo—were exploring, mapping and surveying, and Purdy was made its first head.[26] He had little time to enjoy his new responsibilities, however, for very shortly he was needed for another assignment and one which was quite likely to involve fighting. The British explorer Sir Samuel Baker, governor of the khedive's "Equatorial Provinces," had antagonized the local warlords and had been driven back into Gondokoro on the White Nile in the far south of the Sudan. Outnumbered, and short of ammunition and supplies, he sent an urgent appeal to Cairo. Stone at once started to form a relief expedition to be led by Purdy. Stone's plan, agreed with the khedive, was that rather than simply taking the obvious route up the Nile, the expedition would go down the Red Sea, out into the Indian Ocean and then down the coast as far as Zanzibar, after which it would cut across country to the Nile and follow the river north. The reason for this curiously roundabout route was presumably to allow the expedition to combine relieving Baker with carrying out a useful bit of additional exploration. For four months—from November 1872 until March 1873—Purdy and his men waited daily for the order to move, but each time some new impediment made its appearance, until finally Baker received his supplies and reinforcements by the usual route instead.[27]

There was thus no longer any need for Purdy's relief force. Not wishing to waste all the organization which had gone into preparing for the expedition, however, Stone now came up with an ambitious plan of exploration, which he presented to the khedive. Purdy and his men, starting from Suez, were to proceed by steamer down the Red Sea to the ancient port of Berenice, where they were to survey the harbor and explore the country around. Meanwhile, a second group, under the command of the former Confederate brigadier general Raleigh Colston, was to travel some 400 miles up the Nile to Kenneh and then strike out southeast across the desert in order to survey the overland route to Berenice. Here the two groups were to link up and move together across country southwest to Berber on the Nile, seeing on the way whether they could establish a suitable route for a railway. Ismail being in agreement, the two parties started off on September 19, 1873.[28]

Travelling with Purdy as his second-in-command was Alexander McComb Mason, scion of an old Virginia family and a former lieutenant in the Confederate Navy, a hardworking, dedicated man who could always be relied upon to carry out his orders conscientiously; he was also one of the few Americans who took the trouble to learn Arabic. Unfortunately, he did not like Purdy, whom he found too talkative and too pleased with himself. Nevertheless, by the time Colston's party joined them at Berenice in mid–October, Mason and Purdy had between them made a thorough survey of the port.[29]

The combined group spent the next two months carrying out further explorations in the area. The three Americans, at least, celebrated Christmas in Berenice, and then finally, on January 11, 1874, their camel train started slowly off across the desert on the long trip south. The need to make accurate surveys of the route and the country on either side meant that the journey took longer than it might otherwise have done, but at the beginning of March, the expedition reached the Nile. Amongst the discoveries which they had made along the way were several large wells, Greek ruins from the time of the Ptolemys and an ancient gold mine. A relatively easy journey down the Nile now brought them to Berber, which unfortunately failed to live up to their expectations. However splendid its setting might be, most of its buildings were mud huts and its people seemed to the three Americans "strange and hideous specimens of humanity." It was also a center of the slave trade. This had long been forbidden by the khedive—indeed, one of Sir Samuel Baker's tasks had been to suppress it—but orders from Cairo had little lasting effect this far south.[30]

After a month in Berber, the expedition set off again towards the north on April 12, cutting across the great bend of the Nile to take the direct, overland route to Korosko, from where they could take ship for Cairo. This desert, however, was a great deal harsher than the one they had crossed previously. Most of the wells were dry, animal skeletons lay everywhere and the heat was terrible. To make matters worse, Colston, who had had some sort of infection of the bladder throughout the journey to Berber, was now suffering from lumbago and was in some pain. After nine days, however, they reached Korosko at last and, leaving the camels with their drivers, embarked on the steamer which was to take them down the Nile. On May 7, 1874, eight months after they had started out, they were back in Cairo again. During those eight months, they had carried out the first accurate and comprehensive survey of the entire area. They had collected and brought back with them a large number of geological specimens and had established the feasibility of building a railway between Berber and Berenice.

The khedive was naturally very anxious to hear what they had to say. Without waiting for the formal, detailed report, which Purdy, Colston and Mason worked on together for the next months and into the autumn, he summoned them forthwith to the palace, where he questioned them closely. He was particularly interested in Colston's route to Berenice, but Purdy bore out Mason's gloomy predictions by constantly interrupting the other two and attempting to take all the credit.[31]

One or two of the Americans—most notably Charles Iverson Graves of Georgia, formerly executive officer of the CSS *Rappahannock*—lived frugally in Egypt and actually managed to save money.[32] Purdy was not, unfortunately, one of these. In the autumn of 1874, his financial mismanagement caught up with him when an Italian hotelkeeper in Cairo took legal action against him for an unpaid bill of £385, the equivalent at that time of $1,925. Since Purdy was an American citizen, under the system in operation at the time the case could only be heard before the American Consul, who was in fact a local Greek. According to the Louisiana lawyer and historian Pierre Crabitès, who served as U.S. representative in Egypt on the later Mixed Courts, the amount demanded was impossibly high, and Purdy should simply have "checked his hotel charges, item by item, and then have divided the corrected total by two or three." Instead, Purdy's defense was that he was an officer in the Egyptian Army, that the bill represented expenses connected with his recent expedition to Central Africa and that it should therefore be settled by the Egyptian government. Unfortunately for Purdy, the Consul was not swayed by this argument. On November 25, 1874, he found in favor of the plaintiff, holding Purdy liable for the total amount plus costs. It is unlikely, though, that the bill was ever paid. In April 1875, the hotelkeeper wrote, in Italian, to the Consul stating that he had never received payment and requesting that Purdy's pay be stopped. By that time, however, Purdy was many hundreds of miles to the southwest, far beyond the reach of his creditors.[33]

For the khedive's imperial ambitions were still not satisfied. He had lived and been educated in France, had been friendly with Napoleon III and had come to feel, as be said, that Egypt belonged more properly with Europe than to Africa; as such, she had a civilizing mission in Africa. The province of Kordofan, in Central Sudan, had long been under Egyptian control. Now Ismail was eyeing the wild, uncharted region of Darfur, roughly the size of Spain, to the west of Kordofan. In 1874, he was given his excuse. Fighting between Sultan Ibrahim of Darfur and the slaver tycoon Sebehr Rahma spilled over into an attack on an Egyptian trading post, whereupon the Egyptians moved into Darfur and occupied the capital, El Fasher.[34]

This provided Stone, in turn, with an opportunity to find employment for some of his officers. The khedive was known to be keen to continue the railway right down into the Sudan. Stone now came up with a plan for another two-pronged exploration, once again involving Purdy and Colston. Colston was to make a thorough survey of Kordofan, while Purdy, with Mason again as his second-in-command, was to explore Darfur. The two groups left Cairo on December 5, 1874, travelling up the Nile by steamer and railway as far as Wadi Halfa, where they separated. Colston now continued due south, while Purdy and Mason followed the Nile until they struck the old camel trail across the desert to

Darfur. Two days out, they had already lost some 10 percent of their camels, but they persevered, pushed on into Darfur and finally reached El Fasher, where they established their base.

For the next 18 months or so, Purdy and Mason explored the furthest reaches of Darfur, surveying, mapping and collecting scientific data. Mason, in fact, penetrated as far south almost as Lake Albert. Finally, in the late summer of 1876, they returned in triumph to Cairo, where they were able to present the khedive with a detailed map of the region and a comprehensive report of their expedition.[35] Once again, though, Purdy seems to have taken all the credit, leaving Mason, who had done a large part of the actual work, aggrieved and embittered, pouring out his story to anyone who would listen.[36]

But time was now running out for the Americans. As we saw in the previous chapter, Ismail's European creditors, increasingly concerned about their money, had called upon their governments for help, and the khedive had to face the ignominy of having foreign financial representatives foisted upon him and being ordered by them to rein in his spending. One condition made was that he dramatically reduce the size of his army and dismiss his American officers. On June 30, 1878, then, all of the remaining Americans except Charles Pomeroy Stone were paid off and dismissed. Most then started to make their way home, but both Purdy and Mason managed to find civilian employment in the same field. While Mason went on to have a successful career in Egypt as both explorer and administrator until his death in 1897, Purdy was less successful. He was appointed to an administrative post on April 20, 1879, but was dismissed on January 18, 1881, and died bankrupt and alone on June 21 of that year, apparently of "inflammation of the bowels." He was buried in the American Protestant Cemetery in Old Cairo, which had been established in 1877 by khedival decree. Three years after his death, the Khedival Geographical Society finally recognized his services by erecting a marble obelisk over his grave, with an inscription in French.[37]

It is clear that Purdy was not universally liked. Mason loathed him, not without some justification, and even the mild-mannered, tolerant Raleigh Colston found it impossible to warm to him. Hesseltine and Wolf, having ridiculed his Civil War record, describe him as "a meddler … something of a braggart, both loquacious and boring."[38] Nevertheless, he cannot have been entirely without his good points. His obituary (admittedly in a California newspaper) calls him "one of the most affable and companionable gentlemen, and of unusually prepossessing personal appearance."[39] Pierre Crabitès describes him as having "a heart of gold" and relates a story of Purdy's honoring the dying request of a faithful Sudanese servant and taking responsibility for the upbringing and education of the dead man's son.[40] It is only fair, too, to quote the view of the former Confederate General William Wing Loring, whose 1884 memoir of his Egyptian service is surprisingly temperate and impartial. After referring to Purdy as "one of those laborious officers" who had done so much to extend Ismail's empire, and alluding to his "constant and dangerous service" in Egypt, which had won him the khedive's "highest consideration," Loring finishes, "It is with sorrow that I record the death of this martyr to duty."[41]

Erastus S. Purdy's grave, Cairo (author's photograph).

For many years, Purdy's grave was forgotten, until in 1997 the Cairo historian Samir Raafat wrote an article lamenting its current condition and suggesting that Americans then working on various projects in Egypt might consider restoring the grave.[42] The hint was taken, and on November 6, 2000, the restored grave was rededicated with a color guard of U.S. Marines, while a marine bugler played Taps.[43] A visit to the cemetery in March 2012, however, revealed that the Cairo undergrowth had started to reclaim its own.

I was there with my daughter, who spent a year working in Cairo and speaks good Egyptian Arabic. The gate of the little cemetery was shut, but the caretaker was squatting outside. At my daughter's question, his face brightened. "Burdy Basha!" he exclaimed. He opened the gate, ushered us in and pointed to an obelisk just inside and to the left. Removing from the plinth a glass jar and a faded picture of the Virgin Mary, he stood back to let us see. The cemetery was heavily overgrown, wild plants and creepers were starting to encircle the monument, and there was a large, jagged crack down the front. Nevertheless, the inscription, though faded, was still legible. On the front, it reads:

À
ERASTUS SPARROW PURDY
PACHA
———
LA
SOCIÉTÉ KHÉDIVIALE
DE
GÉOGRAPHIE

On the other side is a brief summary of Purdy's life and service:

NÉ DANS NEW JORK STATE [sic]
1838
EXPLORATION DU COLORADO
1857–1860
DARFOUR ET HOFRA-EN-NAHASS
1875–1876
DÉCÉDÉ AU CAIRE LE 21 JUIN
1881

The grave, and the rest of the cemetery, would presumably have continued to deteriorate had not a group of Americans resident in Egypt happened to visit the cemetery a few years ago and been appalled by its state of neglect. The result was the formation of the Friends of the American Cemetery. Since then, steps have been taken to arrest the cemetery's decline, and plans are apparently afoot to clear it of vegetation and to repair and restore the various grave markers—including, one hopes, Purdy's. The cemetery is situated in the south of the city, just north of Coptic Cairo, and is next door to the beautifully maintained Commonwealth Cemetery. It is a short walk from El-Malek El-Saleh Metro station (Line 1).

Our final veteran, Henry Anker Irgens, was born on December 19, 1838, in Ullensaker, Akerhus, Norway, some 25 miles northeast of Oslo. Precisely when and how he arrived in the United States is not clear, but we do know that he enlisted on July 3, 1863, in New York City and that on August 2 that year he was mustered in at Camp Sprague, Staten Island, for three years as a private in Co. A of the 17th New York Veteran Volunteer Regiment. This regiment had been formed by the consolidation of the 9th (Hawkins's Zouaves), 11th (Ellsworth's Fire Zouaves), 17th (Westchester Chasseurs) and 38th New York Infantry Regiments, together with Colonel Achille M.B. De Villarceau's Union Sharpshooters. A bounty of $550 ($70 in advance) was paid to all who re-enlisted, while new recruits like Irgens received $175. The Colonel was the English-born William T.C. Grower.

Leaving New York in October 1863, the regiment participated in Brigadier General Andrew Jackson Smith's unsuccessful pursuit of Nathan Bedford Forrest in December of that year before being sent to join Sherman at Vicksburg on

January 24, 1864, where it was assigned to the 2nd Brigade, 4th Division, XVI Corps. Nine days later, the regiment was on the march again, this time east across Mississippi on the Meridian campaign. A soldier of the 15th Illinois left the following description of it at Meridian:

> This regiment was composed of Wilson's old zouaves [incorrect; that was the 6th New York] and roughs from New York City, and they were a rough set. Their officers claimed that in order to keep them in subjection, they had to use harsh measures. I never before saw men tyrannized over as they were. In the first place, they started out with heavy knapsacks and half rations. After marching hard, the Colonel, before he would allow them to sit down or rest, had a camp guard detailed and picket also, if required. They went through the regular formula of guard mounting with knapsacks still on. The Colonel kept a guard walking back and forth before his tent, with his load still on, for two hours. The poor fellows looked completely drilled out, but yet there was not a better fighting regiment in the whole division than the 17th New York.[44]

April found the regiment skirmishing around Decatur, Alabama, with the troops of Brigadier General Philip Roddey, the famous "Defender of North Alabama," after which it set off again on the Atlanta campaign. At Jonesboro, by now part of the 1st Brigade, 2nd Division in Jefferson C. Davis's XIV Corps, the regiment lost 100 men, including Colonel Grower, but proudly claimed to have broken Cleburne's hitherto unbroken lines—ignoring the inconvenient fact that the salient held by Govan's lone Arkansas brigade had been attacked by three Union divisions. After the fall of Atlanta, the men took part in the pursuit of Hood but were back just in time to participate in the March to the Sea. Their final battle was at Bentonville, where, although surrounded, they helped to beat off Confederate attacks on the left wing.[45] In his farewell address at the end of the war, Brigadier General William Vandever, commanding the 1st Brigade, said of the regiment:

> In all the essential qualities which distinguish the heroic citizen soldier, the Seventeenth New York has been excelled by none. Representatives as you are of the great city of New York, your association with the men of the northwest, composing the balance of the brigade, has been of the most pleasing and genial kind.[46]

Irgens was mustered out as 1st sergeant on August 2, 1865, at Louisville, Kentucky. Military life seems to have appealed to him, however, since on August 30 he enlisted in the Regular Army. He was described at this time as being 5 feet, 7 inches in height, with blue eyes, light hair and a fair complexion; his profession was given as surveyor. Initially assigned to Company B of the Engineer Battalion, he applied for a commission in 1867 and in November 1867 was appointed second lieutenant in the 27th Infantry.

He never actually joined the regiment, however. For the next year or so, he was on detached service at various different posts. From February 1869, he was on special duties at Fort Omaha, Nebraska. Shortly after this, the 27th Infantry was consolidated with the 9th Infantry. In April 1870, still unattached, Irgens was assigned to the 7th Infantry, despite requesting assignment to the 2nd Cavalry, with which he had been serving at Fort Omaha. He finally joined the 7th Infantry in September 1870. From then on, he was stationed in Montana Territory, chiefly at Fort Shaw. Much of his work here involved surveying and mapping.

A typical example of his duties at this time can be found in the Engineer Department's *Report upon United States Geographical Surveys West of the One Hundredth Meridian* (1889):

> Major Barlow assisted by Second Lieut. Henry A. Irgens accompanied the Northern Pacific Railroad engineers in their surveys in 1872 eastward from Fort Ellis, which they left July 27, to the Yellowstone, thence after a few days' work northward to the Muscleshell, up this valley, across the Belt Range, and down Sixteen-Mile Creek to the Missouri. Maj. J.W. Barlow, Corps of Engineers, commanded the expedition. Bvt. Col. E.M. Baker, major Second Cavalry, commanded the escort of three hundred and seventy-six men, cavalry and infantry. The survey disbanded at Fort Ellis about September 29, 1872. A map of the country and a survey of the camp where an Indian battle occurred were made.[47]

Another typical assignment, in July 1874, involved his escorting a train of supplies from Fort Burton, Montana, to the British Boundary Commission on the Milk River, on the border with Alberta.

From the letters of reference used in support of his application for a commission, it is clear that Irgens was, by any standards, a thoroughly steady and reliable soldier. Like Tevis, though, he too found himself at one point under arrest. A court martial held in August 1873 found him guilty of failing to sign his company's muster and pay rolls on March 1 that year "on account of excessive use of intoxicating liquors." He was sentenced to forfeiture of six months' pay and to suspension of rank and command for the same period, but since the majority of the court recommended mercy, the sentence was reduced to one month.

In May 1875, Irgens applied successfully for five months' leave of absence from August 1 in order to visit his family in Norway, at the same time tendering his resignation from the army, to take effect from the end of the period, in other words from December 31.[48] By that time, however, he was a captain in the Egyptian Army on his way down the Red Sea, one of 11 Civil War veterans assigned to take part in the initial stages of the Egyptian invasion of Abyssinia.

We do not know exactly when Irgens arrived in Egypt, but the Egyptian expeditionary force left Suez on December 6, 1875. From then on, there are frequent references to Irgens in the diary of Colonel Henry Clay Derrick, a former captain of engineers in the Army of Northern Virginia and now Chief Engineer of the Egyptian Army. Irgens was not officially assigned to the Engineers until the general orders were published on December 14, three days after the army had landed at Massawa on the Red Sea coast, but the diary records that on December 7, one day out from Suez, Derrick had already put Irgens and an Egyptian officer to work copying maps of Abyssinia.[49]

Most of Irgens's work during the following weeks, however, was to be rather more active, and on occasion a great deal more dangerous, than tracing maps. Presumably because of his experience with the U.S. Army in Montana, he was regularly chosen to carry out assignments involving scouting and reconnoitering. Derrick sent him out, for example, on Christmas Day and the two following days to make a reconnaissance around Massawa, in the area within the picket lines and on one of the roads leading out, after which he had to produce a detailed map of what he had discovered. When the army started to move out into the interior on January 11, the engineers travelled with the advance guard, surveying the route, building roads and fortifying strategic points. Once again, Irgens's services were frequently called upon, in particular on January 18, when he and the former Confederate general Charles W. Field, now a colonel of engineers in the Egyptian service, led a reconnaissance in force.⁵⁰ His most dangerous assignment, however, came on February 3.

Having passed through the mountains, the army was now encamped in the valley of Gura, on the road leading to the Abyssinian capital of Adowa. Loring, chief of staff of the invasion force, summoned Irgens and introduced him to the Abbé Duflot, a French Jesuit missionary who had lived in the

Colonel Henry Clay Derrick in Egyptian uniform (Henry Clay Derrick, image P-432/88, folder PF-432, Samuel Henry Lockett Papers, Southern Historical Collection, The Wilson Library, University of North Carolina at Chapel Hill).

region for some years, knew the country well and had his own reasons for wishing for an Egyptian victory. Loring proposed a daring and ambitious plan, very probably at the suggestion of the Abbé. Irgens and Duflot were to set out from the camp together in an attempt to ride right round the Abyssinian army, in order, as Loring put it, "to enable us not only to get a map of the country, but to bring us valuable information of the movements of the king."⁵¹

On the afternoon of February 3, then, the two men set off on their mission, accompanied by a lone Abyssinian. To allay suspicion, Irgens, too, had put on a priest's robes, although he was doubtful that this would prove much of a safeguard if they were captured. The Abyssinians were in the habit of stripping naked those prisoners whom they had not already killed, castrating them and then setting them loose, and Irgens joked that the second stage of this process was likely to prove rather harder on him than on a Catholic priest. Although they tried to avoid the main routes and the more inhabited areas as much as possible, they had to come into the villages from time to time, if only in order to find food for themselves and their horses, and here they were often subject to searching questions. They managed to bluff their way through, however, although at one point towards the end of their mission they had to resort to killing some chickens and scattering the blood and feathers on the trail in order to avoid pursuit, correctly calculating that the superstitious Abyssinians, suspecting witchcraft, would not dare to follow. They returned successfully to camp in the evening of February 6, having penetrated to within 30 miles of Adowa and brought back vital information.[52]

Hardly was he back, however, when Irgens was given the task, under Derrick, of superintending the work of fortifying the army's position, for which he was provided with a force of 1,000 men.[53] Further scouting assignments followed in late February and into March, before the disastrous battle of Gura on March 7, which saw the Egyptians caught in the open by the huge Abyssinian force and driven back into the fort, Irgens and Derrick with them.[54]

Here they remained for more than six weeks while peace negotiations were started. The army started moving back to Massawa in stages towards the end of April, and in late June orders came at last for the staff officers to embark for Cairo, which they reached on July 3. On July 8, Derrick and Irgens went up to the Citadel and reported to Stone, who put Derrick in charge of the Third Section and assigned Irgens to the same section. Much of their work there now involved collating and recording all of the information brought back from the Abyssinian expedition and, in particular, preparing and copying accurate maps. The work does not seem to have been especially onerous, however; Derrick's diary for August 1, for example, records "Capt. Irgens at Citadel to-day, but left about 12," and on August 9 "Irgens not there to-day."

After the big Christmas Eve party at General Stone's, things continued much the same into 1877, until on July 18 Irgens left for the United States on a six-month furlough.[55] Part, at least, of this must have been spent in Milwaukee, since Derrick wrote to him there on October 7—although unfortunately the letter was returned, undelivered, five months later.[56] Irgens reported for duty again at the Citadel on January 12, 1878, having just missed the banquet which General and Mrs. Stone gave on January 8 for Ulysses S. Grant—and which Derrick, referring to the general as "the humbug Grant," refused on principle to attend.[57] From now on, though, there was very little work for the Americans to do, and as a result they spent most of their time socializing together without regard to rank or region, talking, smoking, sightseeing and having their photograph taken. On June 30, Irgens, like the others, received his discharge from the Egyptian service. He and Derrick went up to the Citadel the next day to arrange their affairs and then went on to the Finance Bureau to draw their final pay, which they deposited in the Bank of Egypt. On July 6, Irgens left Cairo for Alexandria, where he was to take one of the Moss Line steamers for Liverpool.[58]

Irgens must have felt that once he had reached Liverpool the worst part of the journey would be behind him and that he would soon be home. It was not to be. Having survived Confederate bullets, Indian arrows and Abyssinian spears, Henry Irgens succumbed to disease. He died in the Northern Hospital, Liverpool, on August 1, 1878, the cause of death being recorded as "Dysentery—Abscess of Liver."[59] He was buried in Anfield Cemetery, in grave 138, section 7, Nonconformist plot; the grave can be found just inside the Priory Road entrance, to the left.

My indefatigable colleague Maurice Rigby of the American Civil War Round Table (UK) has discovered that it was originally a public grave and thus unmarked. At some later stage, however, someone—former comrades, family

Henry A. Irgens's grave, Liverpool (author's photograph).

members or concerned compatriots—paid for a fine tombstone to be erected over the grave, with an inscription in Norwegian. Irgens's year of birth is wrongly given as 1839, and he seems to have been posthumously promoted to major, but the inscription reads as follows:

>Herunder hviler Stovet
>af
>MAJOR HENRICH ANKER IRGENS
>FODT I NORGE DEN 19 DECEMBER 1839
>DOD I LIVERPOOL DEN 1 AUGUST 1878
>
>(Beneath here lies the dust
>of
>Major Henry Anker Irgens
>Born in Norway the 19th December 1839
>Died in Liverpool the 1st August 1878)[60]

Henry Irgens, veteran of the United States and Egyptian armies, was not yet 40 years old.

14

An Officer's Payslip

Sometime in the early 1970s, I bought from a rather strange shop in north London a Confederate officer's payslip. It was a standard Confederate States of America form, printed on poor-quality paper and with the entries completed in faded black ink. It was dated November 4, 1863, covered the period from August 31 to October 31 and was for a total of $180, or $90 per month. The recipient's details I deciphered as "Geo. W. Ward, 1st Lieut Co 'B' 3rd S.C. Troops." For some time, I kept it in a display case with my collection of Civil War artifacts, but as it seemed to be becoming increasingly fragile, I finally put it carefully away in a large album with other Civil War documents—letters, postal covers, banknotes, etc. There it would probably have stayed, had it not been for Fold3.

Possibly rather shortsightedly, I had never subscribed to this organization, but at the beginning of April 2018 I received an email from Fold3 offering free access to its collection of Civil War documents for the first two weeks of the month. "Discover Your Civil War Ancestors," the email urged me. Not having any Civil War ancestors, I was at first inclined to ignore this. Then I remembered Lieutenant Ward and his payslip. This seemed the perfect opportunity to find out something about him. I therefore got onto the website, went into the section for South Carolina infantry units and quickly found the 3rd Regiment—to discover that Co. B appeared to have no Lieutenant Ward. I then wondered if the B, which was written in typically florid nineteenth-century fashion, could possibly be intended for a K. Co. K, however, had no Lieutenant Ward either and nor did any of the regiment's other companies. Finally, in desperation, I decided to try the 3rd *North* Carolina, even though what I had always taken for an S did not look as if it could possibly be intended as an N. Immediately, I found my man and was able slowly to copy out all the various documents from the National Archives relating to him.

Having done this, I decided to see what information there might be about him on the internet and was rewarded with a message posted on the Civil War Talk website by a Bruce Vail, an American history enthusiast whose wife and son were apparently direct descendants of Lieutenant Ward. What was more, there was actually a photograph of the lieutenant. Some diligent sleuthing on the internet finally led me to Mr. Vail's address in Baltimore, Maryland, and I wrote to him there, giving my email address. Almost by return, I received a very friendly

George W. Ward's payslip (author's collection).

and helpful reply, and since then we have remained in correspondence. Apart from helping me with further information about Ward's wartime career and supplying me with additional leads, Bruce has been invaluable in filling in for me the facts of the lieutenant's life before and after the Civil War. Much of Bruce's information, in turn, has come from *A History of Alfred and Elizabeth Robinson Ward, Their Antecedents and Descendants* (1945), by Herman Ward Taylor—Bruce's wife's grandfather. Details of Lieutenant Ward's earlier and later life, then, come largely from these sources.

George Washington Ward was born on August 12, 1832, in Rockfish township, Duplin County, North Carolina—a county which is today one of the world's largest centers of pig farming. He was the sixth of eight children of Alfred and Elizabeth Robinson Ward. His grandfather, William Ward, had been a North Carolina Minuteman in the American Revolution. According to his pension claim, he had taken part in the defeat at Moore's Creek Bridge on February 27, 1776, of the Highland Scots Loyalists, who included Allan MacDonald, husband of the Jacobite heroine Flora MacDonald.[1]

Whether or not inspired by his grandfather's exploits, the young George Washington Ward was a keen member of the state militia from an early date. He was commissioned 3rd lieutenant in the Rockfish Company of the 31st Regiment North Carolina Militia on July 16, 1850. The U.S. Census for that year shows him as living with his parents and lists his profession, like that of most men in the area, as "farmer." He was promoted to 1st lieutenant on September 23, 1852, and continued to serve in the militia right up to the outbreak of the Civil War, when his unit became a part of the North Carolina State Troops. At the time of the last pre-war census, he was still living with his parents; this time, however, his profession is given as "teacher."[2]

The chief authority for Ward's Civil War career is his file in the National Archives, which contains extracts from muster rolls, payslips, hospital and medical reports, recommendations for furlough and so on. Apart from that, I have consulted chiefly Manarin's *North Carolina Troops 1861–1865*, Clark's *Histories of the Several Regiments and Battalions from North Carolina* and Moore's *Roster of North Carolina Troops*,[3] as well as the revised edition of the Ward family history referred to above and two manuscript letters written by officers in the regiment.

Unfortunately, as is often the case with Civil War documentation, these different sources not infrequently contradict each other; even Ward's National Archives entries are sometimes mutually contradictory. Where there is disagreement, then, I have carefully compared all the various sources, identified certain obvious errors and chosen what seems the most probable version. I have also benefited hugely, of course, from discussing doubtful points by email with Bruce Vail. The account which follows is, I hope, as accurate as I can make it.

Ward's unit became Co. B of what was to be the 3rd Regiment, North Carolina State Troops, he and his comrades having enlisted "for the war." The regiment began organizing in May 1861 in and around Garysburg, Northampton County, up near the Virginia state line. As the companies gradually arrived, they were each drilled individually, moving on to regimental drill once all were assembled at Camp Clarendon. The regiment was officially mustered in to State service on July 20, 1861. Three days later, George Washington Ward was appointed 2nd lieutenant, to rank from May 16, 1861. Gaston Meares was named colonel, while Robert H. Cowan became lieutenant colonel.

At around the same time, the regiment moved by companies up to Richmond, from where it was immediately sent to the Aquia Creek area, reporting to Brigadier General Theophilus H. Holmes. Here it was to remain until late March 1862. On August 31 and September 1, 1861, the various companies were transferred into Confederate service, after which, together with the 1st North Carolina, the 30th Virginia and the 1st Arkansas, it was formed into a brigade commanded by John G. Walker. The regiment's orders were to act in defense of the Confederacy's Aquia Creek batteries, which commanded the Potomac at that point. Since the Union forces seemed disinclined, however, to undertake any further action against the batteries after the naval attack of May 29–June 1, 1861, most of the regiment's time continued to be taken up with drill.

It is easy to forget what an enormous part drill played in the training of these new armies, North and South. The soldier had not merely to learn the standard musket drill; he had to learn to act as part of a cohesive whole, able to recognize and respond to the various bugle calls and to perform often highly complicated maneuvers even while under fire. Nor was this any less true in the South than in the North. Colonel Fremantle of the Coldstream Guards witnessed a dress parade of the 3rd Texas Infantry at Brownsville in April 1863 and reported that they "really drilled uncommonly well."[4] Very many men on both sides, in fact, must have echoed the words of Oliver Norton of the 83rd Pennsylvania: "The first thing in the morning is drill, then drill, then drill again. Then drill, drill, a little more drill. Then drill, and lastly drill. Between drills, we drill, and sometimes stop to eat a little and have roll-call."[5]

When the Confederates evacuated the line of the Potomac and abandoned the Aquia Creek batteries in March 1862, the regiment was moved, with the 1st North Carolina, to the area of Goldsboro, in order to meet a threatened advance from New Bern on the part of Burnside. It remained there for two months, during which time it lost its lieutenant colonel, Robert H. Cowan, who was elected colonel of the 18th North Carolina. Major William L. DeRosset was therefore promoted to lieutenant colonel to take his place. At the end of May, the regiment was ordered to Petersburg and then sent out from Richmond along the Williamsburg Road, where it spent most of June on picket duty. This was just after the battle of Seven Pines, and DeRosset recalled later, "The march from Richmond was most trying to the raw troops ... who had not then received their baptism of fire. Passing thousands of dead and wounded from the time they left the cars until they arrived on the battlefield, the groans and cries of the wounded were not calculated to inspire the boys with a martial spirit."[6] While here, the regiment was assigned to a new brigade commanded by Brigadier General Roswell S. Ripley, in D.H. Hill's Division. Once again, it found itself with its old comrades from the 1st North Carolina, but this time they were joined by two Georgia regiments, the 44th and 48th. Here, too, the 3rd North Carolina took part in a brief skirmish on June 15 near Seven Pines, its first taste of action.

The regiment's first actual battle, however, took place on June 26 at Mechanicsville, and under the eyes of Lee, Jefferson Davis and George Randolph, the Confederate Secretary of War, who were watching from a nearby hill. Late in the afternoon, D.H. Hill ordered Ripley to send two of his regiments to support Pender's brigade in an assault on the very strong Union position across Beaver Dam Creek at Ellerson's Mill and with the other two to attack a battery in his front. Accordingly, Ripley dispatched the 1st North Carolina and the 44th Georgia to the right to aid Pender and sent the 3rd North Carolina and the 48th Georgia forward against the battery. The first two regiments suffered very heavy casualties in the disastrous attack at Ellerson's Mill before being withdrawn; the 44th Georgia, indeed, lost 71 men killed and 264 wounded. The remnants of both were then sent back to the rear to regroup. The 3rd North Carolina and 48th Georgia, meanwhile, advanced at the double-quick under very heavy fire throughout and succeeded in reaching the millrace a mere 80 yards from the battery's position, but could make no further progress. After nightfall, and under the covering fire of Rhett's South Carolina Battery, they were withdrawn a few hundred yards, where they held their position.[7] The 3rd North Carolina had lost eight killed and 39 wounded.

At Gaines's Mill, the following afternoon, the bulk of the regiment was not engaged, but with the rest of the brigade "was exposed to a musketry and a very severe artillery fire"[8] for nearly two hours. Fortunately, the heavily wooded country provided protection, and casualties were light—one killed and 15 wounded. Things were very different on July 1 when the regiment took part in the unsuccessful assault on Malvern Hill, moving up through what both Ripley and DeRosset described in their reports as "a jungle" and advancing "under a most terrific fire of musketry and canister."[9] Colonel Meares was killed by a shell fragment, and the regiment's total loss at the end of the day amounted to 23 killed, 112 wounded and seven missing. According to DeRosset, in the confusion "several volleys were fired into us by a regiment of our own troops in the rear, from which we suffered much."[10]

Moved back, with the rest of the brigade, to its old camp nearer Richmond, the regiment was joined towards the end of July by 400 conscripts, who were at once divided into squads and put to drilling under the command of noncommissioned officers. This was just as well, since D.H. Hill's Division, with the rest of the army, was soon to move north. By this time, the 4th Georgia had replaced the 48th Georgia in Ripley's brigade. The division arrived too late to participate in Pope's defeat at Second Manassas but crossed the Potomac into Maryland on September 4–5, 1862. Ripley was censured by Hill, first in his report and then, more severely, in a later article, for his failure to engage the enemy at the battle of South Mountain on September 14.[11] In a letter of September 27 to Governor Zebulon Vance, however, Major Stephen D. Thruston of the 3rd North Carolina stated simply, "My Regt. did not get an opportunity of meeting the enemy on this day, owing to some unfortunate error of position."[12] Certainly the regiment more than made up for this at Sharpsburg, three days later.

The morning of September 17 found the men in position some 100 or 200 yards in the rear of the Mumma Farm. Since they were in full view of the Union artillery on the other side of the creek, the regiment and the rest of the brigade were subjected for an hour to "a heavy and destructive crossfire, from which we suffered much in wounded; yet the men kept their posts, quietly and calmly awaiting orders to move forward to the attack."[13] During this enforced and uncomfortable wait, the call went out for volunteers from the 3rd North Carolina, which was on the right of the brigade, to set fire to the farmhouse in order to prevent its being used by enemy sharpshooters. The regimental sergeant major, James Foreman Clark, and three men from Co. A[14] stepped forward. Its mission accomplished, the little squad returned safely to the ranks, although Clark was slightly wounded in the arm. (More than 40 years later, he wrote to the postmaster at Sharpsburg, seeking information on the family who had occupied the farm. By a pleasing coincidence, the postmaster turned out to be Samuel Mumma, Jr., the son of the house. Not only was he able to answer all Clark's questions, he also sent him some photographs of the battlefield and forgave him for an action which had, after all, been carried out under orders.)

When the command finally came and the line moved forward, the troops were briefly impeded by the burning buildings, lost alignment and had to reform under fire. While Ripley was directing this, he was hit in the throat and had temporarily to leave the field, relinquishing command to Colonel Doles of the 4th Georgia.[15] Having advanced beyond the farm, the brigade now received orders to change front and move some 500 yards to the left in order to extend the line in front of the Dunker Church and to support Hood's famous charge into the cornfield. These maneuvers were "executed under a heavy fire of infantry and artillery."[16] Shortly afterwards Colonel DeRosset[17] of the 3rd North Carolina was seriously wounded and permanently disabled, command of the regiment therefore devolving upon Thruston.

The 3rd North Carolina maintained its position here for some three hours, during which it made a number of charges itself into the cornfield, retiring reluctantly only when the men had fired their last cartridge and the arrival of reinforcements under McLaws and Walker finally made it possible for them to be withdrawn in order to reorganize. The three hours of fighting against odds had taken a heavy toll. The regiment was now "reduced to a mere handful,"[18] and at this point we have our first official mention of 2nd Lieutenant George Washington Ward; Thruston reports him as one of several officers "borne from the field severely wounded."[19] No sooner had the remaining men refilled their cartridge boxes, however, than a request was received from Longstreet for them to relieve Colonel Cooke's 27th North Carolina, which was out of ammunition but still holding on behind a rail fence. Here, again, the remnants of the regiment maintained their position, this time from 2 o'clock until nightfall. So few were they now that Thruston was at one stage forced to send Lieutenant Cicero Craige of Co. I to ask Longstreet for reinforcements. According to Thruston, Craige delivered the message as follows: "Captain[20] sends his compliments, and requests re-inforcements, as he has only one man to every panel of fence, and the enemy is strong and very active in his front." Longstreet's reply was succinct and unequivocal. "Tell Captain Thruston he must hold his position if he has only one man to every sixteen panels of fence. I have no assistance to send him."[21] The 3rd North Carolina did not let Longstreet down.

The tenacity of the 3rd North Carolina in holding its position until its ammunition was exhausted, retiring in good order and returning to the front once the men had replenished their cartridge boxes was recognized by the division commander. Riding with Thruston on the morning after the battle, Hill (not a man to pay a compliment unnecessarily) told him, "Your regiment fought nobly yesterday."[22] That night, the army crossed the Potomac again and bivouacked on the Virginia shore. The regiment's losses during the Maryland campaign were 46 killed and 207 wounded.

As for the soldiers themselves, the evidence is that for the officers at least the regiment's stand in front of the Dunker Church was their supreme moment of the war. Writing after the war, Thruston described the 3rd North Carolina as "the pivot upon which success or annihilation turned" and claimed "every man seemed to know … that he must do or die until relief had time to reach him from the rear, or Lee's army was doomed."[23]

Although specific medical reports survive on Ward's two later wounds, we have no direct details of this first wound. We only know that in the week ending September 27 he was received into the General Hospital at Staunton, Virginia, in the charge of Assistant Surgeon Jean Charles Martin Merrillat, born in France in 1811 but now resident in Virginia. From a much later medical report on him, however, we can deduce that this initial wound was almost certainly to the left forearm and therefore perhaps not quite as severe as Thruston had implied. Nevertheless, the company muster rolls from now until at least March 1863 show Ward as recovering at home in Duplin County. Meanwhile, he had been promoted on September 21 (or possibly September 22) to 1st lieutenant, probably because the senior lieutenant in the company, Thomas Cowan, Jr., had been wounded and captured.[24]

Ward returned to duty sometime in the spring, since he signed the roll for March 1 to May 15 as commanding the company. In the meantime, the regiment had been present at Fredericksburg but not actually engaged, and had then gone into winter quarters on the Rappahannock near Port Royal. Here there was another reorganization. The two North Carolina regiments were now moved to Jackson's old division, commanded by Major General Isaac R. Trimble. They lost their comrades of the 4th and 44th Georgia and were brigaded instead with the 10th, 23rd and 37th Virginia regiments under Brigadier General Raleigh E. Colston. In this capacity, they took part in Jackson's flank march at Chancellorsville on May 2, 1863, and in the decisive victory of the following day in which Thruston was wounded; he had been promoted to lieutenant colonel on March 26 to rank from December 10, 1862. The victory at Chancellorsville was a costly one for the army as a whole and no less so for the 3rd North Carolina; the regiment's losses in the campaign were 39 killed, 175 wounded and 17 missing.

Following Jackson's death, the army was divided into three corps. Colston's brigade was now part of Major General Edward "Allegheny" Johnson's division in Ewell's Second Corps. On May 20, however, Lee relieved Colston from duty, and Brigadier General George H. "Maryland" Steuart was assigned to command the brigade. He would remain with it for a year. Lee had given as his chief reason for removing Colston from command of the brigade in Special Order No. 144, dated May 28, the supposed opposition on the part of the two North Carolina regiments to serving under a Virginian. A letter to Colston of May 29, however, from a committee representing the officers of both regiments, rejects this absolutely, stating that their only wish from the start of the war had been to be brigaded with other North Carolina regiments under a North Carolina brigadier but making it clear that if this was impossible, they were "entirely satisfied" with Colston. The letter ends, "Wishing for you, General, new laurels, and that your path to glory may not be darkened by a single cloud."[25]

As a result of Thruston's wound, Major William M. Parsley, at the age of only 23, took command of the regiment and remained in command during the forthcoming Pennsylvania campaign. Breaking camp on June 5, the regiment moved north down the Shenandoah Valley with the rest of Ewell's Corps as part of Lee's plan to clear the valley of Union forces. After Milroy had been surrounded and cut off at Winchester by Ewell's pincer movement on June 13–14, Johnson sent

Steuart's and Nicholls's brigades, with the Stonewall brigade in support, on a night march round to the northeast of the town in order to block his retreat. In a short but sharp engagement early on June 15, Milroy's attempt to break out was halted and his troops routed. The division claimed to have captured some 2,500 prisoners. These were sent off to Richmond under a guard from the Stonewall brigade, which led to some grumbling on the part of the 3rd North Carolina that Steuart's brigade had done the fighting and the Stonewall brigade had gained the credit.[26] The regiment's losses were four killed and ten wounded.

With the valley cleared, the division crossed the Potomac at Shepherdstown on June 18, camping that night near the Dunker Church on the old battlefield of Sharpsburg, the scene of the heroic stand of the 3rd North Carolina nine months before. A detail of men under Lieutenant James I. Metts of Co. G fired a volley over the spot where their comrades lay buried, and later that night, when all was quiet, the men of both the 1st and the 3rd North Carolina regiments marched with reversed arms and muffled drums back onto the battlefield, where the Chaplain of the 3rd North Carolina, the Rev. George H. Patterson,[27] read the burial service. In the words of the regimental history, "Many tears stole down the bronzed cheeks of the old veterans, and all heads were bowed in grief."[28]

As the division moved into Pennsylvania, Steuart's brigade was detached to gather up horses, cattle and other necessary supplies, rejoining the rest of the division at Carlisle. The division then moved off towards Gettysburg on June 29, arriving at about 7:30 in the evening of July 1, too late to play any part in the first day's fighting, and taking position on the left of Ewell's other two divisions. At about 6 the following evening, the division was finally ordered forward across Rock Creek to assault the Federal position on Culp's Hill. Steuart's brigade was on the left of the line, with the 3rd North Carolina on the brigade's right. During the advance up the hill, the regiment became partially separated from the rest of the brigade and was left exposed to a heavy fire from the enemy's second line of entrenchments after the first had been captured. Nevertheless, it held its position, the men refilling their cartridge boxes from those of the dead and wounded. Attempts to take the second line of entrenchments failed, but the Confederates maintained their hold on the lower slopes of the hill until fighting stopped at about 10 p.m. The attack was renewed the following morning, with the 3rd North Carolina once again on the right of the brigade. Unfortunately, the left of the advance failed to maintain its position, and the regiment, unsupported, was once more exposed to the concentrated fire of the Union defenders. Finally the whole line wavered and fell back behind a stone wall, where it remained until ordered to withdraw to Rock Creek.

The regiment's losses during the Gettysburg campaign were 29 killed and 127 wounded. So heavy had been the fighting on Culp's Hill that the authors of the regimental history could claim, "Colonel Parsley,[29] Captain E.H. Armstrong and Lieutenant Lyon were the only officers, perhaps, not killed or wounded."[30] It will be noticed that Ward's name does not appear in this list of survivors. Certainly Moore's *Roster* states that Ward was among those wounded at Gettysburg,[31] as does the Ward family history. The only other evidence for this is a single Roll of

Honor entry, undated, in Ward's National Archives file, which states that he was "wounded in battle at Sharpsburg and Gettysburg." In a letter to his father dated July 10, however, the Captain Armstrong referred to above specifically mentions Ward as another of those officers who escaped injury at Gettysburg, together with Lieutenants Cowan, McClammy and Stone.[32] Ward was less fortunate, however, at Payne's Farm, later that year, as we shall see.

With the rest of Ewell's Corps, the 3rd North Carolina crossed the Potomac again at Williamsport, Maryland, during the night of July 13–14. Although the river had subsided a little and could now be forded, it was still swollen by the recent heavy rains to the extent that the men had to hang their cartridge boxes on their bayonets in order to keep them out of the water. After Lee's withdrawal to the line of the Rapidan, the regiment participated in the various maneuvers in October aimed at turning Meade's flank but was not present at Bristoe Station. The army was just getting ready to go into winter quarters on November 26 when the report came that Meade had crossed the river.

Meade was well aware that Longstreet's Corps was still absent in East Tennessee. He planned to attack Lee's right, held by Ewell's Corps, with overwhelming force, and then overrun A.P. Hill's Corps on the left. It was a solid enough plan, but Major General William H. French, commanding Meade's III Corps, badly mismanaged the river crossing. He took an entire day to get his corps over the Rapidan and managed, in addition, to cause a traffic jam which prevented other units from getting across. Apprised of Meade's movements, Lee ordered Early, temporarily in command of the Second Corps as a result of Ewell's indisposition, to "take up a line perpendicular to the river and prepare to meet the enemy,"[33] and Early disposed his divisions accordingly. So it was that, early on November 27, the men of the 3rd North Carolina found themselves moving out, with the rest of Johnson's division, on what they assumed was a fairly straightforward reconnaissance in force. Jones's brigade led, followed by Stafford's. Then came the Stonewall brigade, now under Brigadier General James A. ("Stonewall Jim") Walker, then the artillery and ambulances. Steuart's brigade brought up the rear.

They crossed Mine Run at Bartlett's Mill and set out east along Raccoon Ford Road towards Locust Grove, where they were to link up with Rodes. Confident that there were no enemy troops in the vicinity, the men were peacefully chatting and joking together as they marched along the little country road with dense woodland on either side. Passing two or three gray-clad men sitting quietly on their horses by the side of the road, whom they naturally assumed to be Confederate cavalrymen but who were later thought to have been Union scouts, they were assured that there were "no Yankees within miles." It was therefore something of a shock when, at about midday and some two miles down the road, the train of ambulances came under sudden attack from the woods to the left.[34]

Hastily sending a courier up the column to alert Johnson, Steuart directed his four regiments to deploy their skirmishers in order to cover his left flank and protect the ambulances.[35] Thruston, who had recovered from his wound and had been promoted colonel to rank from October 3, was now back in command of the

3rd North Carolina. "I immediately received orders to load and throw out skirmishers to feel the enemy," he reported later. "This order was accordingly obeyed by sending forward First Lieut. George W. Ward with the regular detail of skirmishers, connecting his line with that of the regiments on my right. This line pushed forward until it came upon a heavy line of the enemy's skirmishers, when Lieutenant Ward informed me of the fact and of his inability to hold his position. I then ordered my left company, commanded by Capt. John B. Brown,[36] to his support.... Captain Brown, assuming command of the first and second detachments of skirmishers, ... vigorously pushed forward and discovered the enemy drawn up in force in the edge of a field and under a rail fence. Captain Brown here received one volley from the main line and was in turn driven in."

It was now clear that Johnson's division was facing, not dismounted cavalry, as had been supposed, but a strong line of infantry. Accordingly, the division formed a line of battle to the left of the road. At about 4 o'clock Johnson ordered a general advance. Thruston was in the process of closing up on the 37th Virginia, the left-hand regiment, when the order came. "My regiment immediately moved forward in as perfect order as the thick undergrowth and nature of the ground would permit," he reported. On reaching the enemy, "the men with a yell charged their position, driving in confusion three strong lines of the enemy before them." Finding himself outflanked, however, and almost out of ammunition, he was forced to retire to his original position.

The right and center, meanwhile, had driven French's men back through the woods and across an open field belonging to Madison Payne. The extraordinary thickness of the woods and undergrowth, however, made it impossible to maintain the line as each brigade emerged, and as the men had now more or less exhausted their cartridges, they were halted at the fence. When night fell, the division was pulled back to the road and at about midnight was ordered back over Mine Run again to take position on the west bank. As for the 3rd North Carolina, "The accompanying list of casualties," as Thruston put it in his report, "will show with what determination the men entered the contest."[37]

Unfortunately, a footnote on the relevant page of the *Official Records* notes simply of this list of casualties "Not found." We know, however, that one of these casualties was George Washington Ward. The company muster roll for November and December 1863 lists him as "Abs. Wounded at Paynes Farm, Va., Nov 27, '63." A Register of General Hospital No. 4 in Richmond shows that Ward was admitted on November 27 and gives the cause of injury as "VS Rt. Arm & Thigh." "Rt. Arm & Thigh" is clear enough, of course, but "VS" had me stumped. I started by asking two recently retired doctors—one of them a distinguished member of the American Civil War Round Table (United Kingdom)—but with no success. Finally, I turned to Bruce Vail. He had had exactly the same problem as I had when he first examined George Ward's file, so he had posted his query online, and the Civil War fraternity had come to his aid immediately. "VS," it turns out, stands for the medical Latin term "Vulnus Sclopeticum"—"Gunshot Wound"—and was apparently a piece of medical jargon much favored by Civil War surgeons on both sides.

Registers of the Medical Director's Office in Richmond dated December 10, 1863, show that Ward had been given a 40-day furlough and that he was due to return to duty on January 14, 1864. It seems doubtful that he did so, however. A certificate dated February 20, 1864, and signed by Assistant Surgeons Davis and Woodson of the Examining Board at Kenansville, North Carolina, reads as follows: "We certify that we have carefully examined Lieut. Ward of Co. B. 3^d. N.C. Regt. Gen. Stewarts [sic] brigade & find him unable to perform the duties of a soldier because of partial anchylosis of left elbow & also partial adhesion of the bones of right arm impairing its usefulness both resulting from Gun Shot wounds. We declare our opinion that he will not be able to resume duty in a period less than thirty [30] days & respectfully recommend that his leave of absence be extended for that period." The mention of the left elbow is significant; since we know that he was wounded in the *right* arm at Payne's Farm, the implication is that the two doctors are referring to an earlier wound, in other words that he received at Sharpsburg.

Ward came before the Medical Examining Board again at the end of March. This time, the board found him "suffering from Partial anchylosis of both forearms" and recommended a further extension of his furlough for 20 days. The certificate recommending this extension is of some interest, since it shows the many levels through which such a recommendation had to pass in order to be approved. Dated March 29, it went first to Captain John B. Brown, commanding Co. B of the 3rd North Carolina, arriving on April 12. He approved it and forwarded it immediately to regimental headquarters. Lieutenant Colonel Parsley, in command at the time, approved and forwarded it in turn to the headquarters of Steuart's brigade. From there it went to Johnson's divisional headquarters, arriving on April 13, and the next day to the headquarters of Ewell's Corps.

Finally, on April 14, it reached army headquarters, where Lee's aide Colonel Walter Taylor signed it on behalf of the commander-in-chief. It is not clear when exactly Ward returned to duty, but he must certainly have been back with the regiment by the beginning of May since he was wounded again at Spotsylvania Court House on May 12.

After the Battle of the Wilderness in which the two North Carolina regiments captured over 100 men of the 146th New York and two guns in the first day's fighting, the brigade was marched on May 8 to Spotsylvania Court House, arriving after dark. At about 10:30 p.m., the men were put into position on the right (east) side of what was known as the Mule Shoe salient and at once started entrenching. When Upton's innovative attack in column broke through on the left of the salient on May 10, Steuart's brigade played a key role in the successful counterattack which recaptured that portion of the line. Colonel Thruston was seriously wounded here, and Lieutenant Colonel Parsley once again took command of the 3rd North Carolina. It rained heavily during the night of May 11, but Johnson and Steuart could clearly hear, through the storm, troops moving about, which led them to expect a possible attack. Unfortunately, the guns protecting Johnson's division had been withdrawn from that part of the line at nightfall and moved elsewhere, and it was therefore without artillery cover that the troops in the Mule Shoe salient would face the mass onslaught on May 12 with which Grant planned to capitalize on Upton's inspired innovation.

The rain gradually stopped, to be replaced by a thick fog. At about 4:30 a.m., just as this was starting to lift, Hancock's II Corps burst out of the woods, "a rectangular mass of twenty thousand Federal troops … in column of regiments doubled on the centre," as the colonel of the 1st North Carolina put it.[38] Hancock's men charged into the Confederate works, overran Jones's brigade, which was on the left of the two North Carolina regiments, and sweeping on captured the greater part of Johnson's entire division, including Steuart and Johnson himself. Only some 30 men of the 3rd North Carolina escaped capture, although men returning to the colors and conscripts assigned to the regiment would later increase its depleted ranks to some extent.

Once the Confederates, in one of the bloodiest fights of the war, had finally managed to drive back the attackers and retire to a hastily prepared second line of works some 500 yards behind the salient, a reorganization took place of the survivors of Johnson's division. The three Virginia regiments of Steuart's brigade, together with the Virginia regiments from the other brigades in the division, were consolidated on May 15 into a new brigade under Brigadier General William Terry, while the remnants of the 1st and 3rd North Carolina were assigned to Dodson Ramseur's North Carolina brigade in Rodes's division. The two regiments had thus at last had their wish granted; they were in a North Carolina brigade and under a North Carolina brigadier, and there they would stay until the final surrender.

Ward, meanwhile, was admitted on May 17 to Jackson Hospital. We do not know precisely at what point in the day he was wounded, but the hospital's report for the day of his admission gives the cause succinctly as "VS Abdomen Min Ball." He was examined on May 22 by Surgeon A.J. Semmes and two other surgeons, who certified that he would not be fit for duty "in a less period than 60 days." Ward himself was clearly well enough to write, however, since on the same day he "respectfully" requested "leave of absence for 60 days, to go to Teacheys Depot, Duplin Co, N. Carolina," and the following day he signed a statement of account confirming receipt of pay of $270 for the period of February 1 to April 30, 1864.

On May 29, Ward was transferred to Camp Winder, Richmond, known as "the largest hospital in the Confederacy," and on June 7 he was moved again, this time to General Hospitals Nos. 4 and 5 in Wilmington, North Carolina. The Wilmington Hospitals' Register of August 27 shows him as returned to duty that day, but an Inspection Report of Rodes's Division at Bunker Hill, Virginia, dated September 3 lists him as still absent wounded. However, he was certainly back with his regiment again in time to sign the company muster roll for September and October 1864 as the lieutenant commanding the company.

In his absence, Ramseur had been promoted to major general on June 1, and Colonel William R. Cox of the 2nd North Carolina promoted to brigadier general and given command of the brigade. Ward's comrades had taken part in the Battle of Cold Harbor and had followed Early in his Valley campaign and on his advance into Maryland, penetrating as far as the defenses of Washington before retiring back into the Valley. Since the 3rd North Carolina, with the rest of the Second Corps, remained in the Valley until December 14, 1864, it seems probable that Ward was with the regiment when it fought in the third battle of Winchester and at Fisher's Hill and Cedar Creek. Certainly the rolls list him as present for duty from September through to the end of the year. In addition, a requisition order for what appears to be paper, dated October 25, shows him as commanding Cos. A, B, C, D and E.

The men went into winter quarters just north of Petersburg in mid–December 1864. Ramseur, who had been given command of Rodes's division after Rodes was killed at Winchester, had himself been mortally wounded at Cedar Creek. Command of the division had therefore passed to the senior brigadier, Bryan Grimes, another North Carolinian. For the remainder of the war, then, the 3rd North Carolina was officially in Cox's brigade, Grimes's division, Gordon's (Second) Corps. The men were ordered into the trenches at Petersburg around the middle of March 1865, shortly after which the division took part in the initially successful surprise attack on Fort Stedman on March 25. When the lines were breached in the area round Fort Mahone in the early morning of April 2, Grimes's division counterattacked, retook their trenches and remained in possession of them until the Union breakthrough elsewhere made a general withdrawal inevitable. The men then covered the army's rear on the long retreat which led finally to Appomattox.

At Sayler's Creek, on April 6, the 3rd North Carolina lost its youthful Lieutenant Colonel William Murdock Parsley, shot through the head. He had been captured at Spotsylvania Court House, like most of the regiment, on May 12, 1864, but had been exchanged on August 3 and had immediately returned to duty. Since Colonel Thruston had been wounded at Winchester and left unfit for field service, Major William T. Ennett, who had similarly been captured and exchanged, succeeded Parsley in charge of the regiment's depleted ranks.

Grimes's division reached the little village of Appomattox Court House in the evening of April 8 and bivouacked. At around midnight that night, the three divisions of Gordon's Corps were marched through the village and positioned to the west of it in readiness to clear the Lynchburg road. This was found to be blocked by two lines of dismounted cavalry behind breastworks, supported by two guns. Forming up with Clement Evans on the left, "Stonewall Jim" Walker in the center and Grimes on the right, the remnants of the three divisions advanced with a yell shortly after daybreak, carrying the breastworks, driving the cavalry before them, clearing the ridge and opening the road. At the same time, Brigadier General William P. Roberts's small brigade of North Carolina cavalry, on the right, captured the two guns, the last taken by the Army of Northern Virginia.

There were to be no further successes, though, because now Gordon's temporarily victorious men could see the long blue lines of the newly arrived Union infantry sweeping steadily towards them from the west and south. Nevertheless, they held their position and continued firing on the enemy until the inevitable order came to cease fire and fall back on the village. Only Cox's little North Carolina brigade, on the far right of the line, remained in position, either because

Cox had not received the order or (as Grimes later wrote) because he had been ordered to cover the rear of the rest of Grimes's division.[39] Whatever the case, it was Cox's brigade, including what was left of the 3rd Regiment, North Carolina State Troops, which fired the final volley of the Army of Northern Virginia before being summoned back by a messenger from Gordon. Three days later, the remaining 58 men of the regiment, Major Ennett among them, were paroled and started for their homes.[40]

George Washington Ward was not one of them, however. An inspection report on the brigade dated February 25, 1865, at the Dunn House, Petersburg, lists him as absent from February 19 and back in Duplin County "on furlough of indulgence for 18 days" by authority of General Lee. We have no information as to why he was given a furlough of this sort so late in the war, but the logical assumption is that it was to do with his wounds. Certainly there is no evidence that he tried to return to his regiment on the expiry of the 18 days, but by that time Sherman was well into North Carolina, and it would have been impossible in any case for Ward to rejoin the Army of Northern Virginia. What we do know is that for the rest of his life he remained proud of his service in the 3rd North Carolina. Ward's name is one of those on a surviving official roster of the Association of Officers of the 3rd North Carolina Infantry, formed on February 2, 1866, and he was apparently a regular attendant at reunions.[41]

Nor was he the only member of his family to serve in the war. His younger brother, Alfred Charles Ward, enlisted as a private on November 14, 1861, in what became the 3rd North Carolina Cavalry (41st Regiment, North Carolina Troops) and ended the war as Captain of Co. A, while at least two of his elder brothers, William Robinson Ward and James Edward Ward, were in the North Carolina Home Guard.[42]

The war over, George Washington Ward gradually settled down again to life as a farmer. On September 19, 1867, he married the 19-year-old Mary Priscilla Alderman, from Delway in neighboring Sampson County. Their first child, Mary, was given the second name of Vance, and their eighth and youngest child, born in 1882, was Livingston DeRosset. The U.S. Census of 1870 shows Ward as the owner of a farm valued at $1,000. As Bruce Vail points out, "Some of this acreage would have been unimproved swampland or woodland, but even those acres could have generated income through the sale of timber rights, or other uses." Living with Ward and his wife and their two eldest children at this time were his widowed mother and his younger brother, Alfred Charles.[43]

Ten years later, in 1880, the census shows him, aged 47, as still living on his farm, but now with five more children. That same year, he attended the 15th reunion of the Association of Officers of the 3rd North Carolina Infantry. Four years after that, on November 10, 1884, he was helping to fight a forest fire when he was overcome by the heat and died. He was buried in the little family cemetery at Teachey.[44]

There is a tendency today—understandable, perhaps, in the light of modern attitudes, but no less unhistorical for that—to emphasize the extent of disaffection in North Carolina at the expense of the wider picture. Certainly there was a substantial degree of disaffection in the state (as, indeed, there had been during the Revolution). Yet the fact remains that North Carolina contributed more men[45] to the Confederate Army than any other state but Virginia. George Washington Ward's story is a reminder to us of the thousands of ordinary North Carolinians unknown to history—junior officers, noncommissioned officers and men—who enlisted for the war and remained faithful to the end, justifying their state's proud boast to have been "first at Bethel, farthest at Gettysburg and Chickamauga and last at Appomattox."

15

A Postmaster in the Cavalry

It is easy, at times, to forget how important the mail was to the Civil War soldier, North and South. Certainly paintings, prints and photographs occasionally show soldiers in camp reading or writing letters, but they give little indication of what a major part of the soldier's life this constituted. For this, we need to turn to the soldiers' letters themselves. When he was not drilling, marching or fighting, the Civil War soldier spent much of his spare time reading letters from home, waiting for letters from home and, of course, writing letters home. Those soldiers who could read and write read and wrote; those who could not read or write depended upon the help of their more literate comrades. Whether written or dictated, though, their letters show us clearly how vital this link with home was to them. Reading these letters, we find the same theme recurring again and again. In letter after letter, North or South, the soldier complains bitterly at not having received any mail and begs his family to write and write often.

Some of the officers may write rather more elegantly and spell rather more conventionally than the average common soldier, but they express exactly the same feelings as the men in the ranks, and their complaints about delays to the mail tend to be even stronger. Nor were things any different for those who, for whatever reason, had to seek work or service overseas after the Civil War; letters remained one of their chief preoccupations. We have already met Henry Clay Derrick of Halifax, Virginia, who spent the Civil War as a captain of engineers in the Army of Northern Virginia. After the war, finding his prospects limited, he joined other veterans in the army of Khedive Ismail and served as chief engineer in the Egyptian expeditionary force which invaded Abyssinia in 1875. In his diary of his Egyptian service, which consists of two manuscript volumes of some 250 pages each, he lists and numbers every letter written to his wife back home in Halifax and every letter received from her and complains constantly about the slowness of the mail. A typical entry reads:

> At 12½ a steamboat arrived; but, strange to say, brought us no letters. We have been here over two weeks, three weeks since we left Suez, & although more than 6 or 7 steamers have arrived here none of our letters has been forwarded from Cairo. We cannot but feel

that we have been treated with shameful neglect & indifference when our letters could have been forwarded so easily & have not been sent.[1]

Any Civil War officer reading this would have nodded in recognition.

It would be difficult, then, to overestimate the importance of letters to the Civil War soldier. From the point of view of the student of the Civil War, however, the problem is that all too many of these letters are in themselves of no great interest. All too often, men who had experienced some of the most dramatic events of the Civil War make, at best, only passing reference to these, choosing instead to concentrate on more mundane details. An old friend recently sent me copies of a dozen letters written by a New York infantryman called John Helmer, an ancestor of her husband's. Helmer enlisted in Co. A of the 16th New York Infantry on September 13, 1862, at the age of 34. The regiment was mustered out on May 11, 1863, when the two-year men went home, and Helmer and the other three-year men were then transferred to Emory Upton's 121st New York in the same brigade, although he was temporarily attached to the 1st Independent Battery, Massachusetts Light Artillery. He lost an arm in Upton's attack on the Mule Shoe salient at Spotsylvania on May 10, 1864, and died in hospital. He must therefore have been present at Fredericksburg, taken part in Burnside's "Mud March" and in the Chancellorsville and Gettysburg campaigns and been in the bloody battle of Rappahannock Station. In his letters home, though, there is very little hint of any of this, apart from occasional reference to long marches ("i gess that Jo Hooker means to kill us for we have to carry 5 Days rasens … this is a big load a nough for a mule")[2] or to being about to cross the Potomac after Gettysburg. Far more space is devoted to a description of his job as a volunteer laundryman, first washing the clothes of the men in his company and later graduating to laundering and ironing the officers' clothes, with a list of the money which he has been able to make; this may well have been of interest to his family, who were going to benefit financially from it, but it is less so to the military historian.

Nevertheless, there is still something thrilling about holding in one's hand an original letter written by a Civil War soldier, followed inevitably by the enjoyable challenge of first trying to decipher the handwriting and spelling and then trying to find out something about the man himself. So it was that I recently found myself the purchaser of a letter written to his wife on November 25, 1863, by George R. Adderton, a private in the 63rd North Carolina and postmaster of Hill's Store in Randolph County.

In transcribing Adderton's letter, I have not attempted to correct his spelling or to add punctuation, preferring to keep the original flavor of the letter; I have merely inserted four words in order to make the sense clear. (Despite the number of letters passing through his hands, it does not look as if anything more than a fairly basic degree of literacy was required of a Confederate postmaster.) The letter reads as follows:

> Dear wife I resume my self this pleasent evening to rite you afew lines to inform you of my helth I am well an I hope when thes few lines come to han tha may fine you all well at home I am fare very well iamgit aplenty to eate you want to know if ihave drown over cot I hant drown yet I will drow one i nafew days I want to [know] how much wheat you have

sode an how much oates you have sode an how much corn you made an how our hogs is fat ting Tel [me how] Joseph an Troy an sons an the baby [are] git tin along Tel them to rite soon I want you to rite soon an I want you to rite one aweak I reseve your leter was rote 20 November I was glade to her from you I will come to aclose by saing pray for me

I remai your husban
G R Adderton
to A N Adderton

In other words, it seems on the face of it to be in every way a typical Confederate private soldier's letter, of no real interest to the historian whatsoever—except for one very curious fact, which is not immediately apparent but which will become clear later.

Fortunately, there is a surprising amount of information available on George Adderton. He was born on November 21, 1830, in Davidson County, the son of Jeremiah Adderton and the former Abigail Coggin. Jeremiah Adderton died in 1844, and the census of 1850 lists George as a 19-year-old farmer living at home with his widowed mother, who in turn is listed as the owner of an 18-year-old male

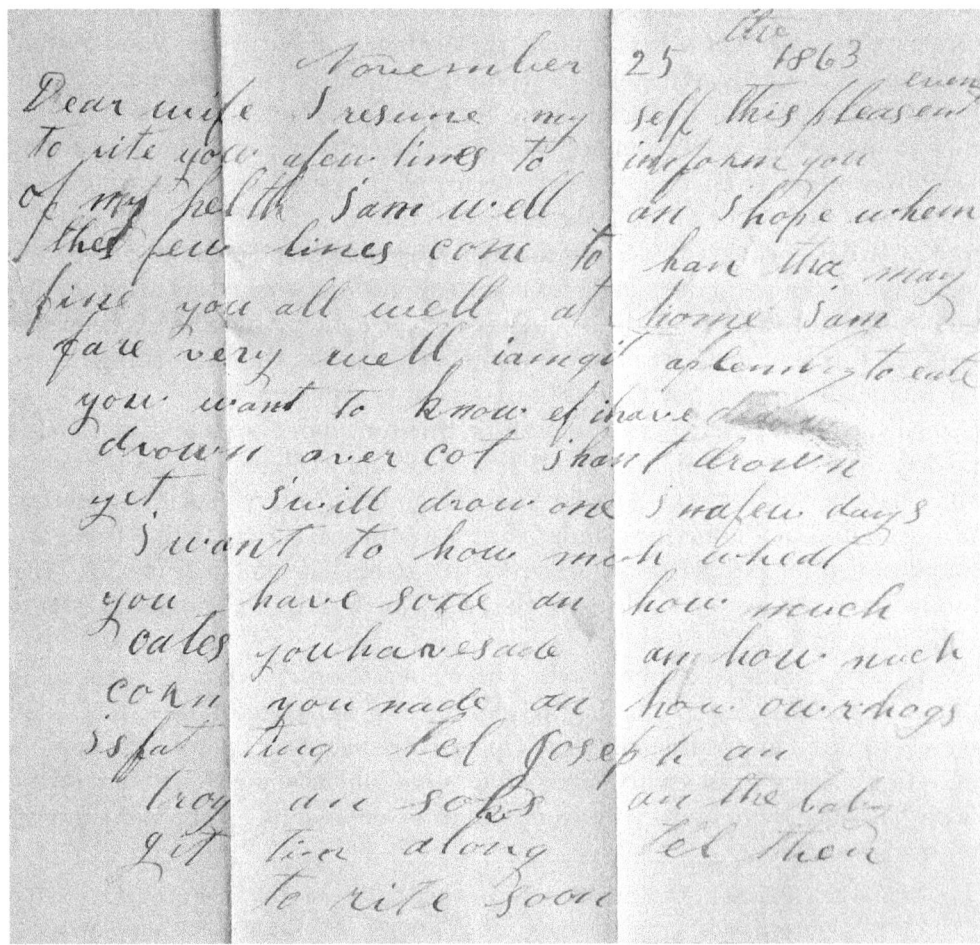

George R. Adderton's letter (author's collection).

slave. By 1860, George had become the main householder. He was now married to Adaline Norwood Kearns (whose name also appears spelled variously as Adeline and Adline), and they had moved, together with his mother, to neighboring Randolph County. He is listed on the 1860 census as the owner of three slaves—a 28-year-old male (presumably the 18-year-old of the earlier census), a 25-year-old female and a one-year-old male baby. His profession is shown as "F" (Farmer), and he is stated to own real estate worth $3,000, with a personal estate of $3,470.

On December 16, 1861, Adderton was appointed postmaster of Hill's Store, so called because the first postmaster had been Samuel Hill in 1823. Although postal clerks and mail carriers were supposed to be exempt from the Confederate draft, postmasters (even in North Carolina) were not, unless appointed by the president and confirmed by Congress.[3] Whatever the case, though, George Adderton enlisted for the war in March 1863, leaving Adaline to take over the duties of postmaster and, with the help of the two slaves, to continue to run the farm. On March 23, he was mustered in to Company K of the 63rd North Carolina by Captain J.E. Wharton.[4]

This regiment had been formed in October 1862 by the amalgamation of a number of different elements. Companies A and C had been independent partisan ranger units. Companies B, D, E, F and G had all been assigned to Major Peter Gustavus Evans's Battalion, North Carolina Partisan Rangers. Company K, originally known as Captain John E. Wharton's Company of Partisan Rangers, together with Companies H and I, had been a part of Major Robert White's Battalion of Partisan Rangers. White, although apparently resident in North Carolina, was a Virginian, and his battalion consisted of both Virginia and North Carolina companies. The three North Carolina companies, however, objected as usual to having to serve with Virginians, with the result that the battalion never completed its organization. Since the 63rd North Carolina in fact served as regular cavalry rather than as partisan rangers, its official title became 63rd Regiment North Carolina Troops (5th North Carolina Cavalry). Peter G. Evans was appointed colonel, to rank from October 1, 1862.

Manarin's *North Carolina Troops 1861–1865: A Roster* contains a useful summary of the regiment's history, while Clark's *Histories of the Several Regiments and Battalions from North Carolina in the Great War 1861–'65* has two separate accounts, a fairly short one by the regiment's major, John M. Galloway, and a very much longer one by Paul Barringer Means, a private in Company F.[5] Despite its somewhat melodramatic style, Means's "Additional Sketch" is of some value. Besides his own earlier writings, he was able to draw on the memories and reminiscences, written or otherwise, of a large number of former members of the regiment. He also quotes extensively from both Confederate and Union reports in the *Official Records*. Finally (although he does not mention this), he was a nephew of General Rufus Barringer, who was the regiment's brigade commander for the last year of the war. Quite apart from what he may have learned from his uncle, Means served during the latter part of the war as a courier at brigade headquarters and thus had the opportunity to see rather more of the battlefield than his comrades in Company F would have been able to do.

The regiment was organized at Garysburg, North Carolina, and brigaded with the 59th North Carolina (4th North Carolina Cavalry) under Brigadier General Beverly H. Robertson. Robertson, a West Pointer, was described by Major Galloway as "very strict, and sometimes irascible on military points" although "in social intercourse a pleasant, polished gentleman."[6] Lee considered Robertson "a good organizer and instructor,"[7] and certainly he proceeded to drill and train his new command both vigorously and thoroughly. As Sergeant Daniel Branson Coltrane of Company I recalled, "It was our good fortune to be under his direction, for we were green country boys and it was necessary for us to have very strenuous drilling."[8] The 63rd then spent the next six months or so in eastern North Carolina, either on picket duty or on various minor operations such as a successful raid on Union-held Plymouth in December. A portion of the regiment also took part in D.H. Hill's abortive move against New Bern in March 1863, where Robertson's failure to cut the railroad gave Hill an opportunity to indulge his notorious dislike of the cavalry by unjustifiably blaming the "woefully inefficient" brigade for his expedition's lack of success.[9] In this context, it is only fair to the 63rd North Carolina to quote the words of Colonel J. Richter Jones, of the 58th Pennsylvania Infantry, who encountered the regiment near Kinston on March 7. "They are a different class of troops from those I have hitherto met," he reported the following day, "contesting successively every strong position and giving way only to my superior numbers."[10] Robertson seems to have done his work well.

In early May 1863, a few weeks after Adderton had joined the regiment, Robertson's brigade was ordered to Richmond for the horses to be shod and the men re-equipped before joining the Army of Northern Virginia. The brigade arrived with the army just in time to take part in the grand cavalry review before Lee at Brandy Station on June 8, where the newly-equipped men and horses stood out among "Jeb" Stuart's veteran regiments. It was not directly involved in the great battle of the next day, although Stuart reported afterwards, "General Robertson's command, though not engaged, was exposed to the enemy's artillery fire, and behaved well."[11] It was not many days, however, before the regiment was very definitely engaged. On June 17, at Middleburg, Robertson's brigade came up against the French-born Colonel Alfred Duffié's 1st Rhode Island Cavalry. Duffié had dismounted his men and positioned them strongly behind stone walls, leaving a small force in the road as a decoy. The leading squadron of the 63rd North Carolina fell into the trap, but the rest of the regiment, coming up, charged down the main street and, in Duffié's words, "surrounded the town and stormed the barricades."[12] Most of his regiment was captured. The 63rd lost two men killed and some 20 wounded.

Skirmishing continued over the next two days. An attack on June 19 by three Union brigades under Brigadier General David McM. Gregg was, as Stuart put it, "met in the most determined manner" by Robertson's and W.H. F. "Rooney" Lee's brigades.[13] Gregg's commanding officer, Brigadier General Alfred Pleasanton, claimed in his report of June 20: "Our cavalry is really fighting infantry behind stone walls. This is the reason of our heavy losses."[14] There were, of course, no infantry with Stuart. At Upperville, on June 21, Pleasanton was able to throw five fresh brigades, including an infantry brigade under Vincent, against four Confederate cavalry brigades. As the Confederates fell back, "the enemy attacked Brigadier-General Robertson, bringing up the rear in this movement, and was handsomely repulsed."[15] Part of this repulse involved a mounted charge by the 63rd North Carolina in which the Colonel, Peter G. Evans, was mortally wounded and captured. Having successfully screened Lee's movements from the enemy, the Confederates then retired unmolested to Ashby's Gap, where Stuart placed Lieutenant Colonel James B. Gordon, of the 9th North Carolina (1st North Carolina Cavalry) in command of the 63rd; Gordon was to command it throughout the Gettysburg campaign.

When Stuart began his famous ride north on June 25, he left behind the two brigades of William E. "Grumble" Jones and Robertson. The reason for his choosing these two brigades to leave behind may simply have been that Jones and Robertson were Stuart's least favorite officers.[16] Although Stuart respected Jones as a soldier, he considered him prone to "opposition, insubordination, and inefficiency,"[17] while he described Robertson as "by far the most troublesome man I have to deal with."[18] His dislike of Robertson may well have had a more personal basis. Robertson had served before the war under Philip St. George Cooke in the 2nd U.S. Dragoons and at one point had been engaged to Cooke's daughter Flora, who later married Stuart. At any rate, Stuart's order of June 24 to Robertson read: "Your own and General Jones' brigades will cover the front of Ashby's and Snicker's Gaps, yourself, as senior officer, being in command. Your object will be to watch the enemy; deceive him as to our designs, and harass his rear if you find he is retiring.... After the enemy has moved beyond your reach, leave sufficient pickets in the mountains ... cross the Potomac, and follow the army."[19] The brigade crossed the Potomac at Williamsport on July 1, reaching Gettysburg in the morning of July 3 and going into position on the army's right flank. At Fairfield that afternoon, Robertson's two regiments arrived in time to complete Jones's rout of the 6th U.S. Cavalry and to gather up prisoners.

The following day, as the army started to retreat, the 63rd North Carolina formed part of the rear guard. Robertson's instructions from Stuart were "that it was essentially necessary for him to hold the Jack Mountain passes" with his own and Jones's brigades in order to protect the withdrawal of the wagon trains.[20] When the lead company of the regiment reached the top of one of these passes that night, it met a Union cavalry regiment riding up with the obvious intention of occupying the pass. The rest of the regiment coming up then charged the enemy and drove them off, encamping on the pass.[21] July 6 found the enemy cavalry in possession of Hagerstown, with the wagons at Williamsport "congregated in a narrow space ... near the river, which was too much swollen to admit their passage to the south bank." Robertson's North Carolinians, with Jenkins's Virginia brigade, secured the road to Williamsport by charging and routing the enemy, an attempt at a counter-charge being "gallantly met and repulsed by Colonel James B. Gordon, commanding a fragment of the Fifth North Carolina Cavalry." "Without this attack," Stuart reported, "it is certain that our trains would have fallen into the hands of the enemy."[22] The 63rd North Carolina finally crossed the

Potomac at Williamsport on July 14, the last unit of Lee's army, according to Galloway, to do so.

On July 15, immediately after the return to Virginia, Robertson asked to be relieved from command of the brigade on the grounds that "in consequence of casualties, detached service, sickness &c," it was "reduced to less than 300 men," and his services "would be of more avail elsewhere."[23] Shortly after this, he fell ill. His request was granted on August 5, and he was ordered to report to the adjutant general for orders. On September 9, there was a major reorganization of the cavalry. The 63rd North Carolina (5th Cavalry) and 59th North Carolina (4th Cavalry) were now joined by 9th North Carolina (1st Cavalry) and 19th North Carolina (2nd Cavalry) in a new North Carolina brigade, initially under Laurence S. Baker and then, in consequence of his wounds, under James B. Gordon, who was promoted to brigadier general. Divisions were formed at the same time, and the new brigade was assigned to Wade Hampton's. The brigade had its baptism of fire at Jack's Shop a few days later, on September 21, when Stuart's force, heavily outnumbered, was surrounded by Union cavalry under Buford and Kilpatrick. One of Stuart's staff rode along the lines calling out, "Boys, it's a fight to captivity, death or victory!" A voice from the 63rd North Carolina answered him: "We'll get out of here if there isn't but one of us left!"[24] And, with the aid of the six guns of Captain William McGregor's Battery, get out they did.

Then came the Bristoe campaign. From October 9 to October 20, the regiment, with the rest of the brigade, was heavily engaged with the Union cavalry at Russell's Ford, James City, Culpeper Court House, Auburn Mills and Manassas Junction. At Culpeper Court House, it lost its adjutant, Lieutenant James Turner Morehead, shot in the mouth and neck, the bullet narrowly missing the spinal column; the wound was thought to be mortal, but Morehead eventually recovered to serve in the Invalid Corps. The campaign ended with the "Buckland Races," where, as Gordon put it, "the enemy fled in great confusion and were pursued for several miles with unrelenting fury."[25] The regiment's only real fighting during the Mine Run campaign, the last of the year, was on November 29 at Parker's Store, where part of the regiment was dismounted and, with the 19th North Carolina (2nd Cavalry), "ordered to charge the Yankee skirmishers, which was done in handsome style, driving them from the railroad cut … and scattering them through the woods, capturing a number of prisoners."[26]

The army now went into winter quarters. As mentioned above, the regiment's final brigade commander of the war was Rufus Barringer. Many years later, when on the faculty of the University of Virginia, the general's son, Dr. Paul Barringer, wrote to his widowed stepmother from Charlottesville: "It is strange, but a fact, that of all the men of father's brigade buried at this place, the old Sixty-third furnished more than the other three regiments put together."[27] These were the dead of the battles of 1863.

Meanwhile, what of George Adderton? The company muster rolls for the year list him as present throughout from the time of his enlistment in March. The roll for September and October, however, while listing him as present, has, under "Remarks," the phrases "No horse 40 days" and "Absent without leave 24 days."

We know that the Confederate cavalryman had to provide his own horse, but perhaps we fail to think how often these horses had to be replaced. Horses could become sick or disabled, and of course horses could be killed; after all, a cavalry horse is a much bigger target than his rider. Nathan Bedford Forrest, for example, had no fewer than 29 horses shot under him (though, as he also killed 30 Union soldiers in hand-to-hand combat, he was able famously to claim that he was "a horse ahead at the end"). If a Confederate trooper lost his horse, he was expected to go home and find a replacement and was apparently given 60 days to do this. It could be, then, that in this case Adderton simply stayed at home rather longer than the time allowed before returning with a fresh horse. He may also have used the time to return temporarily to his duties as postmaster. Certainly he is never again shown as being absent without leave. He had enlisted "for the war," and we know that he continued with the regiment right up to the last moment. Indeed, there is only one other, very small, piece of evidence to suggest that Adderton was in any way other than a sergeant major's ideal soldier; the roll for November and December 1863 records, rather censoriously, "one wooden canteen carelessly lost."

On February 18, 1864, the regiment was temporarily disbanded at Henderson, North Carolina,[28] "that each man might go to his home for a new horse, or the recuperation of the one he had and himself," as Paul Means put it.[29] The men were to rejoin their companies at one of three designated locations on April 10. This period of leave must have been welcome to Adderton, who is recorded on the roll for March and April as having had "no horse from Jany 20 to Feb 20 1864." The men reported at their various rendezvous on schedule and then marched by companies to Richmond, where the regiment was reorganized. From there, they were ordered on May 2 back to the brigade, which on April 30 had been transferred from Wade Hampton's division to that of Rooney Lee. On May 9, Sheridan started his great raid on Richmond. While Stuart moved to intercept the head of his column at Yellow Tavern, Gordon was ordered to attack the rear. Having burned the bridge over the South Anna near Ground Squirrel Church, Sheridan was confident that he was safe from pursuit. This was not the sort of thing to deter a man like Gordon, however. Shouting "Forward!" he plunged down the steep banks, through the river and up the hill on the far side, the 63rd and the rest of the brigade following him. Of this dangerous river crossing, Private Paul Means recalled later, "Some were seriously hurt, but we were out there expecting to get hurt."[30] Sheridan's rear guard was formed by the 1st Maine, which fired upon Gordon's men as they approached. Accordingly, Gordon dismounted the bulk of the 63rd and sent them in. The brigade returns for the Union Second Brigade record: "First Maine as rear guard. It became necessary to dismount the whole regiment to hold back a strong force of the enemy while the column moved on.... The enemy charged, both mounted and dismounted, and caused the regiment to fall back with some confusion and considerable loss."[31] David McM. Gregg, commanding the Second Division, reported: "On the 11th, near Ground Squirrel Church, the division, marching in rear, was attacked by Gordon's brigade of rebel cavalry. The attacks of the enemy were repeated during the entire day."[32]

In a series of charges, both mounted and dismounted, Gordon gradually pressed Gregg's men back until they reached the church itself, where they had artillery support.

Having found the defenses in front of Richmond too strong for him, and with his rear under constant pressure from the Confederate cavalry, Sheridan realized that his only option was to attempt to cross the swollen Chickahominy in order to return to Union lines. In the morning of May 12, therefore, he set about repairing Meadow Bridge, which the Confederates had partially destroyed. At the same time, Gordon once again attacked his rear guard under Gregg, who now occupied a strong position on the Military Road near Brook Church, protected by artillery. Galloping out alone at one point to reconnoiter the enemy lines, the impetuous Gordon was shot and mortally wounded. His men continued the attack, nevertheless, but as soon as the bridge was successfully repaired, Sheridan was able to disengage and to withdraw over the river across it. On June 4, Brigadier General Rufus Barringer was assigned to the command of the North Carolina brigade. Writing after the war, Major Galloway described him as very different from Gordon, "brave enough, but of a prudent, methodical, cautious temperament."[33]

In the weeks following Sheridan's raid, the men were in action almost daily. George Adderton, however, missed much of this. On May 26, he was admitted to hospital in Richmond, suffering from "dysentery chronic."[34] He was finally returned to duty on June 17 and thus may have been back with his regiment in time to be present at the repulse on June 21 of Barlow's infantry division at the Davis Farm on the Petersburg & Weldon Railroad, in which the 63rd North Carolina, fighting dismounted, played a key part.

The following day, June 22, saw the start of another Union cavalry raid. This involved the divisions of James H. Wilson and August V. Kautz, and the object was "to strike the railroad as close as practicable to Petersburg and destroy it in the direction of Burkeville and the Roanoke River."[35] Rooney Lee at once set off in pursuit, taking with him Barringer's Brigade and the brigade of James Dearing, as well as McGregor's Battery. On June 23, at Blacks and Whites, what Galloway refers to as "a serious contest" took place. Kautz having gone on ahead, Lee caught up with Wilson, who had taken the wrong road. Dearing's Brigade, in advance, broke under the Union attack and retreated precipitately, leaving McGregor's guns dangerously exposed. Lee hastily ordered up the North Carolina Brigade, which went in with the 63rd, dismounted, on the right, drove back the advancing Unionists and saved the guns. Still pursued by Lee, the raiders then veered south and on June 25 attempted to attack and destroy the Staunton River Bridge on the Richmond and Danville Railroad, but were repulsed by Captain Benjamin L. Farinholt and a hastily gathered force of "some boys and old men and furloughed soldiers." By now, according to Galloway, "our force had been much decreased, chiefly by breaking down. It was decided to pursue with a few choice men and horses and let the others, a very large majority, proceed leisurely to camp."[36] This force, however, was enough to drive the Federals towards Wade Hampton's waiting division and to their defeat and dispersal.

After this, Barringer's tired men enjoyed a 30-day period of rest, or "a few

15. A Postmaster in the Cavalry

weeks comparative rest," as Galloway put it.[37] From the end of July on, however, they were frequently called upon to help counter Union demonstrations north of the James or attacks on the Petersburg & Weldon Railroad. In mid–September, the 63rd North Carolina took part in Wade Hampton's celebrated Beefsteak Raid, which brought back almost 2,500 head of cattle, and in October it was on a number of occasions in "some very severe fighting," culminating on October 27 in the Battle of Boydton Plank Road, described by Means as "one of the most important actions and greatest victories that the Sixty-third North Carolina was ever engaged in."[38] This was Grant's last attempt of the year at a flanking attack on the Petersburg defenses. Hancock was sent with his Second Corps and elements from other corps, as well as Gregg's cavalry, to seize the Boydton Plank Road on the Confederate right and to destroy the Southside Railroad. Opposing him, though heavily outnumbered, were the infantry divisions of Heth and Mahone and the cavalry under Wade Hampton. Hancock succeeded initially in gaining a lodgment on the Boydton Plank Road, but the Confederates, infantry and cavalry, swiftly counterattacked. While Hancock was able finally to hold them back, his position was dangerously isolated, and that night he withdrew, leaving the Boydon Plank Road in the possession of the Confederates for the rest of the winter. The cavalry pursued him until he "fell back behind his infantry lines."[39] As for the 63rd North Carolina, Gregg, in his report, referred to "the enemy cavalry dismounted, attacking strongly,"[40] while Robert E. Lee, in a letter to Wade Hampton, repeated his "gratification at the conduct of the troops in general and the cavalry in particular."[41]

Purely by chance, I discovered very recently that the Stuart A. Rose Library at Emory University had a copy of a letter which George Adderton had written to his mother on October 30, shortly after this battle.[42] It turned out to be only on microfilm and of fairly poor quality. In view of this, the library does not normally supply copies, but Kathy Shoemaker of the library staff very kindly made an exception and sent me a scanned copy of both the letter and a typed transcript. Much of the letter is indeed very faint, but by enlarging it and examining it very closely I was able in the end both to confirm that the transcript was in general very accurate and to fill in the only blank in it. This, as near as I can judge, then, is what it says:

> Der muther it is throu the ten[der] mercey of god that iam permit[ted] to drop you afew lines to let you no that iam on the pled groun of mercy an iam well i hop when thes few lines come to han tha may fin you all well an hartey i want you to rite to me i hante herde from home lone time senc i le[f]t home i want you to rite soon i hante bin in no fight sen i le[f]t home isen[t] home bey Rusel one par pant an shert an drawrs an some apounes[?] of cofey will close
>
> G R Adderton

If we can be reasonably sure that is what Adderton wrote, what is less certain is what exactly he meant. First, there is the question of the rather cryptic phrase "on the pled groun." This section of the microfilmed letter is in fact fairly clear, and there seems little doubt that this is what Adderton wrote, but what does it actually mean? "Pled" is an old form of "pleaded" and "groun" is obviously "ground." Is

Adderton perhaps saying something to the effect that he had begged God to keep him safe and that his prayers had been answered? Secondly, when he says that he has not been in a fight since he left home, he clearly cannot mean since he originally joined the regiment in March 1863. The answer may well lie in the company muster roll for July and August 1864, which lists Adderton as present but adds that he had had "no horse since Aug 25 1864." Possibly Adderton had been sent home to get a new horse. At any rate, we know that he was back with the regiment on September 26 since on that day he drew clothing for the third quarter of the year. (He is also shown as having drawn clothing for the final quarter of the year on October 29.)[43] Whatever the case, he seems to have missed the Battle of the Boydton Plank Road. Finally, there is the coffee—if it really was coffee. We know that coffee was almost impossible to obtain in the Confederacy, so if Adderton was indeed sending some home, he can only have got it by trading with the Union pickets. Such trading was, of course, very common at periods of quiet. Daniel Coltrane of Company I records a typical instance from the winter of 1863:

> When we were on picket duty on the Rapidan one day, I went down to where the Yankee pickets could see me and held up a paper. That was the signal which meant: "No fighting here now; trading at hand." They motioned for me to come over. Our army had issued tobacco to the soldiers that day, so I went over to trade mine for sugar and coffee. While I was sitting on a log talking, a fellow came dashing up to me and threw his blue overcoat around me. "The general is inspecting our pickets. Keep this coat on, and he won't notice you." I kept the coat on until the general passed. Then I went back over to my side of the river with my sugar and coffee and they had their tobacco.[44]

Adderton must have obtained his coffee in the same way. "Rusel," incidentally, by whom Adderton sent home these items, must be Sergeant Whitson Russell of Adderton's company, a neighbor from Randolph County.

The year ended with Gouverneur K. Warren's Belfield Raid. On December 7, 1864, Grant sent Warren with his V Corps and Gregg's cavalry to destroy the Petersburg and Weldon Railroad as far as Belfield, just above the North Carolina state line. As soon as Lee heard of this, Wade Hampton was sent off in pursuit, with A.P. Hill's infantry following. Warren managed successfully to tear up some 16 or 17 miles of railroad, although the Confederates were eventually able to get this back into operation again. Unfortunately, many of the wreckers came upon a large quantity of apple brandy along the route, with the result that they got drunk and ran amok, looting and burning farms and houses and thus inadvertently giving the expedition one of its several other names, the Applejack Raid. Warren reached Belfield on December 9. The bridge over the Meherrin was guarded by a scratch force under Colonel John J. Garnett, consisting largely of boys from the North Carolina Junior Reserves. Strengthened by the 63rd North Carolina, which Hampton had sent on in advance, Garnett's force "opened fire rapidly and with effect, driving [the enemy] back promptly."[45] With the arrival of the main Confederate force, Warren retreated back north in bitterly cold weather along the line of the railroad, pursued and harassed by Hampton's cavalry. The bulk of Hampton's men returned to camp on December 11, but the 63rd continued the pursuit until Warren had crossed the Nottoway.

That winter was a particularly hard one, and the cavalry suffered no less than the infantry. "Our cavalry has to be dispersed for want of forage," Lee wrote to Secretary of War James Seddon on February 8, 1865.[46] Barringer's brigade, for example, had been sent into winter quarters near Belfield, some distance from the army, so that when called upon to picket, the men had to travel for 30 miles. Evidence of the lengths to which the cavalry had to go in order to find forage can be found in a handwritten receipt dated January 2, 1865, at Guinea Station, signed by Captain Robert E. Cochrane, Assistant Quartermaster of the 63rd North Carolina, and George Adderton and showing that Adderton had been paid $12.10 for supplying one bushel of corn and 270 bushels of fodder.[47] Presumably Adderton—and, by implication, other members of the regiment—had been sent home for this purpose.

One final letter from Adderton survives somewhere, because a partial transcript of it, with the spelling and grammar corrected, can be found on the Olive Tree Genealogy website, having been posted there on September 10, 2004.[48] It was apparently dated March 2, 1865, "at Camp Near Stoney Creek Virginia" and reads (in the corrected version):

> I hear that all you in North Carolina are all scared to death about the Yankees. I don't think there is much danger. I recon the home guards are scared to death but I think they will hear the eleventh bellow before this war comes to a close. I hear there is a good many ? in Randolph County, but I think they will be caught and punished.

Whoever posted the partial transcript suggests, in the accompanying introduction, that by "the eleventh" Adderton is referring to the 11th Battalion, North Carolina Home Guard. This seems unlikely, first because of Adderton's previous remarks about the Home Guard in general and secondly because the 11th Battalion apparently operated in Watauga County, in the mountains of the west of the state. The 5th Battalion was Randolph County's Home Guard unit. Unfortunately, without seeing the original letter, it is impossible to know what exactly Adderton wrote. I contacted Lorine McGinnis Schulze, who created the website, but unfortunately she was unable to tell me, at this distance, who had submitted Adderton's letter. A useful article by William T. Auman in *The North Carolina Historical Review* covers the subject of disaffection during the Civil War in Randolph County, which had a sizeable community of both Quakers and Germans.[49] It is possible that Adderton wrote "seventh," since on February 26, 1865, at Governor Vance's request, Lee sent the 7th North Carolina, with a detachment from the 46th, into Randolph County "for the purpose of arresting and returning deserters from the army to their proper commands," as the regimental history puts it.[50] The missing word in the transcript, then, could in that case be "deserters."

In the meantime, there had been a reorganization of the command of the 63rd North Carolina. On January 5, 1865, Major James H. McNeill was promoted to colonel, to rank from November 24, 1864, while in March Captain Elias F. Shaw of Company C was promoted to lieutenant colonel to rank from January 28. Then on March 31 came the battle of Chamberlain Run (Dinwiddie Court House), described by Means as "the most fearful and fiercest battle we were ever in."[51] A 1999 article by Mark Crawford gives a full description of this battle, largely from the Union point of view.[52] The battle is naturally also covered in some detail in Sheridan Barringer's book on Rufus Barringer and his brigade.[53]

On March 29, Grant sent Sheridan and his cavalry off on a flanking movement towards Dinwiddie Court House on the Confederate right. To counter this, Lee swiftly ordered up Pickett's division to protect his right, while Rooney Lee's men, including Barringer's brigade, were summoned from the Stony Creek area to unite with Fitzhugh Lee and the rest of the cavalry at the crossroads of Five Forks, a short distance north of Dinwiddie Court House. Having had to make a detour around Sheridan, Rooney Lee finally arrived at the rendezvous early in the morning of March 31. As the cavalry, on the right of the Confederate line, advanced at about 11 a.m., they discovered that a small advance force of the enemy had already crossed Chamberlain Run, in their immediate front. These they quickly drove back to the far side, where the rest of Sheridan's left hastily began to dig in. Barringer had three of his four regiments with him. Together with the 63rd North Carolina were the 9th (1st Cavalry) and 19th (2nd Cavalry) regiments. With these he was ordered to attack. Chamberlain Run was normally no more than a small stream flowing south into Stony Creek. At this time, however, according to Colonel William H. Cheek of the 9th North Carolina, it was "very swollen by recent heavy rains, and at places was impassable by reason of briars and swamp undergrowth."[54] Sergeant Coltrane of the 63rd recalled being "dismounted with cartridge box in one hand and rifle in the other struggling to stay on our feet in the current."[55] Nevertheless, the two regiments waded through the water "by fours" and took up position on the far side, the 9th North Carolina on the left and Colonel McNeill and the 63rd on the right. While the 19th was waiting to cross and form up between them, through some error a small detachment of Virginia cavalry was ordered across the ford, mounted, ahead of it. The Virginians splashed through the water and up the hill on the far side, where they were swiftly driven back by Sheridan's men, the bulk of whom were armed with 16-shot Henry repeating rifles. Rushing back down into Chamberlain Run in their haste to find safety, the Virginians became entangled with the 19th, which was just attempting to cross. The men standing their ground on the far side, meanwhile, were rapidly running out of ammunition. In the 63rd, both Colonel McNeill and Lieutenant Colonel Shaw were killed, and eventually the whole line was forced to retire and struggle back across the stream.

There was now a lull in the fighting, broken only by some sharpshooting across the creek from both sides. At one point, a regimental band appeared behind the Union lines and struck up "Yankee Doodle," which the Confederates received, a Union soldier reported, "with yells and shouts of derision."[56] In the meantime, Pickett's infantry had succeeded in crossing Chamberlain Run on the left, a mile upstream, threatening Sheridan's right and center. Barringer was now ordered to attack again, and at about 4 o'clock the men went forward once more. The 9th North Carolina crossed first on the left in order to draw the enemy's fire. The 19th then crossed at the ford, followed by the 63rd, now under the command of Captain John R. Erwin of Company F. As the North Carolinians stepped into the water, a Union officer heard one of them shout, "Wind up them guns, Yanks!"[57] This time, however, even the 16-shot Henrys could not stop Barringer's men. The 19th deployed to the left and the 63rd to the right, and finally both swept forward and drove Sheridan's men from their position and right back to Dinwiddie Court House, where his reserves were entrenched, in what one Ohio trooper admitted was "a pell mell retreat."[58] A member of McGregor's Battery who witnessed the attack wrote later that he "never saw such a splendid charge. They simply swept everything out of their way."[59] Barringer himself described the battle as "the last marked victory won by our arms,"[60] but it had been won at a terrible cost; his three regiments had only two field officers left between them. George Adderton's company commander, Captain Wharton, had been captured and was not released from Johnson's Island until June 17, when he finally agreed to take the oath of allegiance.

Learning that Federal infantry was advancing on his left, at about 3 a.m. the following morning, April 1, Pickett ordered the men back to their original position at Five Forks. Here the 63rd was dismounted and placed in shallow earthworks to the right of Pickett's infantry, with the rest of Barringer's brigade, mounted, on its right. Late that afternoon, Sheridan sent the V Corps against the left flank of Pickett's infantry, while Pickett himself was unadvisedly absent at a shad-bake. The Union attack overwhelmed his division, capturing numbers of men and forcing the rest to retreat. McGregor's artilleryman remembered it as "a stampede."[61] The cavalry on the right, however, mounted and dismounted, continued to resist until the last moment, thus allowing the remnants of the infantry to escape. They then withdrew in good order. Rooney Lee's division, with Barringer's brigade forming the rear guard, continued to cover the retreating column until it reached Namozine Church. Here, on April 3, Rooney Lee ordered Barringer to hold the position "to the last"[62] while the remainder moved on. Barringer's three regiments between them could now muster only 800 men. He placed the 9th North Carolina, mounted, on the left, the 19th, also mounted, in the center and the 63rd, dismounted, on the right. A single gun from McGregor's Battery was with them. Barringer's men drove back the initial attacks by Custer's division but were finally overwhelmed, the 63rd, still under Captain Erwin, being the last to retire. Barringer said later that it "fought with obstinacy and seemed slow to give up the contest" when ordered to withdraw.[63] Some of the men, recalled Captain Charles W. Pearson of Company H, "got into a large body of timber which shielded us. By walking all day, all night and all the next day, almost without stopping, we got out."[64] They were at Pannell's Bridge on the Staunton River when they heard the news of Lee's surrender. "We went to Danville," wrote Captain Erwin later, "but without orders, and after we reached there each Captain took command of his company and inquired the nearest way to their respective homes."[65] The war was over for the 63rd North Carolina.

Exactly how and when George Adderton returned to Randolph County we do not know, but we do know that he eventually reached home safely. The 1870 census shows him back on the farm, together with his wife and his mother. He was no longer postmaster of Hill's Store; the Confederate post office there had closed down by the end of April 1865, and on February 14, 1866, Susannah L. Keenous had been appointed the new U.S. postmaster. The value of his assets had changed, too, since before the war; the census now lists him as worth $2,500 in real estate, with a personal estate worth $1,000. This was still a substantial enough figure, however, and he and Adaline were able to afford a cook, a 14-year-old white girl called Mariah Peacock. Living next door to him were Joseph and Troy Adderton and their, by now, four sons, and it is at this point that George Adderton's short letter to his wife of November 25, 1863, suddenly becomes interesting.

Having discovered initially from a brief entry on the internet that their surname was Adderton and that they were born respectively in 1832 and 1835, I had naturally assumed from the tone of George Adderton's letter that Joseph and Troy must be his younger brother and his sister-in-law. The 1870 U.S. Census, however, has a column headed "Color," the options given being "White (W.)," "Black (B.)," "Mulatto (M.)," "Chinese (C.)" and "Indian (I.)." While "W" appears in this column against the names of George, Adaline and Abigail Adderton and their cook, opposite the names of Joseph and Troy Adderton and their sons is the letter "B." In other words, Joseph and Troy Adderton, now aged 38 and 35, are the 28-year-old and 25-year-old slaves shown in the 1860 census. What we have, then, in George Adderton's November 1863 letter to Adaline, is a Confederate private soldier not just asking after the welfare of his two slaves and their children but asking them to write to him.

At the very least, this provides us with a glimpse of a rather unexpected side of Southern slavery. When we think of slavery, most of us probably have a mental picture of the big plantations like Tara in *Gone with the Wind*. Yet the owners of these vast plantations represented only a tiny proportion of the total number of slaveholders. Far more numerous (although still a minority in the population as a whole, given that most Southern families actually had no slaves) were small famers like George Adderton, owning just one or two slaves. Here, the family members would naturally have worked in the field alongside their slaves. It would not be totally surprising, then, if in these circumstances a feeling of mutual trust, and even almost of friendship, developed in time between master and slave. This, of course, does not justify slavery, but it does remind us that nothing involving human relations is ever quite as simple and straightforward as it may appear on the outside. George Adderton's case is unlikely to have been unique.

In the 1880 census, George Adderton's profession, "Farmer" in the previous census, appears as the more specific "Grain Farmer." His mother, aged 77, was still living with him and Adaline. Living with them also at this stage were the two eldest sons of Joseph and Troy Adderton, Adam, aged 21, and George C., aged 16. George C. must therefore be the baby mentioned in George Adderton's 1863 letter. Their relationship to the head of the household is shown as "Servant" and their profession as "Farm Laborer."

George Adderton died on November 8, 1893, and was buried in Farmer United Methodist Church Cemetery. He had drawn up his will on March 8, 1888. In this, he left "to Joseph Adderton and his heirs absolute and forever all the balance of the tract of land on which he now lives" and "to Adam S. Adderton and his heirs absolute and forever all that tract of land on which he now lives." These two tracts of land consisted of 150 acres and 115 acres respectively. The rest of the land, some 414 acres, he left to Adaline, but the bulk of this was to go on her death to the various other sons of Joseph and Troy Adderton "and their heirs, jointly and severally absolute and forever." In other words, George Adderton had left everything to the family of his former slaves.

Unfortunately, he had also left substantial debts. A sale of farm animals and equipment on March 2, 1894, raised $121.09, of which a single mule accounted for $60.00. A further sale of mainly household effects on June 24, 1898, produced only $31.83. Since this and the proceeds of the sale of Adderton's interest in a mill left some $1,500 of debt still outstanding, Adaline and her co-executor, B.W. Steed, petitioned the Superior Court on May 5, 1899, for authority to sell the land by public auction. While the various individual tracts of land are listed specifically in the petition, the 150 acres bequeathed to Joseph Adderton are not mentioned; the executors' case is listed simply as being "vs Adam S. Adderton & Others."

We know that a Joseph Adderton died sometime before August 31, 1893, and that a G.R. Adderton bought an axle and some lumber at the sale of his personal effects the following month, so we can presume that this was the same man.[66] What, though, happened to the land left to him and his heirs "absolute and forever"?

In any case, the court having granted permission, the rest of the land was finally sold at auction on January 2, 1900, the court stipulating that the executors use the proceeds to pay off the various debts and administrative charges "after first deducting the cost of this suit." Any surplus was to be "regarded as real estate" and "paid out under the direction of this Court, to and among the persons who would have been entitled to the land itself according to law."[67] It would be good to think that the black Addertons received something in the end, as George Adderton had wished. Certainly Adaline can have made no profit from the sale, because on July 6, 1908, now living in Asheboro, she applied for a Confederate widow's pension.[68] She died in 1918.

Chapter Notes

Preface

1. Juliet Wilson-Bareau with David C. Degener, *Manet and the American Civil War* (New York, 2003).
2. Jean-Pierre Deloux, *Le Corsaire Alabama* (Paris, 2001): "que la guerre de Sécession n'est pas terminée et qu'elle concerne directement l'Europe contemporaine, menacée par les rêves mondialistes de l'impérialisme yankee." The book consists largely of extracts from the 1864 French translation of *The Cruise of the Alabama and the Sumter*, with a linking commentary.

Chapter 1

1. *Dictionary of National Biography*.
2. W.W. Rouse Ball and J.A. Venn, *Admissions to Trinity College, 1851–1900. Admissions to Trinity College, 1901–1989*.
3. *All Saints, Margaret Street* (Pitkin Pictorials, Andover, Hampshire, 1990).
4. *The Times*, October 21, 1887.
5. A.J.B. Beresford Hope, *A Popular View of the American Civil War* and *England, the North, and the South*, published together as *England, the North, and the South: Being a Popular View of the American Civil War* (fourth edition, London and Maidstone, 1862).
6. Letter to the Rev. Benjamin Webb, 1851, quoted in John Newman, *The Buildings of England: West Kent and the Weald* (London, 1969).
7. A.J.B. Beresford Hope, *The Social and Political Bearings of the American Disruption* (second edition, London and Maidstone, 1863).
8. General Sir Henry Havelock was one of the great British heroes of the Indian Mutiny of 1857. He died at Lucknow of dysentery in November of that year.
9. *The Times*, October 17, 1863.
10. See *The Index*, October 15, 1863 and January 14, 1864. Wharncliffe's splendid London residence, Wharncliffe House, Curzon Street, is today the Embassy of Saudi Arabia.
11. *Liverpool Daily Post*, October 18–19, 1864.
12. *The Times*, October 21, 1887.
13. Gordon W. Batchelor, *The Beresfords of Bedgebury Park* (Goudhurst, Kent, 1996), pp. 114–115.
14. *The Daily Telegraph*, October 1887, quoted in Batchelor, p. 114.
15. Batchelor, pp. 115–117; James M. Morgan, Jr: *The Jackson-Hope and the Society of the Cincinnati Medals of the Virginia Military Institute* (Verona, Virginia, 1979).
16. He received an LL.D from Washington and Lee in 1881. His Honorary Doctorate in Civil Law from the University of the South was awarded in 1874 (information from Vaughan Stanley, Special Collections Librarian, Washington and Lee University, Lexington, Virginia and Annie Armour, Archives, Rare Books and Preservation, the University of the South, Sewanee, Tennessee, September 2002). The obituary in *The Times* states erroneously that both awards were made in 1881.
17. Hudson Strode (ed.), *Jefferson Davis: Private Letters 1823–1889* (New York, 1966, reprinted 1995), pp. 293, 550.
18. Strode, p. 304.
19. Strode, p. 510.
20. Strode, p. 550.
21. *The Times*, October 27 and 28, 1887.

Chaper 2

1. G.F. Russell Barker and Alan H. Stenning, *The Record of Old Westminsters*, Vol. I (London, 1928).
2. Information from Yvonne Sibbald, Librarian of the Alpine Club, May 2005.
3. Russell Barker and Stenning.
4. The Russian Emperor Nicholas I had invaded Moldavia and Wallachia, then part of the Ottoman Empire, in 1853, thus precipitating the Crimean War.
5. Latin, literally "On the threshold."
6. Joseph Barker, the controversial former Methodist preacher and freethinker, published his *Review* in 1861–1863. He had spent the years 1851–1859 in the United States and had bought

land in Nebraska before returning to England. Although originally a fervent abolitionist, he was one of the Confederacy's most effective propagandists in England during the first two years of the war, speaking on behalf of the South all over Lancashire and in other parts of the country as well.

7. Alexis de Tocqueville's *Democracy in America* was published in two separate volumes in 1835 and 1840.

8. *The Saturday Review* was started in 1855 by Alexander Beresford Hope in partnership with John Douglas Cook.

9. This is William, son of the U.S. politician and orator Edward Everett; William Everett had gone up to Trinity in 1859, aged 20, and was elected President of the Cambridge Union Society for the Michaelmas Term, 1862. The elder Everett gave the principal speech at the dedication of the National Cemetery at Gettysburg on November 19, 1863, followed by Abraham Lincoln.

10. Fernando Álvarez de Toledo, Duke of Alba or Alva, put down the revolt of the Netherlands in 1567–1568.

11. Latin, "Among the first."

12. "He softens their passions and controls their anger" (Virgil: *Aeneid* Book I, line 57).

13. Charles Henry Tawney had been at Rugby School with Sidgwick and had gone up to Trinity in 1856, the same year as Cowell. Elected a Fellow of the College in 1860, he joined the Bengal Department of Education in 1864.

14. Unidentified.

15. Melville's *Directory of Sussex* for 1858 gives it as the residence of a Walter Gower; of the 23 buildings in Grand Parade listed in the *Directory*, no less than 14 were lodging houses. Both No. 21 and No. 3 were still standing in 2005.

16. Information from the Office of Hastings Crematorium and Cemetery, April 2005. The grave is in Division A, Section W, Row G, Number 9.

17. A.L. Mumm's *Alpine Club Register* states that Cowell had contracted an illness while climbing in Italy in 1861 "from which he never entirely recovered."

Chapter 3

1. As far as Lancashire was concerned, at least.

2. Royden Harrison, "British Labour and the Confederacy," *International Review of Social History*, April 1957.

3. Mary Ellison, *Support for Secession: Lancashire and the American Civil War* (Chicago, 1972). Professor Jones's comment above appears in his Epilogue to Dr. Ellison's book).

4. Michael Brook, "Confederate Sympathies in North-East Lancashire, 1862–1864," *Transactions of the Lancashire and Cheshire Antiquarian Society*, Vols. 75 and 76, 1965–6.

5. Douglas Maynard, "Civil War 'Care'; the Mission of the *George Griswold*," *The New England Quarterly*, Vol. 34, No. 3 (September 1961); "The Manchester Operatives; a Turbulent Meeting in Manchester," *The New York Times*, March 29, 1863, copied from *The Manchester Guardian*.

6. Amanda Foreman, *A World on Fire* (London, 2010), p. xxxv.

7. R.J.M .Blackett., *Divided Hearts: Britain and the American Civil War* (Baton Rouge, 2001).

8. See above, Chapter 2, note 6.

9. T.E.A. Verity, "Edward Arundel Verity, Vicar of Habergham," ed. J.T. Ward, *Transactions of the Lancashire and Cheshire Antiquarian Society*, Vol. 79, 1977. Royden Harrison (see above) refers to Verity as a "Tory Democrat."

10. Simon Rennie, "'This 'Merikay War': Poetic Responses in Lancashire to the American Civil War," *Journal of Victorian Culture*, 2020, Vol. 25, No.1; http://cottonfaminepoetry.exeter.ac.uk.

Chapter 4

1. Mary Boykin Chesnut (ed. Ben Ames Williams), *A Diary from Dixie* (Cambridge, MA, 1949), p. 126.

2. Frank Lawrence Owsley, *King Cotton Diplomacy* (2nd edition, revised by Harriet Chappell Owsley, Chicago, 1959), p.77.

3. Don H. Doyle, *The Cause of All Nations* (New York, 2015), pp. 39–40.

4. Edwin De Leon (ed. William C. Davis), *Secret History of Confederate Diplomacy Abroad* (Kansas, 2005), p. 50.

5. Owsley, pp. 51–52.

6. The Bath Hotel was at 25 Arlington Street, on the corner of Piccadilly. The Ritz now covers the site.

7. Thomson was U.S. Consul at Southampton from 1859 to 1861 and then from 1869 to 1876. He died in Southampton in 1887. He was presumably removed from his post in 1861 because of his Confederate sympathies.

8. The Westminster Palace Hotel was at 6 Victoria Street, on the corner of Tothill Street and diagonally opposite Westminster Abbey. The building no longer survives.

9. The house, which is still standing, is listed in the London Directory for 1861 as owned by one Arthur Newman Dare.

10. *Official Records of the Union and Confederate Navies in the War of the Rebellion* (Washington, DC, 1894–1927), Series II, Vol. 3, p. 273.

11. Caleb Huse, *The Supplies for the Confederate Army: How They Were Obtained in Europe and How Paid For* (Boston, MA 1904), pp. 29–30.

12. *The New York Times*, November 25, 1861. The version in *The Illustrated London News* is exactly the same, except that it omits the audience's reaction.

13. *The Saturday Review*, November 16, 1861.

Chapter 5

1. *Dictionary of National Biography* (hereafter cited as *DNB*); *Oxford Dictionary of National Biography* (hereafter cited as *ODNB*). The original entry on Hobart Pasha, by Stanley Lane-Poole (1891), was revised for the *ODNB* in 2004 by Andrew Lambert.
2. *Burke's Peerage*, 107th Edition (2003).
3. *DNB*.
4. Hobart Pasha, *Sketches from My Life* (London, 1887).
5. [J.K. Laughton], "The Adventures of Hobart Pasha," *The Edinburgh Review*, No. 337, January, 1887, pp. 150–181.
6. *The Times*, Monday, June 21, 1886.
7. *The Edinburgh Review*, p. 153.
8. "Captain Roberts," *Never Caught* (London, 1867, reprinted North Carolina, 1967), p. 58.
9. *The Times*, Monday, June 21, 1886.
10. *The Edinburgh Review*, p. 174.
11. Glen N. Wiche, ed., *Dispatches from Bermuda; the Civil War Letters of Charles Maxwell Allen, United States Consul at Bermuda, 1861–1888* (Kent, Ohio, 2008), p. 99.
12. "Captain Roberts," pp. 11, 13.
13. Wiche, p. 112.
14. "Captain Roberts," p. 40.
15. *The New York Times*, January 8, 1893.
16. Wiche, p. 143.
17. Among the passengers was the Southern spy Rose O'Neal Greenhow, who drowned, weighed down by the gold she was carrying, when the boat in which she was trying to reach the shore overturned.
18. "Captain Roberts" p. 44.
19. Eric J. Graham, *Clyde Built: Blockade Runners, Cruisers and Armoured Rams of the American Civil War* (Edinburgh, 2006), p. 117.
20. "Captain Roberts," pp. 49–51.
21. Graham, p. 203.
22. *The New York Times*, January 8, 1893.
23. Hobart Pasha, pp. 186–189.
24. Dilara Dal, *The Modernization of the Ottoman Navy during the Reign of Sultan Abdülaziz (1861–1876)* (doctoral thesis, University of Birmingham, April 2015), pp. 88–92. I am grateful to Emir Yener for kindly supplying me with a copy of this very useful source.
25. Hobart Pasha, pp. 190–198.
26. *The Times*, June 21, 1886.
27. Dal, p. 95.
28. Dal, pp. 1, 48, 247, 264. Dr. Dal is careful to specify "the third largest navy *of Europe*" [my italics], but in practice that would mean, at that period, "of the world."
29. Dal, pp. 83, 96.
30. Hobart Pasha, pp. 204–208.
31. Hobart Pasha, p. 218; *The Times*, January 21, 1886.
32. Hobart Pasha, p. 200.
33. *DNB*.
34. *The Times*, Tuesday, June 29, 1886.
35. *The Daily Telegraph*, Monday, June 21, 1886.
36. Author's visit, 2007, 2009.
37. Author's visit, 2009.
38. Author's visit, 2008.

Chapter 6

1. Lieut. Col. Fremantle, *Three Months in the Southern States* (Mobile, 1864), p. 79; Walter Lord (ed.), *The Fremantle Diary* (Boston, 1954), p. 122.
2. Craig L. Symonds, *Stonewall of the West* (Kansas, 1997); Mauriel Phillips Joslyn (ed.), *A Meteor Shining Brightly* (Milledgeville, Georgia, 1997).
3. Sue Cliborn Forbes, "Dr Christopher James Cleborne," *Claiborne Clan Newsletter*, Vol. 3, Issue 4, December 2002 (The National Society of Claiborne Family Descendants).
4. "A Brief History of Cliburn" (Cliburn Parish website).

Chapter 7

1. Eton College Archives; J.A. Venn, *Alumni Cantabrigienses*, Part II, Vol. II (Cambridge University Press, 1944).
2. "*In England die Löhne der Sache nach niedriger für den Fabrikanten sind als auf dem Kontinent, obwohl sie für den Arbeiter höher sein mögen*"; the translation is mine from the original German.
3. J.A. Venn.
4. W. Marston Acres, *The Bank of England from Within*, Vol. II (Oxford University Press, 1931). The Bank of England Archive has the original agreement, drawn up by Freshfields on October 14, 1834. Cowell's salary was to be £600 p.a.
5. W. Marston Acres.
6. W. Marston Acres. Sir John Clapham, *The Bank of England: a History*, Vol. II (Cambridge University Press, 1944).
7. I am grateful to Sarah Millard and Jenny Mountain of the Bank of England Archive for their help in my researches.
8. This and all subsequent quotations from the pamphlet are translated directly from the French text.
9. Reproduced in full, in translation, in John Bigelow: *Retrospections of an Active Life*, Vol. III, pp. 4–42 (New York, 1909).
10. 21 Grand Parade. The owner was one René Lecieux.

Chapter 8

1. See, for example, "Could the Confederacy Have Won the Civil War?" in *North and South*, Vol. 9, Number 2.

2. Beckles Willson, *John Slidell and the Confederates in Paris (1862–65)* (New York, 1932), pp. 151–153; John Bigelow, *Retrospections of an Active Life* (New York, 1909), Vol. II, pp. 120–121. Willson, quoting from the Eustis Papers, gives the boy's name as Truro and says that he was from New York. Bigelow spells the name "Trouro" and states that he was from New Orleans; this seems improbable.

3. "Proceedings of the Supreme Court Relative to the Death of Justice Ogden and Mr. Dayton," in *The Daily True American*, Trenton, New Jersey, March 3, 1865. The relevant pages are among the William Lewis Dayton Papers, Manuscripts Division, Department of Rare Books and Special Collections, Princeton University Library, Box 4, Folder 8.

4. *American National Biography* (New York, 1999), Vol. VI; *The Daily True American*, March 3, 1865.

5. Frank Lawrence Owsley, *King Cotton Diplomacy* (2nd. Edition, revised, Chicago, 1959), pp. 8–11.

6. Though it was used before him by John Randolph of Roanoke and coined in 1791 by Sir James Mackintosh.

7. W.S. Gilbert, *Iolanthe*.

8. Paul Pecquet du Bellet, *Lettre à l'Empereur: de la Reconnaissance des États Confédérés d'Amérique* (Paris, 1862).

9. See, for example, Slidell's letter of March 26, 1862, to Hunter, *Official Records of the Union and Confederate Navies in the War of the Rebellion*, Series II, Vol. 3, p. 372, and his letter of July 17, 1864, to Mason in the Mason Papers, Library of Congress.

10. See previous chapter.

11. Salwa Nacouzi, "Les Créoles Louisianais Défendent la Cause du Sud à Paris (1861–1865): Latinisme contre Anglosaxonisme," in *Transatlantica* 1, 2002.

12. The phrase was used by the Radical M.P. John Arthur Roebuck at a banquet in his Sheffield constituency on August 14, 1862.

13. Edwin De Leon, *Secret History of Confederate Diplomacy Abroad*, ed. William C. Davis (Kansas, 2005).

14. *American National Biography*.

15. Bigelow, Vol. I, p. 365.

16. *American National Biography*. The author of the entry on Dayton is Professor Norman B. Ferris of Middle Tennessee State University.

17. Bigelow, Vol. II, pp. 237–241. The church was demolished after the site was sold to *The New York Herald-Tribune* in 1931.

18. Damien-Claude Bélanger, "Quebec History," (Marianopolis College, 2004).

19. Later famous as an expert on Christopher Columbus.

20. The late Christopher Dickey was told by Beckles Willson's grandson, Anthony, that the book had been written in great haste in order to meet a ten-week deadline and that there had been "no time" for an index but that his grandfather had been in direct contact with descendants of both Slidell and Caleb Huse. Christopher Dickey, email to author, February 2, 2015.

21. Serge Noirsain, "The Strange Death of Mr. Dayton." The article is available on the Association's website in an English translation by Gérard Hawkins. Despite the kind efforts of Monsieur Hawkins, I have been unable to locate a copy of the original French version.

22. The British call girl whose liaisons with the British Secretary of State for War and an official at the Soviet Embassy led to the former's disgrace and resignation in 1963.

23. Correspondence with Robert L. Folstein of the Jacques Offenbach Society, 2003. See also the Society's Newsletter, Nos. 23 and 24 (March and June 2003).

24. See Note 3, above. The Attorney General of New Jersey at this time was Frederick T. Frelinghuysen.

25. Neither word would be spelled with a capital letter in French, which was therefore presumably the doctor's first language.

26. Dayton Papers, Box 6, Folder 5.

27. Bigelow, Vol. II, pp. 234–235, 237.

28. Maria Monk, *The Awful Disclosures of Maria Monk: the Hidden Secrets of a Nun's Life in a Convent Exposed* (New York, 1836).

29. The Rev. J.J. Slocum was apparently the main author. *The True History of Maria Monk* (London, 1895) contains Maria Monk's mother's affidavit and a summary of Col. Stone's report, which he had published as a pamphlet.

30. Mrs. L. St. John Eckel, *Maria Monk's Daughter: an Autobiography* (New York, 1874).

31. Eckel, *op.cit.*; Leonard Twynham, *Maria Monk's Daughter of Sharon and Amenia: the True Story of Lizzie St. John Eckel and Her Church on the Hill* (privately printed, Flushing, NY, 1932).

32. Christopher Dickey suggests (email to author, January 29, 2015) that this could also have been Henry Shelton Sanford, U.S. Minister to Belgium, who was in charge of Seward's secret service operations in Europe and travelled regularly to Paris. All the evidence, however, indicates that it was Bigelow.

33. Eckel, pp. 108–119.

34. Willson, pp. 76–77.

35. Bigelow, *France and the Confederate Navy 1862–1868: an International Episode* (New York, 1888), p. 168.

36. As Christopher Dickey points out (email to author, January 29, 2015), another possibility, of course, is that the ubiquitous Sanford could have added her to his extensive list of useful informants.

37. Eckel, pp. 111, 115.

38. Dayton Papers, Box 6, Folder 4.

39. Bigelow, *Retrospections*, Vol. II, p. 329.

40. Don H. Doyle, *The Cause of All Nations* (New York, 2015), pp. 297–298, p. 366 note 41. Email to author, July 6, 2015.

Chapter 9

1. *Official Records of the Union and Confederate Navies in the War of the Rebellion* (Washington, DC, 1894–1927), Series I, Vol. 3 (hereafter cited as *ORN* I:3), p. 652: Semmes to Barron, June 14, 1864.
2. *ORN* I:3, p. 674: Extracts from the journal of Captain Semmes, C.S. Navy, commanding the CSS *Alabama*, April 1 to June 16, 1864 (hereafter cited as Semmes Journal), May 21, 1864.
3. *ORN* I:3, p. 676: Semmes Journal, June 11, 1864.
4. Paul Ingouf-Knocker, *Coulez l'Alabama!* (Cherbourg 1976, revised 2002), p. 25.
5. Ingouf-Knocker, p. 22.
6. Service Historique de la Défense, Cherbourg: Le Vice-Amiral Préfet Maritime du 1er Arrondissement, Augustin Dupouy, à Son Excellence Monsieur le Ministre de la Marine et des Colonies, à Paris (hereafter cited as SHD, Dupouy to Minister), June 25, 1864.
7. Ingouf-Knocker, p. 25.
8. Admiral Raphael Semmes, *Memoirs of Service Afloat During the War Between the States* (Baltimore, 1869), p. 751; Ingouf-Knocker, p. 26.
9. Ingouf-Knocker, p. 26.
10. This little building still survives at the end of the rue de l'Onglet. It now houses the offices of a center for watersports.
11. *ORN* I:3, p. 676: Semmes Journal, June 11, 1864; Ingouf-Knocker, p. 27.
12. *ORN* I:3, p. 676: Semmes Journal, June 10, 1864.
13. *ORN* I:3, p. 651: Semmes to Barron, June 13, 1864.
14. *ORN* I:3, p. 676: Semmes Journal, June 12, 1864.
15. Ingouf-Knocker, pp. 27–28.
16. *ORN* I:3, p. 652: Semmes to Barron, June 14, 1864.
17. There has been much confusion over Bonfils's Christian name, probably partly because a number of the men in the Bonfils family appear to have had the same two first names, Joseph Marie, and were therefore known by their third name. Ingouf-Knocker (p. 24) refers to "M. Joseph Bonfils, vice-consul du Brésil" and says that his eldest son, Amédée, "est depuis peu investi de la charge d'Agent consulaire des Etats Confédérés" ("had recently been appointed Confederate consular agent"). Slidell, Confederate Commissioner to France, refers (*ORN* I:3, p. 661) to "Mr. Auguste Bonfils." Semmes, however, writes (*ORN* I:3, p. 648) to "Ad. Bonfils, Esq." and Bonfils signs himself "Ad. Bonfils" in a letter to Slidell (*ORN* I:3, p. 662). The full name of the Brazilian Consul at Cherbourg was Joseph Marie *Adolphe* Bonfils, and he was generally known as Adolphe. There seems little doubt, then, that the same man was also the Confederate consular agent. He was born in 1800 and was thus 64 in 1864. His eldest son Joseph Marie *Gustave* Adolphe (born 1821), known as Gustave, signed the death certificates of the three Confederate dead after the battle of June 19, describing himself as "Agent des Etats du Sud de l'Amérique" ("agent of the Southern States of America").
18. *ORN* I:3, p. 661: Slidell to Benjamin, June 30, 1864.
19. *ORN* I:3, p. 647: Slidell to Semmes, June 12, 1864.
20. Ingouf-Knocker, p. 24.
21. *ORN* I:3, p. 677: Semmes Journal, June 13, 1864.
22. See Penhoat's official report on the battle in *The American Historical Review*, Vol. XXIII (1917–1918), pp. 119–123: "Le *Kerseage* se présente devant la passe de l'Est sans entrer" (p. 121).
23. SHD, Dupouy to Minister, June 15, 1864; Ingouf-Knocker, p. 50.
24. John McIntosh Kell, *Recollections of a Naval Life, including the cruises of the Confederate States Steamers "Sumter" and "Alabama"* (Washington, DC, 1900), p. 245.
25. *ORN* I:3, p. 651: Semmes to Barron, June 14, 1864.
26. Norman C. Delaney, *John McIntosh Kell of the Raider "Alabama"* (University, Alabama, 1973), p. 159; Stephen Fox, *Wolf of the Deep* (New York, 2007), p. 213. Delaney is quoting from the interview given by Kell in 1883 to "Wood Holt" (Alfred Iverson Branham) of the *Atlanta Constitution*, but Fox points out that, in an interview of ca. 1885 with Wood Holt, Kell had recalled Semmes's phrase as "that dirty rag," which Fox feels is more probable.
27. Kell, p. 245.
28. Kell, p. 245.
29. *ORN* I:3, p. 673: Semmes Journal, May 12, 1864; William Marvel, *The Alabama and the Kearsarge: the Sailor's Civil War* (Chapel Hill, NC, 1996), p. 229.
30. *ORN* I:3, p. 664: Semmes to Barron, July 5, 1864; John M. Taylor, *Confederate Raider: Raphael Semmes of the "Alabama"* (Washington, DC, 1994), p. 199.
31. Fox, p. 228 and endnote, p. 297. Breedlove Smith's first name is usually given as William, but according to Maurice Rigby it was actually Wightman.
32. Arthur Sinclair, *Two Years on the Alabama* (London, 1896), p. 261.
33. Douglas French Forrest (ed. William N. Still, Jr.), *Odyssey in Gray: a Diary of Confederate Service, 1863–1865* (Richmond, Virginia, 1979), p. 179.
34. Reproduced in *ORN* I:3, p. 648.
35. Liais lived at 1 rue du Val de Saire and Bonfils at 40 rue du Val de Saire. Both buildings survive today (2013), the former as a savings bank.
36. *ORN* I:3, p. 651: Semmes to Barron, June 14, 1864.
37. Ingouf-Knocker, p. 67 (though he appears

to think that the funds were deposited with Bonfils on June 18, the day before the battle).

38. SHD, Dupouy to Minister, June 15, 1864.
39. *ORN* I:3, p. 652: Semmes to Barron, June 16, 1864.
40. SHD, Dupouy to Minister, June 15, 1864.
41. Reproduced (in translation) in *ORN* I:3, p. 58, enclosure in letter from W.L. Dayton to William H. Seward, June 17, 1864.
42. SHD, Dupouy to Minister, June 15, 1864.
43. Ingouf-Knocker, pp. 18–21.
44. Ingouf-Knocker, pp. 56–60.
45. *Ibid.*
46. Ingouf-Knocker, p. 60, quoting Gaston Maillard of "La Gazette des Étrangers."
47. SHD, Dupouy to Minister, June 16, 1864.
48. Ingouf-Knocker, p. 63.
49. Mme. Octave Feuillet, *Quelques Années de Ma Vie* (seventh edition, Paris, 1899), p. 274 ("un petit homme sec et légèrement voûté, ayant un peu de la tournure du premier Empereur"). See next chapter.
50. Fox, pp. 215, 229; *The Times*, June 21, 1864; Frank J. Merli (edited David M. Fahey), *The Alabama, British Neutrality and the American Civil War* (Bloomington, Indiana, 2004), p. 144.
51. Marvel, p. 247. See also Captain Evan Parry Jones's statement in Sinclair, p. 287.
52. This circular fort still stands in the sea at the west end of the harbor, just below Querqueville.
53. Ingouf-Knocker, p. 66.
54. William Lewis Dayton, Junior, to William L. Dayton, Envoy Extraordinary and Minister Plenipotentiary of the United States at Paris, France, June 22, 1864, in Box 3, Folder 2, William L. Dayton Papers, Manuscripts Division, Department of Rare Books and Special Collections, Princeton University Library (hereafter cited as Dayton).
55. Their names are usually given as Maximilian von Meulnier and Julius Schroeder, but Maurice Rigby of the American Civil War Round Table (UK) has established conclusively that they were in fact Mulnier and Schrader.
56. Marvel, p. 248; Semmes, p. 755; Kell, p. 246.
57. "A.M.F." [Alicia Maria Falls, née Hamond], *Foreign Courts and Foreign Homes* (London, 1898), pp. 281–282.
58. SHD, Dupouy to Minister, June 19 and June 22, 1864; Semmes, p. 755.
59. Ingouf-Knocker, pp. 68, 85; Frank J. Merli (ed.), "Letters on the Alabama, June 1864" in *The Mariner's Mirror* 58:2 (1972), pp. 217–218: George T. Sinclair to Barron, June 19 [misdated as 20] and June 21, 1864. See also Captain T. Saumarez, R.N., quoted in the "British Press and Jersey Times," July 8, 1864: "A very strong feeling existed against the Northerners at Cherbourg."
60. "A.M.F.," pp. 283–285.
61. Ingouf-Knocker, p. 73.
62. *ORN* I:3, pp. 661–662: Bonfils to Slidell, June 18, 1864; Slidell to Bonfils, June 19, 1864.
63. Taylor, p. 201; Marvel, p. 248.
64. Feuillet, p. 275.
65. Taylor, p. 201.
66. Ingouf-Knocker, p. 74.
67. Semmes, p. 755.
68. Merli, "Letters on the Alabama," p. 217.
69. SHD, Dupouy to Minister, June 22, 1864 ("un temps superbe et une mer sans ondulations sensibles").
70. Marvel, p. 249; Fox, p. 218; Semmes, p. 755.
71. Frederick Milnes Edge, *An Englishman's View of the Battle between the Alabama and the Kearsarge* (New York, 1864), p. 22. According to Edge, Rondin succeeded in taking a photograph of the battle. Edge "was only able to see the negative but that was quite sufficient to show that the artist had obtained a very fine view indeed of the exciting contest." No print of this, however, has ever surfaced. See also Marvel, pp. 261 and 313, note 4. Rondin's studio was at 20, place d'Armes (now place de la République); the current building appears original.
72. Ingouf-Knocker, p. 76.
73. Dayton.
74. The painting is in the U.S. Naval Academy Museum, Annapolis.
75. Feuillet, pp. 275–278; "A.M.F.," pp. 287–297. See below, Chapter 10.
76. Marvel, p. 250. The church still stands in the rue du Val de Saire.
77. *ORN* I:3, p. 649: Semmes to Barron, June 21, 1864; *ORN* I:3, p. 667: John Lancaster to the Editor of *The Daily News*, June 27, 1864; Kell, p. 246; SHD, Dupouy to Minister, June 22, 1864; Sinclair, pp. 265–266.
78. SHD, Dupouy to Minister, June 21, 1864.
79. Ingouf-Knocker, p, 76; Marvel, pp. 250 and 311, note 12.
80. Isaiah 9, verse 5 (King James Bible).
81. SHD, Dupouy to Minister, June 22, 1864 ("tous les faits sont tellement dénaturés et interprétés si différemment par ceux qui peuvent seuls m'éclairer, qu'il y a une difficulté extrême à faire constater la vérité avec quelque certitude"); SHD, Sinclair to Dupouy, June 21, 1864, enclosed in Dupouy to Minister, June 25, 1864; Merli, "Letters on the Alabama," p. 218.
82. *ORN* I:3, p. 79: Winslow to Welles, July 30, 1864, and p. 649: Semmes to Barron, June 21, 1864.
83. Semmes, p. 756.
84. *ORN* I:3, p. 64: Abstract Log of USS *Kearsarge*, Captain John A. Winslow, June 19, 1864; p. 79: Winslow to Welles, July 30, 1864; p. 649–650: Semmes to Barron, June 21, 1864; SHD, Dupouy to Minister, June 22, 1864; Dayton.
85. Fox, p. 220 and p. 297, quoting from *Boston Evening Transcript*, June 21, 1922.
86. SHD, Dupouy to Minister, June 22, 1864.
87. *ORN* I:3, p. 79: Winslow to Welles, July 30, 1864.

88. James D. Bulloch, *The Secret Service of the Confederate States in Europe: or, How the Confederate Cruisers Were Equipped* (London, 1883, reprinted 1959), Vol. I, p. 286.
89. William Gowen or Gowin.
90. Sinclair, p. 284; John McIntosh Kell, "Cruise and Combats of the *Alabama*," in *Battles and Leaders of the Civil War* (New York, 1887, reprinted 1956), Vol. IV, p. 609. Mars's real name was Maher; I am grateful to Maurice Rigby for this information. See Norman C. Delaney, "The Alabama's 'Bold and Determined Man,'" in *Naval History Magazine*, August 2011, Vol. 25, No. 4. It was not unusual to sign on under a false name at this time, but it is also possible that the name was simply taken down incorrectly when Mars originally signed on.
91. Kell, "Cruise and Combats," p. 610.
92. *ORN* I:3, p. 665: John Lancaster to the Editor of *The Daily News*, June 27, 1864; p. 65: Abstract Log of USS *Kearsarge*, June 19, 1864.
93. At 12.50, according to the log of the *Deerhound* (*The Times*, June 20, 1864); at 12.24, according to the log of the *Kearsarge* (*ORN* I:3, p. 65).
94. Figure for killed and wounded in Semmes's report to Barron, June 21, 1864 (*ORN* I:3, p. 651; total drowned calculated by Marvel, p. 259.
95. Sinclair, p. 263.
96. Kell, *Recollections*, p. 250.
97. *ORN* I:3, p. 656: Mason to Lancaster, June 21, 1864.
98. *ORN* I:3, p. 653: Lieutenant R.F. Armstrong, C.S.N., to Barron, June 21, 1864. Mars had been entrusted with a part of the ship's papers, the other half being given to Frank Townsend, who was rescued by the *Deerhound*; both sets of papers safely reached Semmes in Southampton (Marvel, p. 256 and p. 312, note 21).
99. Ingouf, p. 85.
100. For the battle, see *ORN* I:3, pp. 64–65: log of the *Kearsarge*, June 19, 1864; pp. 79–81: Winslow's report to Welles, July 30, 1864; pp. 649–651: Semmes's report to Barron, June 21, 1864; Kell, "Cruise and Combats," pp. 607–614; Kell, *Recollections*, pp. 247–252; John M. Browne, "The Duel between the *Alabama* and the *Kearsarge*," in *Battles and Leaders*, Vol. IV, pp. 615–625; Sinclair, pp. 267–271; SHD, Dupouy to Minister, June 19, June 21, June 22, 1864. (Note that Winslow's full report was not written until over a month after the battle and then only after a stern reminder dated July 7, 1864, from Welles; see *ORN* I:3, p. 73).
101. *ORN* I:3, p. 60: Winslow to Welles, June 21, 1864; p. 80: Winslow to Welles, July 30, 1864.
102. Edge, p. 13.
103. Browne, "Duel," pp. 619–621.
104. Semmes, pp. 766–776.
105. The relevant part of the professor's letter is given in a footnote to Browne, "Duel," p. 621.
106. SHD, Dupouy to Minister, June 22, 1864.
107. These are, respectively, Nicholas Adams, James Higgs, Henry Middleton Kernot and John Wilson, and Brent Johnston and George Yeoman. The affidavits are in the Freeman Harlow Morse Papers, 1861–1888, Ms. 823. I am grateful to Maurice Rigby for this information.
108. Semmes, p. 760.
109. In a dispatch to Charles Francis Adams, U.S. Minister to Great Britain; quoted in, e.g., Semmes, p. 762 and Bulloch, p. 291.
110. *ORN* I:3, p. 74, Welles to Winslow, July 8, 1864.
111. *ORN* I:3, p. 653, Armstrong to Barron, June 21, 1864.
112. *ORN* I:3, p. 61, Winslow to Welles, June 21, 1864.
113. SHD, Docteur G.T. Dufour, "Relation Chirurgicale du Combat Naval entre le Kerseage [sic] et l'Alabama," in *Archives de Médecine Navale 1864*, Tome IIe; this contains a full report of the injuries and treatment of the 15 wounded.
114. Ingouf, p. 86; SHD, Dupouy to Minister, June 19, 1864; *ORN* I:3, p. 70, Browne to Whelan, July 23, 1864.
115. Construction started in 1869, and the building was finished in 1871.
116. Correspondence with M. François Zoonekyndt, Service Historique de la Défense, Département de la Marine, Échelon de Cherbourg, January-February, 2011. The abbey was occupied by the Germans, and blown up by them in 1944. The building which housed the main part of the provisional naval hospital, however, although roofless, can still be seen behind the ruins of the abbey church. The well-preserved barracks (la Caserne de l'Abbaye) are now occupied by the Service Historique de la Défense.
117. Merli, "Letters," p. 218. The Appleby and King graves are on a small terrace a short distance up from the lower entrance to the cemetery, but the whereabouts of Robinson's grave are unknown. Gustave Bonfils (see above, note 17) signed the three death certificates.
118. She probably came in through the Outer Dock and landed her passengers in the Inner Dock; the Inner Dock was built over some time ago, but the Outer Dock survives as the Ocean Village Marina. Alternatively, she may have landed them at the Royal Pier, which was opened in 1833 but was badly damaged by fire in 1987 and 1992; its remains still stand in the water next to the Red Funnel Terminal. I am grateful to Geoff Watts, formerly of the Southampton Tourist Information Centre, for this information.
119. *The Times*, June 21, 1864. The Sailors' Home was two buildings to the west of the Canute Castle Hotel, which is still standing. A modern building covers the site of the home.
120. Sinclair, p. 286.
121. *The Times*, June 21, 1864. The building is still standing, extending from 29 Queen's Terrace almost to the corner of Terminus Terrace.
122. The photograph was recently in the collection of Gary Hendershott.

123. Delaney, *John McIntosh Kell*, pp. 179–80, quoting from Kell interview with Wood Holt of the *Atlanta Constitution*, 1883. Wiseman's studio was at 9 Bernard Street and Emanuel's premises at 145 High Street, diagonally opposite the old Star Hotel (which still exists). Neither building survives today.

124. *The Times*, June 21, 1864; Semmes, pp. 787–788. The terminus building is still standing, although it is now a casino.

125. Semmes, p. 787.

126. Semmes, pp. 784–785; Edwin W. Besch, Michael Hammerson and Dave W. Morgan, "Raphael Semmes, the English "Confederate Parson" and his Maiden Sister Louisa: A Cased Presentation Revolver, a Magnificent Silver-mounted Sword, and a "Mammoth" Silk Confederate Second National Flag," in *Military Collector & Historian*, Vol. 53, No. 4, Winter 2001–2002.

127. Meredith to Samuel Laurence, June 20, 1864, in Cline (ed.), *The Letters of George Meredith* (1970), Vol. I, p. 271.

128. Holy Trinity, Easton Royal, can usually be found open, and the former vicarage still stands next to it. Charing Cross Hospital moved in 1973 to Fulham Palace Road, but the Llewellyn memorial moved with it and can be found just inside the Margravine Street entrance to the hospital.

129. Frank E. Vandiver, *Blood Brothers: a Short History of the Civil War* (Texas, 1992), p. 177: "The Confederacy went on to legend and the United States to world power."

Chapter 10

1. William L. Dayton Papers, Box 3, Folder 2, Manuscripts Division, Department of Rare Books and Special Collections, Princeton University Library.

2. These must have been the two German Master's Mates, Mulnier and Schrader, who were eventually allowed to proceed (see previous chapter).

3. Querqueville is about five miles from Cherbourg.

4. The West Pass of the breakwater.

5. 1,040 tons.

6. One 110-pounder Blakely rifled pivot gun, one heavy eight-inch 68-pounder (9,000 pounds), and six 32-pounders. *ORN* I:3, pp. 59, 77, 81; Semmes, *Memoirs of Service Afloat*, p. 753.

7. Officers 19, crew 144. *ORN* I:3, p. 77.

8. 1,030 tons. Besides the armament Penhoat mentions, the *Kearsarge* had a 28-pound rifle. *ORN* I:3, p. 59.

9. The Montagne du Roule (367 feet), behind the town.

10. 173 and 55 respectively. *ORN* I:3, p. 64.

11. It is possible that the Feuillets were staying at the Grand Hôtel, built in 1860, which is right on the quay (the Quai Caligny, known at the time of the battle as the Quai de l'Avant-Port).

Chapter 11

1. Roy O. Hatton, *Prince Camille De Polignac: the Life of a Soldier* (PhD dissertation, Louisiana State University, 1970), pp. 22–23.

2. Hedwige de Polignac, *Les Polignac* (Paris, 1960), pp. 216–224; Hatton, pp. 19–20.

3. H. de Polignac, pp. 247–248.

4. Hatton, pp. 26–31.

5. Hatton, p. 33; Jeff Kinard, *Lafayette of the South: Prince Camille de Polignac and the American Civil War* (Texas, 2001), p. 8.

6. Hatton, pp. 33–37.

7. T. Harry Williams, *P.G.T. Beauregard, Napoleon in Gray* (Louisiana, 1955), p. 4.

8. This is presumably Major John G. Barnard, later a Union general, at that time working on New York's coastal defences.

9. This is a literal translation of Polignac's phrase "un corps de troupes mobile." What exactly Polignac meant by this phrase is not clear, but Daniel Frankignoul of the Confederate Historical Association of Belgium suggests that Polignac probably had in mind something similar to the later French Garde Mobile, a locally raised force responsible for security and public order, especially in the case of invasion by enemy troops—in other words something like the Confederate Home Guard.

10. Kinard, p. 13.

11. Harold Acton, *The Last Bourbons of Naples* (London, 1961).

12. Hatton, p. 34.

13. T.J. Stiles—The Blog, May 29, 2009: *Character Spotlight: Joseph L. White*.

14. Michael Schreiber, "The route across Nicaragua 1849–1868 and plans for a Nicaragua canal 1886–1902" in *Nicarao, the Philatelic Journal of the Nicaragua Study Group*, Vol. 25, Number 2, April 2016 (Revision of May 2016).

15. Schreiber, p. 22; Proyecto de Tratado Cass-Irisarri, 16 de noviembre de 1857, Artículos XIV–XVI.

16. Daniel Frankignoul, *Prince Camille de Polignac Major General C.S.A.* (Brussels, Belgium, 1999), p. 25. Frankignoul email to author, December 17, 2020. Frankignoul cites as his source a letter of August 16, 1861, from Polignac to his brother Alphonse ("J'ai écrit à Edmond dès mon arrivée à N.Y. le 12 juin & à ma mère quelques jours après de Cincinnati") and states that this letter is dated from New York. This must be in error, however, since Polignac had long been in Richmond by August 16.

17. Frankignoul, p. 25. According to *Lloyd's List* for June 26, 1861, the *Glasgow* left Liverpool on May 29 and arrived in New York on June 13. She was due to leave on the return voyage on June 22. (I am most grateful to Tony Margrave for this information). The Master of the *Glasgow*, Patrick McGuigan, in fact submitted the Passenger List to the New York authorities on June 12; possibly the ship had arrived early. In any case, Polignac's

name does not appear on the list, but then it does not seem to appear on any of the other passenger lists of around that date.

18. I am grateful to Tony Margrave for bringing this report to my attention.

19. Mary Boykin Chesnut (ed. Ben Ames Williams), *A Diary from Dixie* (Cambridge, MA, 1949), p. 73. Unfortunately, the entry in the index confuses Polignac with his elder brother Ludovic.

20. National Archives, Civil War Service Records (CMSR)—Confederate, Camillus J. Polignac file.

21. Adolphe Robert, Edgar Bourloton et Gaston Cougny, *Dictionnaire des Parlementaires Français* (Paris, 1889–1891).

22. H. de Polignac, p. 162.

23. H. de Polignac, pp. 164–177; Hatton, p. 11.

24. Polignac Diary, January 10, 1863; National Archives, Camillus J. Polignac file.

25. Alwyn Barr, *Polignac's Texas Brigade* (Texas, 1998), pp. 9, 21–22, 28–29.

26. Barr, pp. 39–40; National Archives, Camillus J. Polignac file.

27. "Polignac's Mission" (*Southern Historical Society Papers*, Vol. 35). The *Washington Post* had alleged (March 14 and 19, 1901) that the reason behind Polignac's mission to Paris was to offer the State of Louisiana in exchange for France's armed intervention in support of the Confederacy. In a long letter to the paper, Polignac effectively demolishes this claim.

28. A copy of Montalembert's pamphlet is in the collection of Daniel Frankignoul of the CHAB.

29. "Celui de M. de Montalembert ... contient à peu près tous les genres d'erreurs qui aident à noircir le Sud, et ... par là, il peut servir de type à tout ce qu'on a fait paraître sur le même sujet" (*L'Union Américaine après la Guerre*, p. 19).

30. The letter was sold through Heritage Auctions for $1,900 on June 8, 2010.

31. Hatton, pp. 192, 201–203; Ancestramil; "Composition du 20ème Corps Octobre 1870."

32. *The New York Times*, December 3, 1882.

33. H. de Polignac, p. 250, quoting Major Roche des Breux; Frankignoul, pp. 61–62.

34. Polignac file, Légion d'Honneur. I am grateful to Tony Margrave for supplying me with a copy of the file.

35. Copies of these two letters are in the collection of Daniel Frankignoul. I am grateful to him for bringing them to my attention. See Chapter 12 for more on this subject.

36. We know that she was certainly back in France some time before August 31, 1862, since the entry for that day in Polignac's diary records: "I heard last night of L. by the French consul; the first news since we parted and L. arrived in France."

37. Kinard, p. 73.

38. See Polignac Diary, e.g., December 18, 1862, February 3, 1863, March 3, 1863.

39. For Edward Eggeling, see the 2004 article on RootsWeb by John L. Maurath of the Missouri Civil War Museum. When Polignac left Richmond for the Trans-Mississippi on April 2, 1863, he chose Eggeling's younger brother, William (Karl Wilhelm), then serving as a private in Captain Parker's Company of Virginia Light Artillery, to come with him as his aide-de-camp.

40. Polignac Diary, November 11, 1862.

41. Polignac Diary, March 16, 1863.

42. The main source for Léda Blanchard's story is *La Justice*, March 10, 1883, which contains a full report of the trial on March 7 of Camille Olivier Blanchard. *La Justice*, founded by Georges Clemenceau, was a Republican paper, and the tone of the report is very much biased against Polignac. Nevertheless, the basic facts of the case appear to be correct.

43. Frankignoul, p. 64.

44. *La Justice*, March 10, 1883.

45. *The New York Times*, December 3, 1882.

46. Polignac's mother, the Dowager Princess, had died in September, 1864.

47. *La Justice*, March 10, 1883; Bérard des Glajeux, *Souvenirs d'un Président d'Assises* (Paris, 1892), pp. 98–104.

48. H. de Polignac, p. 239.

49. Comtesse de Polignac to W.D. Fane, May 1, 1883 (Lincolnshire Archives).

50. F.W. Knight to W.D Fane, May 4, 1883 (Lincolnshire Archives).

51. Comtesse de Polignac to W.D. Fane, May 7, 1883 (Lincolnshire Archives).

52. Marriage certificate in General Register Office, Southport.

53. Birth certificate in General Register Office, Southport.

54. Frankignoul, pp. 69–73.

55. Including to the USA, where he had invested in railroads. On one of these visits, in 1889, he provided the capital for the forerunner of what is today the Erlanger Health System in Chattanooga, Tennessee.

56. This part of the *Gruftenhalle* was badly damaged during two very heavy bombing raids on Frankfurt in March 1944. It was restored after the war, and in 1973 the Baron's tomb was finally moved a little further along to its current position.

57. Author's visit, December 1, 2016.

Chapter 12

1. John P. Dunn., "An American Fracas in Egypt—The Butler Affair of 1872," *Journal of the American Research Center in Egypt*, Vol. 42, 2005/2006, pp. 153–161. This excellent article has the fullest account of the incident.

2. "There is no doubt that Jefferson Davis and other leaders of the South have made an army; they are making, it appears, a navy; and they have made, what is more than either, they

have made a nation" (W.E. Gladstone, speech in Newcastle, October 7, 1862).
 3. John P. Dunn, *Khedive Ismail's Army* (Abingdon, 2005), p. 6.
 4. Dunn, *Khedive Ismail's Army*, p. 1.
 5. *Ibid.*, pp. 8–9.
 6. *Ibid.*, p. 21.
 7. William B. Hesseltine and Hazel C. Wolf, *The Blue and the Gray on the Nile* (Chicago, 1961), p. 30.
 8. In an interview with the British civil servant Charles Rivers Wilson, August 23, 1877. (John Eliot Bowen, "The Conflict of East and West in Egypt," *Political Science Quarterly*, Vol. 1, No. 2, June 1886, pp. 295–335).
 9. Dunn, "An American Fracas in Egypt."
 10. Dunn, *Khedive Ismail's Army*, p. 51.
 11. A copy of Charles Iverson Graves's contract, written in French, is in the Charles Iverson Graves Papers, Wilson Library, University of North Carolina at Chapel Hill.
 12. Dunn, *Khedive Ismail's Army*, p. 56.
 13. Pierre Crabitès, *Americans in the Egyptian Army* (London, 1938), p. 7.
 14. T. Harry Williams, *P.G.T. Beauregard, Napoleon in Gray* (Louisiana, 1955), pp. 263–265.
 15. Hesseltine and Wolf, p. 44.
 16. James Morris Morgan, *Recollections of a Rebel Reefer* (Cambridge, 1917), p. 270. It is highly probable that many of Morgan's stories had become embellished by the time that he wrote this book.
 17. The Gezira Palace is today the Cairo Marriott Hotel.
 18. Hesseltine and Wolf, p. 90. The Harem Palace is today the Egyptian National Military Museum.
 19. Dunn, "An American Fracas."
 20. Dunn, "An American Fracas"; Hesseltine and Wolf, pp. 116–117; *The New York Times*, July 18, 1872; *The Times*, July 15 and 17, 1872.
 21. Dunn, "An American Fracas"; Hesseltine and Wolf, p. 117.
 22. Hesseltine and Wolf, p. 117.
 23. Dunn, "An American Fracas."
 24. Hesseltine and Wolf, p. 126.
 25. *Ibid.*, pp. 154, 167–168.
 26. *Ibid.*, p. 93.
 27. *Ibid.*, p. 60.
 28. Massawa is today in Eritrea.
 29. Charles Iverson Graves, Egyptian Journal, 1875–1878, p. 6 (Charles Iverson Graves Papers, Wilson Library, University of North Carolina at Chapel Hill).
 30. Dunn, *Khedive Ismail's Army*, p. 138.
 31. Hesseltine and Wolf, p. 212.
 32. Dunn, *Khedive Ismail's Army*, p. 58.
 33. Hesseltine and Wolf, pp. 231–233.
 34. Morgan, pp. 266–269.
 35. *Ibid.*, pp. 290–291.
 36. Hesseltine and Wolf, p. 108; Dunn, "An American Fracas."
 37. Morgan, pp. 298–299; Hesseltine and Wolf, pp. 108–109.
 38. Morgan, p. 300.
 39. *Ibid.*, pp. 277–281, 288–289; Hesseltine and Wolf, pp. 109–112.
 40. Morgan, pp. 315–316; Hesseltine and Wolf, p. 112.
 41. Hesseltine and Wolf, pp. 233–234; *The New York Times*, August 11, 1878.
 42. Hesseltine and Wolf, pp. 243–244.
 43. Dunn, *Khedive Ismail's Army*, p. 4.
 44. Hesseltine and Wolf, p. 250.

Chapter 13

 1. James Innes Randolph, "Oh, I'm a Good Ol' Rebel."
 2. William B. Holberton, *Homeward Bound; The Demobilization of the Union and Confederate Armies, 1865–1866* (Mechanicsburg, Pennsylvania, 2001).
 3. In a Memorial Day address, May 30, 1884, in Keene, New Hampshire.
 4. William B. Kurtz, "An American Condottiere: The Antebellum Career of General Charles Carroll Tevis" (Part 1), May 2016; "An American Condottiere: The Civil War Career of General Charles Carroll Tevis" (Part 2), June 2016; "An American Condottiere: The Post-War Career of General Charles Carroll Tevis" (Part 3), July 2016.
 5. Information from Will Kurtz, 2018.
 6. Sarah Agnes Wallace and Frances Elma Gillespie (ed.), *The Journal of Benjamin Moran, 1857–1865* (Chicago, 1948–1949), Vol. I, p. 583 (August 27, 1859) and pp. 258–259 (March 3, 1858). According to the *Richmond Dispatch* of August 15, 1857, however, Tevis had been made a Khan by the Shah and was to be employed by him to reorganize the Persian Army entirely.
 7. See the Belgian LittleGun website for details and photographs.
 8. *Household Words*, Vol. XIII, January 26, 1856, pp. 46–48.
 9. *The War of the Rebellion: A Compilation of the Official Records of the Union and Confederate Armies* (Washington, DC, 1881–1901), Series I (hereafter cited as *OR*), Vol. XXVII, pp. 777–781.
 10. *The Cincinnati Enquirer*, November 17, 1863.
 11. *OR* Vol. XXXIII, p. 386, *OR* Vol. XXXIV, p. 171.
 12. Charles A. Coulombe, *The Pope's Legion* (New York, 2008), pp. 9, 145, 147–148.
 13. Desprez, Adrien, *Histoire de la Guerre de 1870–1871 et du Siège de Paris* (Paris, 1873), pp. 412–415.
 14. Hesseltine and Wolf, p. 260.
 15. Information from Will Kurtz.
 16. Charles Godfrey Leland, *Memoirs* (London, 1893), p. 384.

17. Hesseltine and Wolf, pp. 241, 282.
18. Author's visit, April 2013.
19. *Daily Alta California*, July 29, 1881.
20. Hesseltine and Wolf, p. 84.
21. *Daily Alta California*, July 29, 1881; Francis B. Heitman, *Historical Register and Dictionary of the United States Army* (Washington, 1903), Vol. 1, Part II.
22. *Daily Alta California*, July 29, 1881.
23. *OR* Vol. L, pp. 466, 487.
24. Hesseltine and Wolf, p. 84; Morgan, p. 269.
25. Crabitès, pp. 49–50.
26. Hesseltine and Wolf, p. 84.
27. Hesseltine and Wolf, p. 122.
28. Hesseltine and Wolf, pp. 122–123, 125.
29. Hesseltine and Wolf, pp. 127–128.
30. Hesseltine and Wolf, pp. 131–132.
31. Hesseltine and Wolf, pp. 133–134.
32. Hesseltine and Wolf, pp. 93, 229, 243–244. Graves kept detailed accounts in his journal.
33. Crabitès, pp. 55–58, 63; Hesseltine and Wolf, p. 115.
34. Hesseltine and Wolf, p. 135.
35. Hesseltine and Wolf, pp. 135–139, 148.
36. Hesseltine and Wolf, p. 220.
37. Crabitès, pp. 58–59; *Daily Alta California*, July 29, 1881.
38. Hesseltine and Wolf, p. 127.
39. *Daily Alta California*, July 29, 1881.
40. Crabitès, pp. 58–59.
41. W.W. Loring, *A Confederate Soldier in Egypt* (New York, 1884), pp. 299–300.
42. Samir Raafat, "Adopt a Monument," *Egyptian Mail*, March 8, 1997; *The New York Times*, November 8, 2000.
43. "Civil War Officer Honored in Egypt," Associated Press, November 6, 2000.
44. Lucius W. Barber, *Army Memoirs of Lucius W. Barber, Co. "D," 15th. Illinois Volunteer Infantry* (Chicago, 1894), p. 136.
45. *The New York Times*, July 17, 1865.
46. *The New York Times*, June 17, 1865.
47. G.M. Wheeler, H. Gouverneur Wright, A.A. Humphreys., *Report upon United States Geographical Surveys West of the One Hundredth Meridian* (Washington, 1875–1889), p. 640.
48. Documents detailing Irgens's postwar enlistment, his commission, his assignments, his court martial and his request for leave of absence and resignation can be found in *Letters Received by the Commission Branch of the Adjutant General's Office 1863–1870* (National Archives).
49. Henry Clay Derrick, Egyptian Diary, 1875–1878 (ms., Library of Congress), December 7, 1875.
50. Derrick, Egyptian Diary, December 25, 1875, January 18, 1876.
51. Loring, pp. 379–380.
52. Hesseltine and Wolf, pp. 197–198.
53. Derrick, Egyptian Diary, February 16, 1876.
54. Derrick, Egyptian Diary, March 7, 1876.
55. Derrick, Egyptian Diary, July 17–18, 1877.
56. Derrick, Egyptian Diary, October 7, 1877; March 4, 1878.
57. Derrick, Egyptian Diary, January 8 and 9, 1878.
58. Derrick, Egyptian Diary, July 5 and 6, 1878.
59. Death certificate in General Register Office, Southport.
60. Correspondence with Mrs. Hilde Chapman, Royal Norwegian Embassy, London, June 2013. The local Liverpool stonemason seems to have been unfamiliar with the Norwegian letter Ø.

Chapter 14

1. Lucile Ward Mosback (ed.), *A History of Alfred and Elizabeth Robinson Ward Their Antecedents and Descendants, Edition II, Revision and Supplement to Edition I* (Duplin County, NC, 1971), pp. 16, 512, 514.
2. Mosback, pp. 456, 521.
3. National Archives, Civil War Service Records (CMSR)—Confederate, George W. Ward file. Louis H. Manarin, *North Carolina Troops 1861–1865 A Roster*, Vol. III (third printing, Raleigh, 2014); Walter Clark (ed.), *Histories of the Several Regiments and Battalions from North Carolina in the Great War, 1861-'65*, Vol. 1 (Raleigh, 1901); John W. Moore, *Roster of North Carolina Troops in the War Between the States* (Raleigh, 1882).
4. Lieut. Col. Fremantle, Coldstream Guards, *Three Months in the Southern States* (Mobile, 1864), p. 12. Walter Lord (ed.), *The Fremantle Diary* (Boston, 1954), p. 16.
5. Oliver Willcox Norton, *Army Letters 1861–1865* (Chicago, 1903), p. 28.
6. Clark (ed.), Vol. 1, pp. 180, 217. The chapter on the Third Regiment was written by Captain John Cowan, Co. D, and Captain James I. Metts, Co. G.
7. Chet Bennett, *Resolute Rebel: General Roswell S. Ripley, Charleston's Gallant Defender* (Columbia, SC, 2017), pp. 114–115; Manarin, pp. 136, 481.
8. Clark, Vol. 1, p. 182.
9. *The War of the Rebellion: A Compilation of the Official Records of the Union and Confederate Armies* (Washington, 1881–1901), Series I (hereafter cited as *OR*), Vol. XI, Part 2, pp. 650, 658.
10. *OR* Vol. XI, Part 2, p. 659.
11. Bennett, p. 129.
12. Major S.D. Thruston to Governor Zebulon B. Vance, September 27th., 1862, William L. DeRosset Collection, State Archives of North Carolina, Raleigh.
13. Thruston to Vance.
14. Hopkin Williams, William Eason and John R. Heath.

15. Bennett, p. 134.
16. Clark, Vol. 1, p. 185.
17. Having taken command of the regiment after Meares's death, he was promoted to colonel from July 1, 1862.
18. Thruston to Vance.
19. Thruston to Vance.
20. Thruston had been promoted to major from July 1, 1862, but his commission did not reach him until after the return to Virginia, and he was thus addressed and referred to during the battle as Captain Thruston.
21. Clark, Vol. 1, p. 187.
22. Clark, Vol. 1, p. 188.
23. Clark, Vol. 1, pp. 188–189.
24. Manarin, Vol. III, p. 502 lists Ward as appointed 3rd lieutenant to rank from May 16, 1861, promoted to 2nd lieutenant September 22, 1862, and to 1st lieutenant October 9, 1862. There is no other evidence for this, and it can probably safely be dismissed as an error. Cowan died in a Washington hospital on October 4.
25. Letter to Brig. Gen. R.E. Colston in the Louis Round Wilson Special Collections Library, University of North Carolina at Chapel Hill. The committee of officers consisted of Capt. F. W. Bond, Co. A, 1st. NC (Chairman), Capt. H.W. Horne, Co. C, 3rd. NC, Capt. W.H. Thomson, Co. C, 1st NC and Lieut. John Cowan, Co. D, 3rd NC.
26. Clark, Vol. 1, p. 194.
27. Patterson, of Greek origin and born in Massachusetts., was more than a little eccentric in dress, appearance and behavior. He was an Episcopalian, which most of the ordinary soldiers were not, but he was a brave and dedicated man, generally well liked and, apparently, "very useful towards the men." See Donald B. Koonce, *Doctor to the Front, the Recollections of Confederate Surgeon Thomas Fanning Wood 1861–1865* (Knoxville, 2000), pp. 56–57.
28. Clark, Vol. 1, p. 194.
29. Although promoted to lieutenant colonel to rank from October 3, 1863, Parsley was a major at Gettysburg.
30. Clark, Vol. 1, p. 196.
31. Moore, Vol. I, p. 85.
32. Lieut. Edward H. Armstrong to his father, July 10, 1863, Special Collections, William M. Randall Library, University of North Carolina at Wilmington.
33. *OR* Vol. XXIX, Part 1, p. 831.
34. Clark, Vol. 1, p. 197.
35. *OR* Vol. XXIX, Part 1, p. 862.
36. Captain John Badger Brown, Co. B.
37. *OR* Vol. XXIX, Part 1, pp. 866–867.
38. Colonel Hamilton A. Brown. Clark, Vol. 1, p. 203.
39. General Bryan Grimes, *The Surrender at Appomattox,* Southern Historical Society Papers, Vol. 27. *The Charlotte Observer,* September 17, 1899.
40. William G. Nine and Ronald G. Wilson, *The Appomattox Paroles April 9–15, 1865* (Lynchburg, VA, 1989). Ennett's name is misspelled as Emett.
41. This roster is in the Special Collections, William M. Randall Library, University of North Carolina at Wilmington.
42. Manarin, Vol. II, p. 182; Mosbach, pp. 295, 491, 540.
43. Mosback, pp. 456–457, 522.
44. Information from Bruce Vail.
45. Including at least two companies of Cherokees, in William Holland Thomas's Legion. See Vernon H. Crow, *Storm in the Mountains* (Cherokee, NC, 1982).

Chapter 15

1. Derrick, Egyptian Diary, December 26, 1875.
2. John Helmer to wife, April 14 [1863] (private collection).
3. L.R. Garrison, "Administrative Problems of the Confederate Post Office Department" I, *The Southwestern Historical Quarterly* Vol. XIX, No. 2 (October, 1915).
4. National Archives, Civil War Service Records (CMSR)—Confederate, George R. Adderton file.
5. Manarin, Louis H., *North Carolina Troops 1861–1865 A Roster,* Vol. II (Raleigh, 1968), pp. 367–372; Walter Clark (ed.), *Histories of the Several Regiments and Battalions from North Carolina in The Great War 1861-'65,* Vol. 3 (Goldsboro, 1901), pp. 529–543 and 545–657.
6. Clark, Vol. 3, p. 530.
7. *OR* Vol. XVIII, p. 1088.
8. Daniel Branson Coltrane, *The Memoirs of Daniel Branson Coltrane* (Raleigh, 1956), p. 7.
9. *OR* Vol. XVIII, pp. 891, 188–189.
10. *OR* Vol. XVIII, p. 161.
11. *OR* Vol. XXVII, Part 2, p. 683.
12. *OR* Vol. XXVII, Part 1, p. 963.
13. *OR* Vol. XXVII, Part 2, p. 689.
14. *OR* Vol. XXVII, Part 1, p. 911.
15. *OR* Vol. XXVII, Part 2, p. 691.
16. Patrick A. Bowmaster, *Confederate Brigadier General B.H. Robertson and the 1863 Gettysburg Campaign* (Master of Arts thesis, Virginia Polytechnic and State University, 1995), p. 65.
17. J.E.B. Stuart to Samuel Cooper, October 24, 1862, J.E.B. Stuart Papers, Virginia Historical Society, Richmond, Virginia. I am most grateful to Eric Wittenberg for kindly supplying the source.
18. In a letter to his wife, October 21, 1861; Adele H. Mitchell, *The Letters of Major General J.E.B. Stuart* (Alexandria, 1990), p. 221.
19. *OR* Vol. XXVII, Part 3, pp. 927–928.
20. *OR* Vol. XXVII, Part 2, p. 699.
21. Clark, Vol. 3, pp. 569–570.
22. *OR* Vol. XXVII, Part 2, pp. 701–702.
23. *OR* Vol. XXVII, Part 3, p. 1006.

24. Clark, Vol. 3, p. 573.
25. *OR* Vol. XXIX, Part 1, p. 461.
26. *Ibid.*, p. 903.
27. Clark, Vol. 3, p. 636.
28. Manarin, p. 370.
29. *Ibid.*, p. 591.
30. Clark, Vol. 3, pp. 596–597.
31. *OR* Vol. XXXVI, Part 1, p. 864.
32. *Ibid.*, p. 853.
33. Clark, Vol. 3, p. 538.
34. National Archives, G.R. Adderton file, Register of Chimborazo, Hospital No. 3, May 27-June 17, 1864.
35. *OR* Vol. XL, Part 1, p. 620.
36. Clark, Vol. 3, p. 539.
37. *Ibid.*, pp. 539–540.
38. *Ibid.*, p. 627.
39. *OR* Vol. XLII, Part 1, p. 950.
40. *Ibid.*, p. 609.
41. *Ibid.* p. 954.
42. Civil War Collection, Series 1, Subseries 1.1, Lovett family, letters, 1859–1864.
43. National Archives, G.R. Adderton file, receipt rolls for clothing 3rd and 4th quarters, 1864.
44. Coltrane, p. 26.
45. *OR* Vol. XLII, Part 1, p. 951.
46. *OR* Vol. XLVI, Part 2, p. 1210.
47. National Archives, Confederate Citizens File, G.R. Adderton.
48. Letters Home: Civil War: Past Voices.
49. William T. Auman, "Neighbor against Neighbor: The Inner Civil War in the Randolph County Area of Confederate North Carolina," *The North Carolina Historical Review*, Vol. 61, No. 1 (January 1984).
50. J.S. Harris, *Historical Sketches of the Seventh Regiment North Carolina Troops* (Mooresville, North Carolina, 1893), p. 60.
51. Clark, Vol. 3, p. 638.
52. Mark Crawford, "Battle of Dinwiddie Court House," *America's Civil War*, March 1999.
53. Sheridan R. Barringer, *Fighting for General Lee* (El Dorado Hills, California, 2016) pp. 191–197.
54. Clark, Vol. 1, p. 472.
55. Coltrane, p. 39.
56. Crawford.
57. *Ibid.*
58. *Ibid.*
59. Sheridan R. Barringer, p. 196, quoting from David Cardwell, *Confederate Veteran*, March 1914.
60. Clark, Vol. 1, p. 442.
61. Sheridan R. Barringer, p. 202.
62. Clark, Vol. 3, p. 650.
63. Sheridan R. Barringer, p. 209.
64. Clark, Vol. 3, p. 653.
65. *Ibid.*, p. 654.
66. North Carolina Estate Files, 1663–1979, Randolph County: Joseph Adderton, 1893.
67. North Carolina Estate Files, 1663–1979, Randolph County: George R. Adderton, 1893.
68. North Carolina Office of the State Auditor, Confederate Pension Applications.

Bibliography

Writing this book has involved consulting a large number of quite varied sources, both published and unpublished. Detailed references to all the sources used for each chapter can be found in the endnotes to that chapter. The following, then, is simply a selective list of some of the main published sources consulted.

Adams, E.D. *Great Britain and the American Civil War*, 2 vols. in one. New York: Russell & Russell, 1958. Originally published in London, 1925.

Barringer, Sheridan R. *Fighting for General Lee: General Rufus Barringer and the North Carolina Cavalry Brigade*. California: Savas Beatie, 2016.

Batchelor, Gordon W. *The Beresfords of Bedgebury Park*. Goudhurst, Kent: William J.C. Musgrave, 1996.

Beresford Hope, A.J.B. *England, the North and the South: Being a Popular View of the American Civil War*. London: James Ridgway, 1862.

_____. *The Social and Political Bearings of the American Disruption*. London: William Ridgway, 1863.

Bigelow, John. *Retrospections of an Active Life*. 3 vols. New York: Baker & Taylor, 1909.

_____. *France and the Confederate Navy 1862–1868: An International Episode*. New York: Harper & Brothers, 1888.

Blackett, R.J.M. *Divided Hearts: Britain and the American Civil War*. Baton Rouge: Louisiana State University Press, 2001.

Clark, Walter (ed.). *Histories of the Several Regiments and Battalions from North Carolina in the Great War 1861-'65*. Vol. 1, Raleigh: E.M. Uzzell, 1901. Vol. 2, Goldsboro, NC: Nash Brothers, 1901.

Cowell, John Welsford. *La France et les États Confédérés*. Paris: E. Dentu, 1865.

Crabitès, Pierre. *Americans in the Egyptian Army*. London: Routledge, 1938.

Delaney, Norman C. *John McIntosh Kell of the Raider Alabama*. Tuscaloosa: University of Alabama Press, 1973.

De Leon, Edwin. *Secret History of Confederate Diplomacy Abroad*, ed. William C. Davis. Lawrence: University Press of Kansas, 2005. Originally published 1867–1868.

Desquesnes, Jacky. *Duel au Large: La Guerre de Sécession devant Cherbourg*. Condé-sur-Noireau: Éditions Charles Corlet, 2014.

Doyle, Don H. *The Cause of All Nations: An International History of the American Civil War*. New York: Basic Books, 2015.

Dunn, John P. "'An American Fracas in Egypt': The Butler Affair of 1872." *Journal of the American Research Center in Egypt*, Vol. 42 (2005/2006), pp. 153–161.

_____. *Khedive Ismail's Army*. London: Routledge, 2005.

Dye, William McE. *Moslem Egypt and Christian Abyssinia*. New York: Atkin & Prout, 1880.

Eckel, Mrs. L. St. John. *Maria Monk's Daughter: An Autobiography*. New York: The United States Publishing Company, 1874.

Ellison, Mary. *Support for Secession: Lancashire and the American Civil War*. Chicago: The University of Chicago Press, 1972.

Foreman, Amanda. *A World on Fire*. London: Allen Lane, 2010.

Frankignoul, Daniel J. *Prince Camille de Polignac Major General, C.S.A.* Brussels: C.H.A.B. Publications, 1999.

Graham, Eric J. *Clyde Built: Blockade Runners, Cruisers and Armoured Rams of the American Civil War*. Edinburgh: Birlinn, 2006.

Hesseltine, William B., and Hazel C. Wolf. *The Blue and the Gray on the Nile*. Chicago: The University of Chicago Press, 1961.

Hobart Pasha, Admiral. *Sketches from My Life*. London: Longmans, Green and Co., 1887.

Ingouf-Knocker, Paul. *Coulez l'Alabama!* Cherbourg: Édition La Dépêche, 1976. Revised edition Lassy: Éditions Paoland Connaissance, 2002.

Joslyn, Mauriel Phillips (ed.). *A Meteor Shining*

Brightly: Essays on Maj. Gen. Patrick R. Cleburne. Milledgeville: Terrell House, 1999.

Kinard, Jeff. *Lafayette of the South: Prince Camille de Polignac and the American Civil War* College Station: Texas A&M University Press, 2001.

Loring, W.W. *A Confederate Soldier in Egypt.* New York: Dodd, Mead and Company, 1884.

Mahin, Dean. *One War at a Time: The International Dimensions of the American Civil War.* Washington, D.C.: Brassey's, 1999.

Manarin, Louis H. *North Carolina Troops 1861–1865: A Roster.* Vol. 2, *Cavalry.* Raleigh: North Carolina State Division of Archives and History, third printing, 1989. Vol. 3, *Infantry.* Raleigh: North Carolina Office of Archives and History, third printing, 2004.

Marvel, William. *The Alabama and the Kearsarge: The Sailor's Civil War.* Chapel Hill: The University of North Carolina Press, 1996.

Morgan, James Morris. *Recollections of a Rebel Reefer.* Boston: Houghton Mifflin Company, 1917.

Official Records of the Union and Confederate Navies in the War of the Rebellion. 31 vols. Washington, D.C.: Government Printing Office, 1894–1927.

Owsley, Frank Lawrence. *King Cotton Diplomacy: Foreign Relations of the Confederate States of America.* 2nd. ed. Chicago: The University of Chicago Press, 1959.

Polignac, Le Prince Camille de. *L'Union Américaine Après la Guerre.* Hachette Livre BNF, 2016. Originally published 1866.

Sainlaude, Stève. *Le Gouvernement Impérial et la Guerre de Sécession (1861–1865).* Paris: L'Harmattan, 2011.

_____. *La France et la Confédération Sudiste (1861–1865).* Paris: L'Harmattan, 2011.

Semmes, Admiral Raphael. *Memoirs of Service Afloat During the War Between the States.* The Blue and Grey Press, 1987. Originally published 1869.

Sinclair, Arthur. *Two Years on the Alabama.* London: Gay and Bird, 1896.

Symonds, Craig L. *Stonewall of the West: Patrick Cleburne and the Civil War.* Lawrence: University Press of Kansas, 1997.

The War of the Rebellion: A Compilation of the Official Records of the Union and Confederate Armies. 128 vols. Washington, D.C.: Government Printing Office, 1880–1901.

Wiche, Glen N. (ed.). *Dispatches from Bermuda: The Civil War Letters of Charles Maxwell Allen, United States Consul at Bermuda, 1861–1888.* Kent, Ohio: Kent State University Press, 2008.

Willson, Beckles. *John Slidell and the Confederates in Paris (1862–65).* New York: Minton, Balch and Company, 1932.

Index

Numbers in ***bold italics*** indicate pages with illustrations

Abdul Aziz 45, 201*n*24
Abdul Hamid II 45–46
Abyssinia 143, 163–165, 182
Adams, Charles Francis 26, 38, 72
Adderton, Adaline 183–185, 195–197
Adderton, Adam 196–197
Adderton, George R. 183, ***184***, 185–186, 188–193, 195–197; death and estate 196–197; in hospital 190; letters home 183–184, 191–193; no horse 188–189; slaves 185, 196–197; supplies forage 193
Adderton, Joseph 184–185, 196–197
Adderton, Troy 184–185, 196–197
Adowa 143, 164–165
C.S.S. *Alabama* 2–3, 6, 26, 34, 85–103; armament 90, 109, 111; battle with *Kearsarge* 96–101, 105–113, 115; casualties of battle 101–102, 113; at Cherbourg 85–96, 111; crew rescued 98–101, 113; disadvantages versus Kearsarge 90; need of repairs 85–91; prisoners landed by 85–87, 92, 107, 109
Alba, Duke of 21–22
Alexandria, Egypt 132, 137, 140–141, 145–146, 165
Allen, Charles M. 43
Allen, Henry W. 124
Anson, Talavera V. 103
Antietam *see* Sharpsburg
Appleby, George 101, ***102***, 205*n*116
Appomattox 14, 179–181
Arabi Pasha 145–146
Armstrong, Richard 99, 101
Arrendrup, Søren 143

Badlam, William H. 107
Bahiana 89, 93–94
Baker, Sir Samuel 156–157
Ballincollig 50, ***51***, 55
Bank of England 59–61
Barker, Joseph 20, 22, 27, 29, 33–34, 199*n*6
Barringer, Rufus C. 185, 188, 190, 193–195
Barron, Samuel 87–88, 90, 101
Bartelli, A.G. 99
Beauregard, P.G.T. 82, 117–118, 122–123, 125, 136
Benjamin, Judah P. 2, 70, 73, 75, 82, 117, 119, 121, 123
Berber 142, 157
Berenice 142, 156–158
Beresford, Lord 7–8, 16
Beresford Hope, A.J.B. 7, ***8***, 9–14, ***15***, 16–17, ***18***, 59, 66; contrasts North with South 9, 11; funeral 16; home a refuge for Confederates 14; honored by Southern universities 15; Jackson statue 14–15; and Jefferson Davis 9, 15–16; Laird rams 12–13; lectures on the war 9–11; in Liverpool 11–13; in Parliament 8–9, 13; publications 9, 13, 15, 199*n*5, 199*n*7; *Saturday Review* 15, 20, 38, 200*n*8; on slavery 10–12; Southern Independence Association 13
Beresford Hope, Lady Mildred 8, 13, 15
Bermuda 43–44
Beylard, Edward J. 77–78, 81, 83–84
Bigelow, John 66, 72–73, 75, 78, 81–84, 124
Blanchard de la Bretesche, Armand 116, 125, 128
Blanchard de la Bretesche, Camille Olivier 126–128, 207*n*42
Blanchard de la Bretesche, Cécile Léda 125–128, 207*n*36, 207*n*42
blockade-running 2, 41–45, 48, 153
Bonfils, Adolphe 88–89, 91, 95–96, 203*n*17
Bourbaki, Denis-Charles 125, 153
Boydton Plank Road 191–192
Bragg, Braxton 42, 123
Brazil 22, 41, 88–89, 93–94
Breckinridge, John C. 31
Bricard, Sophie 73–76, 82; *see also* Eckel, Lizzie St. John
Bright, John 26
Bristoe campaign 175, 188
Britain 1–3, 6–7, 9–10, 12–14, 17–18, 22, 25–27, 31–32, 34–38, 45–49, 58–64, 66, 68–72, 116, 119, 122, 129, 135, 140, 145–146; Confederate sympathies in 7, 12–13, 17–18, 25, 27, 29–30, 43, 69–70; dislike of slavery 7, 10, 25, 59
Brown, Patrick J. 56
Browne, Dr. John M. 89, 99–100, 108
Bruce, Sir Frederick 152
Bulloch, James D. 14, 73, 103, 205*n*88
Burnley 6, 25–28, ***28***
Butler, Benjamin 12, 63, 132, 140–142
Butler, George H. 132, 140–142

Cairo 2, 133, 137, ***138***, ***139***, 143–146, 156–159, ***160***, 161, 165
Calais 91, 139–140
Calhoun, John C. 61–62, 70

215

Campbell, William P.A. 132, 139–142
Canada 152–153
Chaillé-Long, Charles 142
Charles II 70
Charles X 66, 116
Chamberlain Run 194–195
Chancellorsville 173, 183
Chasseloup-Laubat, Prosper de 3, 86, 93
Chattanooga 1, 6, 23, 49, 207n55
Cherbourg 2–3, 6, 85, **86–89**, 90–97, 99, 101, 113, 115, 139; Casino des Bains de Mer 92–93, 113
Chesnut, Mary 35, 122
Church of England 27, 34, 69
Cleborne, Christopher J. 56
Cleburne, Dr. Joseph 50–51, 53, **54**, 55
Cleburne, Patrick R. 49–51, **52**, **53**, **54**, 56, **57**, 58, 162
Cliburn 56, **57**, 58
Clifton 58
Collie, Alexander 43–44
Colston, Raleigh 136, 142, 144, 157–159, 173
Coltrane, Daniel 186, 192, 194
Condor 43
Constantinople 44, 133, 140; *see also* Istanbul
Corbin, Richard W. 8
Cork 49–51, 53, 55–57
cotton 30–31, 33, 62–63, 66, 69–70, 134
Couronne 85, 89, 95–97, 101, 110–112
Cowell, John Jermyn 17–**18**, 23–24, 59–60; alleged Union atrocities 21, 23; historical parallels 19, 21–22; letters to Henry Sidgwick 17–24; liberal principles of 18–19, 21–22; reaction to Confederate defeat 23; slavery 20–22; states as sovereign 20–21

Cowell, John Welsford 17, 19, 23, 59–**60**, 61–66, **67**, 71; alleged Union atrocities 62; appeals to France's commercial and political interests 62, 66; considers secession inevitable and justified 61; contrasts North with South 62–63; factory reform 59; meets Calhoun 61; minimizes possible risks in recognition 64–65; pamphlets on the war 59, 61–62; proposes French commercial alliance with South 63–64; on protectionism 61; quoted by Karl Marx 59; represents Bank of England in U.S. 59–61; slavery 66
Cox, William R. 178–180
Crabitès, Pierre 158–159
Crémer, Camille 125, 153
Creoles 71, 73, 116, 124–125
Crimean War 27, 34, 41–42, 45–47, 68, 85, 116, 119, 150, 199n4
Cunliffe, William 27–28, 33–34
Cuyler, Theodore L. 26

Dahlgren, Ulric 23
Darfur 158–159, 161
Davis, Jefferson 9, 15–16, 35, 82, 122, 133, 170, 207n2
Dayton, William L. **69**, 71–74, **75**, 76–78, 80–81, 83–84, 124
Dayton, William L., Jr. 72, 74, 77–78, 81, 94, 96, 104, **105**, 109
Deerhound 94–95, 97–102, 105, 107, 113
de Hoghton, Sir Henry 103
de Hoghton, Lady 103
De Leon, Edwin 14, 35, 71
Denison, the Rev. Charles W. 26, 28, 32–34
DeRosset, William L. 170–172
Derrick, Henry C. 136, 163, **164**, 165, 182
desertion 124, 193
Dickens, Charles 150
Dimitry, Alexander 121
Dinwiddie Court House *see* Chamberlain Run
disaffection 180–181, 193
Disraeli, Benjamin 9, 147
Don 43–44
Doucet, Auguste 99
Drayton, Henri 25
drill 169–171, 186
Drouyn de Lhuys, Édouard 78, 83
Duffié, Alfred N. 186
Duflot, Abbé 164–165
Dufour, Dr. G.T. 3, 101, 108
Duleep Singh 154
Dupouy, Augustin 3, 85–97, 100, 104–105, 107, 110, 114–115

Early, Jubal A. 175, 178
Eckel, Lizzie St. John 77, 78, **79**, 80–83; *see also* Bricard, Sophie

Edge, Frederick Milnes 99, 204n71
Eggeling, Edward 126, 207n39
Egypt 2–3, 125, 132–149, 153, 155–161, 163–165
Ennett, William T. 179–180
Ericsson, John 4, **5**
Erlanger, Baron Frédéric Émile de 126, 129
Ethiopia *see* Abyssinia
Eugénie, Empress 114, 134, 146
Everett, William 20, 200n9
Ewell, Richard S. 173–175, 177

Falcon 43
Fane, W.D. 129
Farragut, David **4**
Fenians 152–154
Feuillet, Madame Octave 92–94, 96, 113–115
Field, Charles W. 136, 164
5th North Carolina Cavalry *see* 63rd North Carolina Regiment
Fishmongers' Hall 35, **36**, 37, **39**, 40
Five Forks 194–195
Flashman, Harry 149
CSS *Florida* 87
Forrest, Nathan B. 42, 161, 189
France 1–2, 6–7, 12–13, 19–21, 59, 61–72, 69, 75, 80–82, 91–93, 96, 98–99, 101, 104, 106–107, 110, 112, 116, 118–119, 121–122, 124–127, 129, 132–135, 151, 153, 158, 173
Franco-Prussian War 125, 127, 152–153
Frankfurt 6, 116, 126, 129, **130**
Franklin, William B. 155
Fredericksburg 173, 183
Fremantle, A.J.L. 10, 49, 170
French, William H. 175–176
Fuad Pasha 44
Fullam, George T. 98–100, 106

Galloway, John M. 185–186, 190–191
Galt, Dr. Francis L. 90–91, 98, 101, 108
Garibaldi, Giuseppe 119–120
Garrison, William L. 27, 29, 31
George Griswold 26, 28
George III 21
CSS *Georgia* 139
Gettysburg 3, 68, 174–175, 181, 183, 187
Gladstone, W.E. 16, 103, 133, 207n2
Gone with the Wind 4, 196
Gordon, Charles G. "Chinese" 142

171–172, 174; Spotsylvania 177–178
Thompson, George D. 26
Thomson, William 35, 200*ch*4*n*7
Thruston, Stephen D. 171–173, 175–177, 179
Tocqueville, Alexis de 20, 92
Tremlett, the Rev. Francis W. 103
Trinity College, Cambridge University 6, 8, 17, *18*, 59, 200*ch*2*n*9
Turkey 44–47, 150, 135, 153; *see also* Ottoman Empire
Türr, István 119–120

University of the South 15, 199*n*16
Upton, Emory 177–178, 183

Vanderbilt, Cornelius 120
Varney, Alphonse 82
Verity, the Rev. Edward A. 27, 29, 33–34, 200*ch*3*n*9
Vignaud, Henry 73, 202*n*19
Virginia Military Institute 14–15

Wadleigh, George 141
Walker, James A. "Stonewall Jim" 175, 179
Walker, William 120
Ward, George W. 167, **168**, 169, 172–181; death 180; family 168, 180; on furlough of indulgence 180; post-war reunions 180; promoted 173, 210*ch*14*n*24; in state militia 168–169; wounded 172–173, 176–178
Washington, George 30
Washington and Lee University 15, 199*n*16
Welles, Gideon 101
Wharncliffe, Lord 13, 199*n*10
Wharton, John E. 185, 195
White, David 99
White, Joseph L. 120–121
Wilkes, Charles 10
Willson, H. Beckles 72–73, 75–76, 82, 202*n*20
Wilmington 43–44
Wilson, Joseph D. 98, 108
Winslow, John A. 86, 89, 91–92, 94, 98–101, 104–109, 111–115; character of 100–101; comes ashore 89, 115; denies sending challenge 112; paroles prisoners 101, 108; reports to Welles 99, 205*nn*99–100; requests supplies and reinforcements 105; visits Dupouy 91–92
Wright, George 155

Yancey, William L. 14, 35–40, 117

www.ingramcontent.com/pod-product-compliance
Lightning Source LLC
Chambersburg PA
CBHW060342010526
44117CB00017B/2934